Navelbine® and Taxotere®

For Arthur, Marguerite, Pierre, Elsa and Charlotte.

Series Editor
Max Malacria

Navelbine® and Taxotere®

Histories of Sciences

Muriel Le Roux
Françoise Guéritte

ISTE PRESS

ELSEVIER

First published 2017 in Great Britain and the United States by ISTE Press Ltd and Elsevier Ltd

ISTE Press Ltd
27-37 St George's Road
London SW19 4EU
UK

www.iste.co.uk

Elsevier Ltd
The Boulevard, Langford Lane
Kidlington, Oxford, OX5 1GB
UK

www.elsevier.com

British Library Cataloguing-in-Publication Data
A CIP record for this book is available from the British Library
Library of Congress Cataloging in Publication Data
A catalog record for this book is available from the Library of Congress
ISBN 978-1-78548-145-1

Printed and bound in the UK and US

Contents

Acknowledgements

We would like to thank Max Malacria for the faith he showed in our work and the support he gave us throughout this research. Without him this book would never have been completed. Along with Max, we must also include our editor, Sami Menascé, for accepting the project, and for the patience he has shown.

The warm reception, interest, help, advice and proofreading provided by Lucile Allorge, Michel Colin, Bruno David, Jean-Louis Fabre, Daniel Guénard, Max Malacria, Pierre Mangeney, Georges Massiot and Renée Ventura-Clapier have helped us to see this project through to the end. We would like to thank them for these friendly exchanges.

We would also like to thank our colleagues at the IHMC and the ICSN, who have listened, advised and helped us at some point or other, both on a material and intellectual level, especially Christiane Marmonteil, who facilitated our access to documents.

Finally, we are infinitely grateful to Marie-Claude and Guy Potier, who, in allowing us to consult their father's "papers and archives", have made this association or *compagnonnage* between history and chemistry possible.

Foreword

I am privileged to have been asked to write the foreword for Muriel Le Roux and Françoise Guéritte's excellent book. By rights, it should have been written by Pierre Potier, one of the scientists who jointly discovered the molecules this book discusses. Unfortunately, he lost his battle with disease in February 2006. He is sorely missed by his family, friends, colleagues and those close to him. Hence, the task is a tricky one.

The publication of the first part of the story recounted in this book is the result of convergence and encounters. To begin with, there has been the coming together of the disciplines of history and chemistry, which, in a manner of speaking, is the subject of this book; on the other hand, there has been the meeting between science as a whole, chemistry and publishers, who are the promotors of knowledge promulgation. Above all, though, there has been the convergence of desires which we all share – scientists, authors and publishers: the desire to make our work known beyond our academic circles. Had it not been for that shared intention, this project would never have come to fruition.

Thus, I must point out how much this work owes to Jean-Charles Pomerol, who offered me the opportunity to coordinate the "Molecular, green, medicinal and pharmacological chemistry" series for ISTE, and introduced me to Sami Menascé, President of ISTE, whose enthusiasm is so contagious! I could hardly refuse to play my part in their project: to promote French research and, at the same time, shine a light on our work, whilst conforming to the very strictest of academic requirements. For me to join the project, as the head of one of France's most important chemistry labs (the *Institut de chimie des Substances naturelles* at the CNRS), was a form of tribute to the internationally-recognized work done at that lab at the CNRS in Gif-sur-Yvette.

Also, it became plain to see that the collection ought to include a book on Navelbine and Taxotere, right at the moment when Françoise Guéritte, one of Pierre Potier's disciples, was retiring. I, of course, suggested that she write the story, in which she was one of the protagonists. Whilst she was interested in the project with a view to preserving the memory of the long and winding road that had led to the knowledge at our disposal today, she accepted my invitation on condition that the historian Muriel Le Roux, who had already been working on the subject for some time, also be involved. Having met both authors, I approved and enthusiastically supported their project based on the combination of hard science and human science, of chemistry and history. They began work on it immediately, with the chemists discovering how complex historical research can be.

I closely followed each stage of the writing of the chapters on chemistry, later discovering the historical context in which each discovery took place; the historical reconstruction and analysis were all the more remarkable in view of the difficulty involved in gaining access to the various documents and archives. I believe this historical contribution is perfectly appropriate in this type of book, because the history offers the best possible illumination of the scientific method, attempting to recreate the conditions and circumstances in which these two molecules were discovered. You hold in your hands a remarkable first instalment (there will be a second), which will undoubtedly become a standard reference in the analysis of the discovery of cancer medications, which have had an undeniable social impact.

Having witnessed the collaboration of the two authors, having seen them at work, I can confidently state that they were both imbued with the same determination, the same scientific rigor, the same will to succeed; when the chemist suffered doubt, she was buoyed up by the experience of the historian, for whom challenges are eventually resolved by patience and time. There is not so great a distance between chemistry – an experimental science in the service of society, based on doubt and rigorous investigation – and history, based on a critical analysis of the facts and documents, whose social purpose is to render the past (that which was) accessible. As a team, the two authors complemented each other perfectly. Here, we are dealing with a completely original project, the like of which is too rarely seen. So seemingly simple when viewed from the outside, this *compagnonnage* (to use the authors' own term) could, in my view, serve as a model for the study of sciences as modern techniques, but the process requires the ability to listen and selflessness.

Max MALACRIA
October 2016
Gif-sur-Yvette, France

1

Co-constructing the Past for a History of the Chemistry of Natural Substances

1.1. A convergence

This book comes at a time when hindsight and maturity of thought prevail over excitement and stimulation, the taste for the quest and the obsession with investigation in one or other of the authors. This is a good thing. Time and detachment – and the critical analysis that comes from these – have made possible the creation of the narrative for this history of navelbine and taxotere.[a]

---

a By general consent, since this book is an academic publication written by French researchers, the words navelbine, taxol and taxotere are not given capital letters, these being generic names of products. A capital letter and/or the symbol ® is used in this publication either when referring to a quote, or the title of an article or paper, etc., or when mentioning the industrial product Navelbine®, Taxotere® or Taxol®. In the latter case, this usage has actually been reserved for the specialty of the pharmaceutical company Bristol-Myers Squibb, since 1992, when this was authorized by the US Federal government in spite of the controversy surrounding the "privatization" of a name used in over 600 scientific publications in the 20 years preceding this authorization, – *cf.* "Names for hi-jacking", *Nature, 373 (6513) 370, 1995.* Likewise, Rhône Poulenc became Aventis after merging with Hœchst, then Aventis-Synthélabo-Sanofi, and finally Sanofi. By general consent, although the name of the company has changed over time, they have kept only the Rhône-Poulenc terminology to designate the industrial partner of the CNRS.

The chemist Françoise Guéritte, an Inserm researcher whose career developed at the *Institut de chimie des substances naturelles* (ICSN) [Institute of chemistry of natural substances] of the *Centre national de la recherche scientifique* (CNRS)[b], has spent her professional life seeking to resolve issues relating to society, to make "chemistry useful to others"[c]. She has experienced the moments of hope, excitement and despondency that characterize the daily life of the researcher, at first under the leadership of the other protagonists in this story: Pierre Potier, Nicole and Yves Langlois, then with her colleagues Zo Andriamialisoa, Michel Colin[d] and friends, among others Pierre Mangeney, or with her ongoing accomplices: Thierry Sevenet and Daniel Guénard[e], and then, of course, as a research director herself.

A researcher of the CNRS at the *Institut d'histoire moderne et contemporaine* [Institute of Modern and Contemporary History][f], the historian Muriel Le Roux studies sciences, technology, innovation and businesses of the 20th Century. Therefore, an attempt to retrace the processes essential to the circulation of knowledge and the people who led to the discovery of two anti-cancer drugs could not fail to interest her. Unlike chemistry, historical research is a solitary activity. She has devoted a considerable part of the last 15 years to the search for and the tracking down of all possible sources, since history requires the gathering of evidence. She has also experienced the moments of excitement historians feel on finding a wealth of sources and original, scholarly support, moments that have been fleeting, given the extreme difficulty of access to the written sources, and the likelihood that they would not prove useful.

---

b CNRS's own laboratory based on the campus at Gif-sur-Yvette; for its history cf. Chapter 2.

c Françoise Guéritte – Muriel Le Roux interview, March 29 2012, in her office at the ICSN. Since 2000, the historian has single-handedly carried out interviews with the various participants of this story. They will be cited according to the discipline history methods that considers the source to be as legitimate as a piece of writing from the moment it is subject to appropriate treatment.

d Engineer from the Rhône-Poulenc company, on secondment to the ICSN *cf.* Chapter 3.

e *Cf.* Chapters 3 and 4.

f Joint laboratory involving the CNRS – ENS – University Paris 1 Panthéon-Sorbonne.

So how did this book come about? What was it that led to the co-writing of this narrative? Why did the motivations of the researchers, very different at the outset, eventually converge? The answer lies within a convergence network, at the heart of which is Pierre Potier[1]. The focus and curiosity of this chemist of international standing, and his taste for precision, led him to take an interest in all forms of inquiry and research beyond the boundaries of chemistry. The co-inventor of the two molecules directed the research teams and negotiated with industrial firms, in order to achieve the creation of two drugs; as director of the ICSN he also founded, and for some time directed, a joint CNRS/industry laboratory, became involved in the development of public policy research as Director of the *Direction générale de la recherche scientifique* (DGRST) [French General Department for Scientific Research], and was elected Professor at the *Muséum national d'histoire naturelle* [French National Museum of Natural History].

Aware of the contributions that others could make to science, Pierre Potier was also a great popularizer, in the noblest sense of the word[2].

Having suggested, in 2000, whilst still director of the ICSN, that she should write a history of Navelbine and Taxotere, Pierre Potier allowed the historian unrestricted access to all the cabinets in his office, where a total of 40 years of documents of all kinds had been outstandingly classified. This remarkable source of archives was only accessible, however, when he was not present. In addition to this intellectual openness based on trust, authorizing the reading of all his professional and personal archives, he made himself available for numerous interviews[g]. Moreover, his great mastery of the research process in fact placed him within the spheres of historical research. He never made the slightest attempt to manipulate the results of the historical work in any way. More than this, it is because of his acting as an impartial witness that this research exists, facilitated by access to other documents and meetings with other participants. However, in

g Interviews conducted by the historian, which took place in Pierre Potier's office at the ICSN, at the *Maison de la chimie* in Paris, or at his home.

order to present a full picture[h], it should be mentioned that it was in his interests that this historical research should succeed.

Firstly, and this is not specific to the chemistry of natural substances, it is clear that the work of French teams has been rarely or scarcely mentioned as it should have been by colleagues/competitors who were publishing in English. Pierre Potier would have liked things to have been different. This incentive sheds some light on his interest in popularization. In this respect, the historian might have become the herald of this story. However, because Pierre Potier was a scientist, proud of his independence, there was never any question of this. At the same time, for a number of reasons specific to the field of history – where access to archives is difficult – French historians had not studied the history of specific drugs as much as their English-speaking colleagues[3,4]. J. Goodman and V. Walsh having studied the American history of taxol[3], the historian wanted to provide her own input and offer a more precise understanding of the contribution made by French scientists in the history of taxol and taxotere. Like Viviane Quirke, historian at Oxford Brookes University, whose work compares the history of pharmaceutical companies in France and the United Kingdom up to 1965[5], far from nationalism, it was to supplement the work of American historian Alfred D. Chandler[6] who also rarely quoted France or the United Kingdom in his work on the history of the pharmaceutical industry. In the end, the authors of this volume witnessed, in spite of their efforts, the frailty of preservation of evidence – testimonies and archives- which sadly disappeared or were scattered, the vigilance of the curator-archivist, which Pierre Potier also was, not having been passed on.[i]

It was initially at P. Potier's request that Françoise Guéritte accepted Muriel Le Roux from the beginning of the project. Because, like her boss, the chemist was interested in the historical approach, she extended the same welcome to the historian, based on trust and mutual

h The historian is the only one to speak.

i His archives, covering over 40 years of ICSN activity, were scattered following his death on February 10 2006. Letters were returned to their senders, files belonging to researchers were sent back to them...

respect[j]. Thus, when, a decade later, Max Malacria, director of the ICSN, asked F. Guéritte to write a history of navelbine and taxotere, she accepted the project on the condition that M. Le Roux would be involved. Unlike some other scientists, F. Guéritte understood that writing the history of scientific facts would be a long and specific process.

Thereupon, Max Malacria agreed and supported their project enthusiastically.

A common desire to present the truth as closely as possible, unvarnished without embellishment, but modestly, since they have not been able to access all the archives and documents they had hoped to consult, thus motivated a chemist and a historian to co-write this book. On the strength of their respective disciplines, and aware of some urgency, the two authors have presented this as original work, at least in its conception[k].

1.2. "A small world"[l]

Let us make something clear. If chance has played a part in the story about to be told here, the discovery of vinorelbine and docetaxel, better known by the trade names Navelbine® and Taxotere®, did not happen purely by chance or luck, so much as by the accumulation of knowledge and the development of a science-based industry, stemming above all from the determination of a few individuals. These discoveries are the fruit and the culmination of exchanges and interactions between various protagonists over a long period of time: naturalists, botanists, anthropologists, chemists, pharmacists, physicians, patients and, more generally, between actors from academia and industry.They also stem

j Such was the case with all researchers, with the exception of Nicole Langlois (Chapter 3) and Andrew Greene (Chapter 4), who for personal reasons denied M. Le Roux access to their archives and declined to be interviewed.

k The historical analyses and interpretations are the sole responsibility of Muriel Le Roux; Françoise Guéritte is responsible for the contents relating to chemistry; but they have joint responsibility for the general scheme and contents of the book.

l With reference to the novel *Small World*, by David Lodge, Secker and Warburg, London, 1984.

from the society generating them. The protagonists of this long accumulation of understanding come and go; they make up an inner circle located at the crossroads between knowledge and economics, fully submerged in a mercantile world. This "small world", difficult to pinpoint for those on the outside, since its outlines are fuzzy and shifting, is nothing new. The area of interest to us here, that of natural substances, emerged in the 19th Century, when one moved from vegetable to synthetic dyes[7]. This world has internal practices whose origins are as old as it is itself. The close alliance between scientific research and industrial practice has thus been driven by synergy and reciprocation. And even if the chemistry of natural substances only underwent a real boom in France during the great "big science" development after 1945, it falls within that area that is rooted in the chemistry appearing in the 19th Century.

If this natural closeness – in a philosophical sense – between academic and industrial chemists is ancient[8], to the point of not always being perceived as specific by those involved, it was after the Second World War that the reciprocation between the approaches of academic and industrial chemists became commonplace.

All the same, this is why, for the sake of accuracy of the intellectual process, it is worth recalling a few principles relating to this activity. Research has long been thought of and experienced as a dual activity, the two forms having a reciprocal relationship. Fundamental research is aimed at determining the general laws of matter, life, the universe or human behavior, and the work is carried out without preconceived ideas about the applications that may result. Applied research produces applicable knowledge that affects reality, resolves practical problems, and changes the world, the work being carried out with a view to a specific "use"[9]. This definition should be completed by mentioning where this occurs: this activity takes place within both academic – in France, research centers and universities – and industrial environments. Sometimes, however, fundamental and applied research is conducted in a single place: academic and/or industrial, or in a shared area. These shared facilities are numerous and occur most often in chemistry, which, by definition, is a hybrid science – at the same time academic and industrial[10] – but which is thereby practiced and experienced by chemists as a continuum[m]. Continuum does not imply that the sole purpose of this discipline is application and industrialization. This continuum is made up of "fuzzy actors and actions"[11], and is therefore common to all kinds of participants, and all kinds of research occur, cohabit and co-produce fundamental and/or applied scientific knowledge. The *Institut de chimie des substances naturelles* (ICSN) [Institute of chemistry of natural substances], a laboratory belonging to the CNRS, to which this book refers, is one example of such a place and such research. As an academic and public location for fundamental, but also "applied" research, this institute has collaborated with industry and contributed to the emergence of joint research units since its creation, producing knowledge that spans the whole spectrum of research.

Subsequently, in the history of these two drug molecules, comes the development phase, which involves making use of the results of the fundamental or applied research (for navelbine and taxotere these were the results of the continuum), in order to bring about new products, materials, systems or procedures. This phase involves moving onto the industrial prototype for a "drug molecule", which will be first of all tested *in vitro*, then *in vivo*, before moving onto the clinical trial phase, and then, in time, after authorization and approval, placed onto the market and sold[9]. The prototype testing, in this case the clinical trials, forms part of the development, but not the launch of the product/drug. This feature has not been included in this book[n]. Why did we create this bias?

First of all, for reasons concerned with the scope of the topic. The pharmaceuticals, scientific products are both health goods – thus public assets – and economic goods – domain of industrial and private conception. They raise questions that go beyond the boundaries of this publication.

The difficulties in gaining access to sources held by pharmaceutical companies, but which are necessary if one is to write a complete history

m Pierre Potier – Muriel Le Roux interview, at his home in Paris, January 5 2006.

n This investigation will not be completed on production of this book. M. Le Roux is working on a history of drugs that will attempt to include these features.

of the process, are accompanied by methodological issues. Firstly, even if the aforementioned interactions between the academic and industrial worlds are known, they are rarely analyzed or explained in detail, since that which is implemented in the process of discovery, invention and innovation is complex. The analyzer needs patience and time, especially when it also involves drugs invented by chemistry, complex structures produced in the utmost secrecy. Furthermore, even if the invention of the two drugs was enabled by a continuum, no one could have predicted the outcome.

An outcome of academic and public research, these molecules, although "usable", were not the result of activity that began with a commercial purpose in mind. In other words, the specific mission of the ICNS researchers was not to produce drugs, but to further knowledge. With the creation of this institute in the 1950s, the intention was to enable the French to catch up in the field of chemistry of natural substances, and potentially develop an applicable science. We will come back to this. Thus, researchers of all kinds, working on a variety of research projects, worked together and collaborated at the ICSN, this being from the time it was set up to the present day. Having met with the majority of those involved[o], and read almost all accessible ICSN archives[p], it can be argued that the researchers who took part in these discoveries will recognize their quest in this extract from the biography of *Magellan* by Stefan Zweig[12], quoted by Etienne Klein to qualify scientific research: "[...] practical usefulness never determines the moral value of an achievement. Only the person who increases the knowledge humanity has about itself and enhances its creative consciousness permanently enriches humanity..."[13]

o The name of each witness will be cited according to the principles of oral history. The interviews conducted by Muriel Le Roux, once transcribed, will be included among the archives of Pierre Potier; the authors hope that these will one day be classified. These interviews may be used as a source, once the agreement of both the interviewee and the interviewer has been obtained.

p Archive references will be quoted in footnotes, while bibliographical references will be included at the end of the book, and presented according to the conventions appropriate to the subject of chemistry. Historians, readers of this book, will find bibliographical references classified in order of citation at the end of the book.

However, the cooperation between some of the ICSN personnel and industry was never denied or prohibited. In fact, one could say that this has also been an invariant of the history of this institute. Nevertheless, although the researchers carried out part of the development of the two molecules in conjunction with industrial organizations, their development was never their responsibility. This book has been thought out and written as a collaboration between a chemist and a historian, who have placed their subjects, chemistry and history, on equal footing. Each entered into the territory of the other. The chemist explained the job done at the ICSN, and the historian applied the methods used by historians to research the past. The question of which sources would be the most conveniently mobilized soon arose. It was the archives of Pierre Potier (1933 – 2006) to which the historian had unrestricted access during his lifetime. Owing to the kindness of his children, Marie-Claude and Guy Potier, she still had access after his death. Some archives of Françoise Guéritte and her colleagues kept at the ICSN were used too[q]. Compared to what was just mentioned, including a history of the industrial development would have made no sense if two other authors, one from Laboratoires Pierre Fabre, and the other from Rhône-Poulenc, had not joined the project with access to the various archives. Since it is the responsibility of the historian to develop an investigation method for consulting all possible kinds of documents, the chemist did not, in this process, feel that she could legitimately refer to the history of the development and industrial production of the two drugs, not having participated, and knowing how to select and analyze the relevant documents for this aspect of the history. Her position is all the more commendable given the complex nature of this exercise in total history[r,14]. It is essential to change one's perspective, leaving the observation of the world of science behind, in order to focus one's attention on the hinge point between the history of science and technology, the history of the devices of development of knowledge, and the history of businesses, medicine and the state[15].

q Access facilitated by the kindness of the director, Max Malacria.

r Aspiration of the *Annales*, a journal founded by Marc Bloch and Lucien Fèbvre. *Cf.* ref. 14.

Moreover, this complex history unfolded in a society whose attitude was changing rapidly. From the 1970s onwards, public health policy henceforth had to contend with opinion, patients and their families who were becoming increasingly informed, exerting a growing influence in the wake of scandals such as thalidomide or diethylstilbestrol, and later, lack of treatment following the discovery of HIV. The 1970s, 1980s and 1990s, crucial in the discovery of our two molecules, were years during which academic knowledge and therapeutic knowledge clashed with the commercial logics of companies who were themselves still evolving; such knowledge therefore had to respond to these changes. The legislation granting marketing authorization became binding, which radically changed the nature of the relationship between the academic and industrial worlds[16]. That is another story[s].

It was thus decided, in concert, to limit this book to a history of the chemistry of the natural academic substances responsible for the origin of these two molecules; the idea being to write a book on the history of the sciences studied and written to make chemistry understandable to historians, whilst chemists would have a work based on scientific archives that have been sought out, consulted, re-read and analyzed using the methods and rigor of scientific inquiry. The process of historical research, additional to the one implemented here, which studies the interaction with industry, therefore represents another inquiry.

This unlikely co-writing was born out of two desires and a wager. For the historian, this meant not simply leaving the chance to write a history of contemporary sciences to the people involved. They are so complex and specialized that only certain members of the scientific community are capable of understanding each other[17,18]. The chemist, who was repeatedly asked to assess research in her field or explain the genesis of her work, wished to collect as much information as she could, in order to lessen the passage of time that deposits an inexorable film over memories and collections. As for the wager, this was simple: would they succeed in writing together?

s This is better known, since this story was written from public sources.

1.3. Incomplete sources on the history of the chemistry of natural substances?

The scientific and industrial environments that collaborate and interact together are the issuers of the necessary documents for this account. At first sight, one might think that these were legion. However, this is not the case. Reality is not as generous as it seems. Knowing who is keeping what and where remains a major problem. Yet, unfortunately, while academic and industrial institutions have sought to monitor their personnel, to organize and determine their collaboration in recent years, it is only in rare cases where, in this context, the status of their joint documents has been determined, at an earlier stage of cooperation, authorizing their preservation as archives. This can be explained. There are increasing demands on the scientific community to support international competition, sometimes guided or structured by ill-concealed commercial purposes, and these have changed the culture of scientists working under greater time pressure. Added to this there is the use of new information technology, which, in removing the paperwork, has made information, if not knowledge, volatile. This change in research practices casts light on the lack of interest in preservation of that which is produced on the part of researchers. Convinced that others will do it for them, they are not the "curators and archivists" that their predecessors were.

Researchers working in academic laboratories, but also organizations: the central services of the academic research centers, the supervising authorities (ministries, national and European funding agencies), produce information that ultimately becomes the sources, archives and the documents necessary for writing history. These documents should be readily available from the time when the statutory 30 years of storage without communication have elapsed; it should be possible to consult them after obtaining a waiver if the document is less than 30 years old. It is not this simple, since the conservation policies in France are not very strictly enforced, for financial reasons. Numerous valuable documents do not become archives because they are simply not all added to the archives, recorded, inventoried...and thus they are not conserved. This is the first pitfall.

For this "360°" and "top-down" view of the history, it is also essential to consult the archives belonging to industrial organization partners (those of the centers for research, development, strategy management, legal affairs, and general management). The conservation of these private files/archives depends on the goodwill of the directors. Although it is desirable to study this issue, which is another problem concerned with the history of sciences, technology and businesses, it requires widespread access to sources (archives and testimonies). Laboratoires Pierre Fabre occasionally granted limited access to Muriel Le Roux, while Aventis, now Sanofi, never acknowledged the many requests for access to the Rhône-Poulenc archives kept by this company[t]. On this subject, it is common practice for pharmaceutical companies to deny access to their archives, even in the case of the oldest. Could it be that this stance results from their frequently being plunged into a media vortex, or is it because of certain questionable practices – the methods of calculating the prices of certain drugs, out of all proportion to the cost of research and development, and the return on investment, for example – that they do not wish to be made public?

Nevertheless, for several years there has been a general climate of suspicion against pharmaceutical laboratories. The more advanced countries, France included, have established solidarity systems, allowing access to healthcare for the greatest number of people, although the cost is high. But, in the past 15 years or so, the pharmaceutical industry, as with other industrial sectors, has seen a renewal of managerial practices that now favor the return on short-term investment for shareholders. In this respect, the drug has become a financial product rather than a healthcare product. And even if the drug-molecules used against cancer are very specific products that had little to do with the criticisms made by citizens, this fact is not true anymore. So some confusion has occurred that could explain the position of the pharmaceutical companies. Whatever it is, this climate of suspicion is not favorable to History.

t *Cf.* Chapters 2 and 4.

The position of Laboratoires Pierre Fabre changed over time. After an initially favorable reception[u], there followed a certain reserve, no doubt related to the tighter economic environment and the change in general management following the recent changeover of the firm into a public limited company, or was it a result of the general stigma that affects this industrial sector? In the case of this company, with so specific a culture, why not allow historians to do some objective work whose results would be known to all?

In any case, in dealing with molecules intended as future drugs, one should, at the very least, consult the files that the pharmaceutical companies have assembled in order to obtain marketing authorization; duplicates are kept by the companies, and the originals by the national, European and American health agencies, etc. However, there is no certainty that these can be found, or that access will be granted. For all these reasons, the industrial history of Navelbine® and Taxotere® will not, therefore, be dealt with here at all. But before that, the scientific work that led to the production of navelbine and taxotere was conducted partly in conjunction with other academic and industrial research centers. There is a joint building of knowledge, a network of participants, institutions, and thereby a co-production of papers, reports and contracts. Who should keep these documents? And if they do, who should maintain the archives that they have become? Are they to be kept under shared ownership? Nothing is less certain, as often no thought is given to their conservation. When these archives exist, gaining access to them depends on the goodwill of the keepers, whose positions will undoubtedly vary from one archive to another. Access to the archives is thus characterized by a lack of continuity; this is the second pitfall[v].

u Although some individuals, who knew Pierre Potier and Pierre Fabre personally, were in favor of hospitality, these people have sadly left the company since.

v For reasons of editorial balance – the reconstruction of industrial development and manufacturing process of both molecules without industrial archives is complicated – the approach to this aspect of the history will be attempted in a subsequent book.

As if this were not enough, technological developments, from the post-it notes thrown away as soon as an idea had been used (papers were previously stuck into laboratory notebooks and therefore preserved) and the non-transcribed telephone conversations (except those of company directors), as well as emails, preliminary drafts and other texts that disappear with the continuous processing of writing by means of word processing software, to the destruction of the hard drives of obsolete computers, all lead to new ways of working for those producing documents. So, like medievalists, present time historians only have incomplete sources. In short, everything has unexpectedly conspired against the recording of scientific activity in recent times[19]. And if writing this story is not as easy as it would appear to be at first sight, this is compensated for by a wealth of information that fleshes out the work of the historian[w]: meetings with the actors.

The vast majority of the protagonists of this story (whether retired or still active) were contacted with a view to discussing the project and requesting an interview. In this respect, Pierre Potier was the first to help the historian. But at this stage more than any other, one cannot make a mistake in making requests. If the historian does not have the assistance of one or two individuals in compiling a list of participants that are willing to be interviewed, then in compiling a list of the necessary documents, especially scientific documents, he or she will lose all credibility and the slim chance of gaining access to primary sources will fade away. Moreover, there begins another job for the historian, which also forms part of the research process: building up oral archives, sources that are indispensable in launching and supporting the quest. Generating, collecting, listening to and making use of the dozens of oral testimonies assembled to write this history of drugs has formed the bedrock of the historian's work and the preamble of the access to written archives. This immersion into the world of "science

w "The good historian is like the giant of the fairy tale. He knows wherever he catches the scent of human flesh, there his quarry lies". Marc Bloch, *Apologie pour l'histoire ou le métier d'historien,* Paris, 1949, trans. *The Historian's Craft*, Manchester University Press, 2008, p. 22.

in action" is similar to the participatory observation of an ethnologist. Like a painter, the historian acts by small touches, and generally carries out several interviews with the same person. Out of these interviews with the active scientific community of scholars and industrialists, scientific, technical, economic and political issues emerge. During cross-checking, a history of the failures emerges, enlightening and coloring what is predominantly a success story. The written sources consulted as a result of the help provided by the people interviewed will validate, invalidate and complement the testimonies, the cross-referencing of the two kinds of sources clarifying the work of critical analysis. In fact, if the interview is the key to the history of the present time, allowing access to the archives, it is even more important in analyzing the scientific archives and the writing of the story in question. So, each of the witnesses questioned provided information, and sometimes documents, archives...... Additionally, scientific publications by French and foreign chemists have been consulted, the archives of the ICSN, of the CNRS[x], the archives of the DGRST and the *Institut national de la propriété industrielle* (INPI) [French national institute of national property].

Speeches/analyses of written documents and speeches/writing are the key events that have enabled the investigation to succeed. This book is the first result of this. If the authors shared a common desire to write in order to preserve the broad pattern of this history[y] they still had to agree on the language, tone and nature of the narrative, knowing that certain scientists wonder if science can really be described by language... So what does this historico-chemical co-construction mean?

x Mr. Laurent Pinon, historian, lecturer at the ENS, in charge of the financial support service for science at the CNRS, Mr. Dominique Massiot, director of the *Institut de Chimie* at the CNRS, Ms. Marie-Laure Bachellerie, head of archive service at the CNRS, and Ms. Isabelle Dujonc, head of archives at the Gif-sur-Yvette campus of the CNRS, are warmly thanked for their help.

y We do not claim to offer a definitive account. We are offering a text written jointly, based on archives and testimonies to which we have had access, and which are not exhaustive.

1.4. An original way of telling the history of chemistry: "a *compagnonnage*"[z]

How does one say in words what chemistry says with formulas? How does one make what chemists observe, describe, analyze, create and re-create understandable to all, whether expert or layperson? How does one link up the present of today with the present of yesterday? On which sources should this narrative be based? In view of that which prevails in the history of the chemistry of more ancient times – about which the historian knows enough science to explore the documents alone – writing the history of the chemistry of the second half of the 20th Century, after 1945, requires a specific methodology and multifaceted language.

If the scientists, industrialists and technologists are legitimately entitled to ask what the "literary scholars" might perceive from their knowledge and practices, the use of interviews is still the main gateway to their world. As a result of an identity of academic position and social status, but also because in writing the history of two molecules, the historian became the sounding board for competition, rivalry, alliances and friendships, the attitudes of the witnesses were more entrenched in comparison with a historian/ engineer *compagnonnage*. But once the process had been understood, support was genuine. This point is crucial, because it is the only way that the scientific content can be accessed by a non-specialist.

It was easy for participants to assess her ignorance about chemistry. It would have been tempting to exploit this. The conscience and ethics of the researchers protected them against such a temptation – it is easier to refuse to meet with the historian than to argue with her in an attempt to direct her thoughts. Explaining these approaches to

z In the sense of workers' organizations (in this case researchers) characterized by mutual aid and training organizations [...] whose qualified members considered themselves companions. Translated from *Le Grand Robert de la langue française* defintion: "The French *Compagnonnage* system is a unique way of conveying knowledge and know-how linked to the trades that work with stone, wood, metal, leather, textiles and food".
http://www.unesco.org/culture/ich/en/RL/compagnonnage-network-for-on-the-job-transmission-of-knowledge-and-identities-00441?RL=00441

history, seeking, at all costs, to thoroughly understand that which was, is not without resonance with the activity of scientists. Out of these regular exchanges over the course of several years emerged respect, trust, goodwill and empathy. This goodwill is even more remarkable given that they had to agree to become an object of study. It is not so easy. Besides, some categorically refused to cooperate, others refused to discuss anything other than scientific facts; these attitudes highlight the importance of the chemist/historian *compagnonnage*, which aims to make major scientific facts from a recent but fragile past intelligible to others.

With each new encounter, the historian built up her network, which was a fair reflection of the one that had previously existed. Then, at some point, without this being anticipated or premeditated, the regular exchanges with some interviewees led to a *compagnonnage* with some of the participants of the story that she is writing. These regular exchanges with the participants, which some historians might criticize, as they could blur the boundaries that are essential between a historian and his/her subject, were nevertheless, for this historian, a significant asset. They were a key part of the methodology that has been developed to write this recent history of science and technology. This is due to the acute problem experienced by science historians trying to understand scientific documents without the necessary training in each discipline. The relentless, growing complexity of disciplines that subdivide into specialties makes an understanding of the scientific content impossible for anyone who is unfamiliar with this specialization.This goes just as well for chemistry as with the other hard sciences.

Should one, for all that, abandon the present time history of science and technology? Should one rely solely on the accounts provided by the actors? If French historians suspect that the biographical genre is partial, what does this mean for autobiographies? Yet again, it is clear that one cannot do without this source[20] which provides both raw facts – *cf.* the autobiography of Edgar Lederer (1908-1988)[aa,21] – and an

aa A biochemist, he was one of the first directors at the ICSN, along with Maurice-Marie Janot. After completing his PhD in Vienna in 1930, he became assistant at the *Kaiser Wilhelm Institut für chemie* in Heidelberg, a fellow at the IBPC, head of

explanation of the choices and the commitments of those involved, – *cf.* the dialog between Pierre Potier on one hand, and François Chast, pharmacist, and Cécile Guérin, journalist, on the other[22]. If this creates a window onto science in action, the scientists who write are only making visible that which is significant to them. As important as it is, this genre rarely provides information on the specific scientific content of the activity of the researchers, who, as autobiographers, change, in this case, into popularizers, campaigners for the scientific cause.

Yet, the history of science, as with that of technology, is not only the history of the modernity of science and technology, it also addresses the need for rationality, knowledge and understanding of various subjects, in distinct geographical regions, at different times, the guiding principle of this quest being the demand for truth, the main basis of the historical discipline[23,24]. Now, to come close to this truth, to practice the exercise of proof, what better than a shared perspective, consultation of sources, and analysis? It is to come close to this truth, without shying away from studying an object on the grounds that she does not understand the parlance of the archives before her, that the historian practices what she calls the *compagnonnage*.

laboratories at the Vitamin Institute in Leningrad, a fellow of the *Caisse nationale de la recherche scientifique*, CNRS attached to the Zoology laboratory at the ENS, naturalized French in 1938, *chargé de recherche* (researcher) at *the Centre national de la recherche scientifique* in 1940, joined the laboratory of biochemistry at the faculty of sciences in Lyon the same year, and was promoted to *maître de recherche* (research fellow) in 1945. Back at the IBPC in Paris in October 1946, he became in 1952 head of the department of chemistry of natural organic substances, and was promoted to *Directeur de recherche* (senior researcher) in 1953 at the CNRS. He applied for a position as *maître de conférence* (lecturer) at the Sorbonne, the status being more stable there than at the CNRS. Then he was appointed Professor without chair in 1956. Appointed director of the ICSN in July 1955 (until 1978), he was appointed Professor at the Sorbonne in 1958, succeeding Pr Fromageot, then at Université de Orsay. He worked for, or was adviser to, the Hoffman La Roche and Firmenich and Ciba companies. Recipient of the CNRS gold medal, the highest scientific disctinction in France in 1974, he was elected to the Academy of sciences in 1982. Arch. CNRS personnel records, partially available with permission.

The chemist adopted the operating methods and codes of history from the outset. During preliminary conversations aimed at establishing the boundaries for the book, they decided, for reasons already explained, to plan the project in two phases: the joint scientific restitution collected in a first volume will be followed by a "total layout of the history" of these findings. After being intrigued by the approach, the chemist was fully involved in this original project, in the sense that the final form of this book does not correspond to what would have been written had she written the book alone, or if she had been questioned by a journalist.

The same goes for the historian, who would have had to circumvent the science itself due to a lack of competence. This co-production did not proceed without some difficulty on both sides.

The chemist, who patiently agreed to work according to the methods used in history, was obliged to go to the library, compile a bibliography, seek out scientific archives (including her own), read them, re-read them, agree to check her memories, discover that her information differed from that of the historian and, indeed, undertake the necessary verifications, listen to the historian's questions, often replying to them many times, find a way of wording a scientific fact that would be understandable by readers who were not chemists, without boring the chemists, etc. All this demanded patience and detachment on her part. As with all multi-disciplinary projects, this book required long hours of dialog, exchanges, and the development of a common language. She agreed that the second book was to be written by the historian, leaving her totally free to analyze and interpret scientific, social and economic networks, free to contextualize the history of the interface between the ICSN and industrial partners.

As for the historian, she was obliged to dare to show her ignorance, repeat questions, explain the reasons for the thorough checks at every stage of the research and writing, to go through the archives again in order to eliminate any doubts emerging from their differences. She also attempted to explain the time differences between chemistry and history, of which there are many.

Indeed, in contrast to the chemist, who is oriented towards the quest and the future, and for whom yesterday belongs to the past, for the historian yesterday still belongs to the history of the present time. However, there are exceptions: Pierre Potier, and his desire to make the work of his teams better understood outside the clearly-defined community of the chemistry of natural substances. This desire can be explained by a double sense of belonging: belonging to a community of chemists that is supranational, since it is academic, but also belonging to the national scientific community as a citizen steeped in classical culture, and thus history, as scholars of his generation often were. To a lesser extent, and with greater restraint, this awareness is also to be found in Françoise Guéritte. This focus of the partner chemists – P. Potier and F. Guéritte – on the past goes back to the work of the historian, which, due to the awareness of the time that it generates around the present time, directs their thoughts.

Thus, if the present time is a dividing line, a segment that characterizes a before and after, the history of their chemistry forms part of this scenario. The line between the past and the future is located somewhere around the discoveries of the molecules, the patenting, and the first clinical applications[25]. It is probably because there have been no new discoveries of drug molecules at the ICSN that we are still in the present, and that the present is multi-faceted. It is precisely this duration of the present that transforms it into a plural sequence, and this is all the more so as each participant is legitimately within his rights to present his own account. Is an historic account not also embodied in personal visions, in the freedom of each person to make his own interpretation[bb,26]? However, far from being beneficial to writing a history of discoveries, this extension of the present time leaves traces, and imposes an adaptation of the institution. This thereby complicates access to public and private archives. Hence, since there is not a new present surrounding such important discoveries, when it comes to access to archives, whether at the CNRS or pharmaceutical laboratories, nothing is certain; the attitude of those in charge fluctuates between indifference, supervision and control...Only the invention of new drugs

bb Theses have been written, as well as articles and other literature on the subject; these will be cited during the course of the book.

at the ICSN, equally important in treating medical conditions[cc] could propel this history into the past, diverting the attention away from all aspects of this story.

Sharing the same ideas about the past, time and chronology with "*compagnons*" on the one hand, and making the chemists' community accept that the past can have a legitimacy other than that of a heroic tale, constitutes a real challenge when working on the history of science. In this sense, the ongoing dialogs between the authors were the basis for a mediation between history and chemistry that is reinforced by the co-writing of the narrative.

Furthermore, the rhythms of writing reports in chemistry are quicker than those of history. To simplify this somewhat, they are organized as follows: hypothesis, experiment, observation, discussion, writing and publication, which usually occurs, except in certain cases, on a shorter time scale than those of history. This was also negotiated and agreed by the chemists.

The custom in science is to publish only the good results, evaluations, funding, promotions and careers being the result. Who would dare to write "I have spent several months and most of my grant for nothing"? This history of science, dependent on scientific publications and testimonials, and in a small part on the individual records of researchers, is no exception to the genre. This is a story of success, and with good reason. Access to all of the academic sources has not been possible, and, with some exceptions, the archives relating to unsuccessful research have not been preserved[dd]. It still remains very difficult to consult those of the CNRS or the industrial

---

cc *Cf.* testimony of Professor Martine Piccart, Professor of oncology at the *Université Libre de Bruxelles*, and head of the Department of Medicine at the *Institut Jules Bordet*, center of the fight against cancer in Belgium, in the film by Jean-Luc Bouvet, *L'if, aux frontières de la vie,* 2010, Le Miroir, ARTE France, CNRS images and the *Muséum national d'histoire naturelle de Paris*.

dd Benoît Dardelet, Head of the CNRS-ICSN partnership, is warmly thanked for the help he has provided. The archives consulted at his recommendation, relating to undeveloped potentials, are unique to the ICSN.

organizations, simply because noone is inclined to raise these issues which would nevertheless enable a much broader contextualization; these documents are very often destroyed. This attitude of academic researchers is not surprising in itself if one considers how the relationships between academic research and pharmaceutical companies have evolved. Although there is a complementarity in the general process of knowledge production and drug molecules, it is nevertheless accompanied by an imbalance in the presentation and use of the results of these collaborations in the public arena, for which, unlike industrialists, academic researchers are not necessarily well prepared[27]. This is why P. Potier, who dealt with this subject in particular, devoted so much time to it[2]. The account presented here is thus not balanced, but is supported by this ideal of total history that has motivated the quest in spite of obstacles.

Curiosity, and the desire to speak out in spite of criticism denouncing “the fanciful stories”– because of their incompleteness or their not making enough of the work of one or the other –, criticizing the chosen subject because it is “easy to write a success story”, never failed the historian, who regularly heard these remarks from researchers of various academic disciplines. She was not, therefore, at all surprised by the reactions sparked by the announcement of the project. She attempted, without always succeeding, to help her chemist co-author to objectify the symbolic violence – as described by Pierre Bourdieu – which runs through the research community. A reflection of the fragile nature of the scientific community in a world of fierce competition, these remote positions of critical analysis – the very foundation of so small a world – sometimes came close to attempted manipulation or destabilization. This book is an answer to those who may have imagined doing this work one day, without daring to do it, or who even tried to alter its course. The *compagnonnage*, the method preferred by M. Le Roux for the study of the history of science and technology of the present day[28], protected them against their respective pressures, enabling them to succeed in their investigation while observing the ethics of history.

Finally, the reader will have noticed that the authors use different pronouns, using either the neuter, commonly used in scientific writing, or the third person singular or plural, to refer to an approach or an analysis common to both of them, which designates them impersonally.

It is the neuter of the narrators, modestly replacing the "I" or the "we" of the historian, or the neuter that the chemist would have used had there been no co-writing. This is not some style clause, or a coquetry on the part of the authors, but a manifestation of the expression of the wager: to write together, a history, a narrative, in several voices. Thus there are at least three voices in this book. In the background, there is that of Françoise Guéritte, the PhD student at the age of 24, researcher at the Inserm, assigned to the ICSN. Then, there is the voice of Françoise Guéritte the chemist, now in retirement and a narrative writer, who, having acted as an observer, is co-writing this book. Her narrative is combined with that of Muriel Le Roux, observing and analyzing historian and narrator, who was behind the historic research and testimonies. Just like her, the chemist of today has examined and looked at the chemist of yesterday. In this work of self-analysis and analysis of the past, she has joined the historian, who has helped her to manage this tension while, in turn, the chemist has helped the historian to approach the science from within ... Thus, there are at least three approaches in this book, that of chemistry, that of history, and that of co-writing, which are shown by the variation in pronouns.

But these strategies make up just one narrative.

The history of navelbine and taxotere could serve as an example, a reflection of what was happening in general in France or Europe between the 1950/1960s and the 2000s, since part of this narrative embraces the developments of the century. The story is based on two axes, the timeline, which is an observation instrument, since without it some facts would remain elusive, and the evidence, which brings out the unique. In combining the chronology and the unique, history offers a setting that reveals the collective, the interactions, movement. But the historical narrative – and not history – in its reproduction, has an arbitrary nature in itself. The facts do not speak for themselves. They must be chosen as one chooses documents[29]. There is a consistency between them in the organization of the narrative. And there, in this narrative, the personality of the authors intervenes; this is to be taken into consideration[30]. At no time did they claim, or even wish, to revive "The" past, still less the idea of forming definite conclusions. Like archaeologists, they have removed some of the sediments deposited by time, and attempted to show the conditions in which the discoveries were made, and the discoveries themselves. As Randy Olson emphasizes[31], science is defined by two activities: seeking and communicating, which is not the same as saying that scientists do not need history. This is what we, the authors, are offering.

2

The *Institut de chimie des substances naturelles* of the CNRS (1955–2000): Emblematic of an Evolving Area of Research?

2.1. Research in France and the CNRS: ambivalent sentiments?[a]

The earliest initiatives which would lead to the founding of France's CNRS took place in the early 20th Century[32,33]. It was a long, complicated road to achieve it. The *Front populaire* – a left-wing political alliance in the 1930s and the establishment of the *sous-secrétariat d'Etat à la Recherche* [Undersecretary of State for Scientific Research], an office first held by Irène Joliot-Curie and then by Jean Perrin, both Nobel Prize winners, heeded and responded to scientists' demands, whilst organizing very quickly for wartime mobilization.

2.1.1. *From the creation of the CNRS in 1939 to its first reorganization in 1959*

The *Centre national de la recherche scientifique* was set up by decree on 19 September 1939, published in the *Journal officiel de la*

a The aim of this chapter is not to offer an exhaustive overview of the history of research in France. Instead, the discussion will be limited to the main facts which contextualize the history of the ICSN.

République française on 24 October 1939[34]. Meeting scientists' demands, in that text, the French State aimed to draw "a higher yield" from the national research effort[b,35]. The organization, entrusted to the leadership of Henri Laugier, was to play an active role in shaping the country's research – in terms of both fundamental and applied research. However, the CNRS leadership could not prevent the proliferation of publicly-owned research hubs during the Second World War[c,36]. Consequently, in 1945, the *Comité national de la recherche scientifique* [National Committee for Scientific Research] – which, at the time, still harbored the ambition of managing all of France's research – refused to accept researchers from these institutions – the *Commissariat à l'énergie atomique* (Atomic Energy Commission), *Institut national d'hygiène* (National Hygiene Institute, which was later to become Inserm, *Institut national de la santé et de la recherche médicale*), etc. Furthermore, at the same time, the CNRS was denied the status of interministerial organization enjoyed by the CEA. In the same vein, research as a "strategic activity" was overlooked by the Plan Monnet (1946–1950), despite the presence of Frédéric Joliot-Curie, who was head of the CNRS from August 1944 to September 1945, on the board which drafted the Plan[37,34]. On the other hand, the second plan attempted to remedy this oversight, and the CNRS directors were included in the drafting process, putting forward a "research plan"[d]. For the first time, it seemed, the question of a set scientific agenda had been raised[34]. However, the action of the politicians, dominated by ministerial instability, focused largely on the international crises, affording very little attention to the questions raised by research. In this unsettled context of the Fourth Republic, Pierre Mendès France's ascendance to *Présidence du Conseil* (the head of the Council) to form a new government, on 18 June 1954, was

---

b This argument would be reiterated, becoming an invariant characterizing State support for natural substance chemistry, as can be seen from the archives.

c The *Institut national d'hygiène* in 1941 (which would later become Inserm), the *Office des recherches coloniales* in 1943 (the future Orstom/IRD), the *Centre national d'études des télecommunications* (CNET), the *Office national des recherches aéronautiques* (ONERA), the *Commissariat à l'énergie atomique* (CEA) in 1945, the *Institut national de recherche agronomique* (INRA), the *Institut national d'études démographiques* (INED) in 1946…

d Interview with Charles Gabriel, J.-F. Picard and E. Pradoura, 13 June 1986, http://www.histcnrs.fr/archives-orales/gabriel-charles.html.

a crucial turning point, because he was one of the only politicians at that level to pay any attention to the issue. One year earlier, on 3 June 1953, he had declared in a speech that "The Republic needs scientists and scholars"[38]. As President of the Council, he set up a sub-directorate for Research[e]. From that point on, scientific and technical research was viewed as one of the possible tools in the drive to modernize the country. The resources set up by P. Mendès France placed researchers at the heart of the system[39].

After relinquishing the presidency of the Council, P. Mendès France's ideas contributed to making research a national cause. The *Conseil supérieur de la recherche* (the high council for research) had established a sort of assessment of the current situation, and evaluated the needs of research, formulating proposals in order to prepare the options of the IIIrd Plan (1957–1961). His successor, Edgar Faure, delegated these questions to others. However, P. Mendès France continued to vigorously defend that agenda, as evidenced by the holding of conferences in Caen, Grenoble and Dakar[40], with the participation of university students, researchers, politicians, civil servants and industrialists. Although the CNRS was not a significant player in these major conferences for the structuring of research in France[34], the analyses produced circulated, so it was difficult for policy not to take notice of the lacks and voids which touched on certain disciplines including natural substances chemistry… Also, the decision to set up a Natural Substances Chemistry Institute, dating from the mid-1950s, fits in wholly with this movement of P. Mendès France's. We shall come back to this point later on.

From the start of the 1950s, the directors of the CNRS requested regular increases in their budget, justified by an agenda to support the center's orientations and development. However, their wish to develop a five-year plan for research did not come to fruition[32]. Furthermore, the creation of the arsenal of committees at the start of the Fifth Republic, with the *Délégation générale à la Recherche scientifique et technique* [General Delegation on Scientific and Technical Research] (1961), under the Prime Minister's authority, definitively stripped the CNRS of any hope of setting a national policy

e The first had been for Irène Joliot-Curie during the time of the *Front populaire*.

for academic research in France. However, it retained the role of a referential authority in the structuring of the arena of French research, serving as an anchor point for the other organizations evolving by comparison, by default or in addition. Alongside the CEA, the CNRS was the largest research organization, with extensive and stable budgets at its disposal, although those budgets were yearly. Unanimously, though, the directors of the CNRS considered that failure to be the death of the CNRS' legitimate aim of coordinating all research done in France. The subject of confrontation within the scientific community, this difficulty in setting an agenda for research was not a temporary problem. It endured for as long as the politicians and the CNRS' directors failed to reach a clear position on that topic; the State's position regarding this question remained ambiguous for a very long time. In fact, developing a structured scientific policy for the whole of the CNRS became a major issue for the successive general directorates, to ensure the CNRS's incontestable authority on the French research scene, from the 1950s to the 2000s.

In the 1950s, France had around 12,000 researchers in public and parapublic establishments, distributed between 14 ministerial departments, heading around 100 organizations with over 1,500 laboratories, in addition to the private and industrial research centers[f]. The researchers' situation was as different as the places where they worked. Their professional statuses varied from one employer to the next. Industrial researchers benefited from the conventions existing in their sector of activities. Academic researchers enjoyed statuses similar to those of public functionaries (1946)[g] and could be assigned

---

f Report of the *Conseil scientifique et du progrès technique*, *La recherche scientifique et le progrès technique*, report to the president of the *Conseil des ministres et au commissaire au Plan*, Paris 1957, *Centre des Archives contemporaines de Fontainebleau*, 92 0547/1(IIIe Plan), p. 9.

g *Statut général des fonctionnaires* (general status of civil servants) adopted by the *Assemblée nationale* drafting the Constitution, written into law on 19 October 1946, replaced by the order of 4 February 1959. See *Code de la fonction publique commenté*, 4th ed., Paris, Dalloz, 2005, p. 3. The status, which pertained only to State-employed civil servants, set up the judicial framework for the pay system, the organization of careers within the different levels of qualification, the institution of a specific social-security regime and a new retirement scheme. That scheme was extended to apply to researchers in 1984. The principle of equality (article 6 of the 1789 *Déclaration des droits de l'homme et du citoyen* [Declaration of the Rights of

to research on more or less a full-time basis, whilst researchers at public enterprises and at the CEA, for example, held a status closer to that of industrial researchers. The other research organizations had implemented recruitment policies and working conditions which varied on the basis of their supervising authority (the Ministries of Health, Agriculture, P&T etc.). The researchers at the CNRS and the *Institut national d'hygiène* (which would become Inserm) were fellows of their institution and were remunerated in accordance with the public work payscale. One never knew, though, from one year to the next, whether one could recruit, keep existing personnel and continue to work in the absence of a medium-term agenda. Indeed, the budgets for these two organizations were re-examined each year. Thus, "mobility only [existed] insofar as those concerned, and particularly the best among them, escape[d] for themselves to find more favorable situations (…)", i.e. to a university and, in the case of chemists, also into industry[h].

The eight decrees published in 1959 specified the attributions of the CNRS, particularly as compared to those of Général de Gaulle's planning and management organizations[i,34]. The DGRST was led by the *Comité consultatif de la recherche scientifique et technique* (Scientific and Technical Consultive Board) a ministry before its time; it was these two organizations that were in charge of the distribution of the civil research budgets[36]. At the beginning, of the 1960s, the State, not the CNRS, defined a programmed scientific policy, based on the Plan. Until the dawn of the 21st Century, the CNRS was placed in an ambiguous position. The State considering it to be the "flagship

Man and of the Citizen] virtues and talents is behind the rule, which stipulates that civil servants be recruited through a competitive process.

h *Report of the Conseil scientifique et du progrès technique*, *La recherche scientifique et le progrès technique*, *op. cit.*

i 1958 saw the creation of the *Comité interministériel de la recherche scientifique et technique*, and the *Comité consultatif de la recherche scientifique et technique*; in 1959, the following were founded: the *Comité de recherches spatiales*, the *Fonds de développement de la recherche scientifique* and the *comités d'études d'actions concertées*; 1961: the *Délégation générale de la recherche scientifique et technique*, and the promulgation of the program law on the *actions concertées coordonnées du Fonds de la Recherche Scientifique et Technique.*

of French research"[j] because its leaders and personnel worked to make it that way. However, on the other hand, that prerogative was increasingly hotly contested over time. The 1959 reorganization contributed to that state of mind because, while the CNRS no longer coordinated all research in France, it still had a permanent contract to carry out research projects of all types and analyze the scientific conditions for the government. In that sense, it remained a singular feature of the French research scene, slowly but surely becoming one more research establishment among so many others. At the request of the Director General, Jean Coulomb, the *Comité national* had to evaluate the center's future needs for each discipline. The document, which is commonly considered the center's first situation report, offers a snapshot of CNRS chemistry and the CNRS itself (see below).

Nonetheless, whilst the CNRS remained the most important of the French research hubs in terms of the number of employees and its budgets, or indeed the number of disciplines represented there, it was during this period that it started to turn in on itself. Thus, from then on, the *Comité national* ceased to evaluate all researchers working in France – even those partially funded by the center. From that point onward, it only evaluated CNRS personnel, confirming the demise of the center's national ambitions. This document was the first situation report, although it devoted less space to collective dynamics and strategy than to the state of affairs in each discipline. The 1959 text also clarified the status of CNRS researchers; it drew a distinction between university lecturers and professors and researchers (in French *attaché*, *chargé de recherche* for researcher, and *maître et directeur de recherche* for senior researcher), offered the possibility of pursuing a career as a researcher, recognizing the principle of the full-time researcher, as in the industrial sphere.

Later on, precisely because of this ambiguous relationship with the State, the CNRS tried to preserve its management role of French research, although the ministry controlled it. This was possible by virtue of the political principle, which was essentially to make no clear

j Expression borrowed from Bernard Larouturou, Directeur Général of the CNRS (dismissed by Minister Goulard on 14 January 2006), letter to CNRS personnel, 17 January 2006.

decisions and publish no medium-term strategic vision. The arrangement endured. As a matter of fact, one observation was inevitable: the CNRS was neither a research establishment independent of patronage, nor the driving force behind French research which its founding fathers had intended it to become.

2.1.2. *From pragmatism to 1979 reform*

Nonetheless, whilst the CNRS was able to develop into a major center for scientific research, doubtless because of this hybrid situation in which it found itself, lending it a certain degree of autonomy, the center was, in fact, a very interesting arena for experimentation with research management, at least before its structures became more rigid, in the 1990s, influenced by the major international (especially European) research agencies. The center saw the development of "RCPs" – *recherches coopératives sur programme* [structured cooperative research] (1963) to address specific questions; and ATPs – *actions thématiques programmées* [planned thematic actions] (1965) to support cross-cutting research over a limited time-period. In 1964, the *laboratoires associés* (associated laboratories) were set up, followed by the *laboratoires mixtes* (joint laboratories) linking university and CNRS, continuing with the creation of the *laboratoires propres* (intramural laboratories entirely funded by the CNRS) and *instituts* (even more important structures which were on an intermediary scale between the center and the laboratory). These evolutions were accompanied by an increase in administrative staff numbers and size, introducing additional complexity and rigidity into the system. In 1966, the CNRS set up scientific departments instituting "sectorialization" or territorialization of research. The CNRS had retained a measure of independence in relation to the nation's general scientific policy, supporting and developing research in promising sectors, with relatively flexible tools, whilst heeding the major decisions and national guidelines such as interdisciplinary programs.

This evolution was approved by the 1979 decree reorganizing the CNRS. However, this new reform was perceived as being an interference with the center's autonomy from the world of university, whether because of the influence of the Universities Minister or of the university personnel appointed to evaluate research at the CNRS, even though the teaching staff and their teaching were not evaluated[k]. The Bernard report in 1973[1], which pointed out that a third of the budget allocated for research at the CNRS served no scientific policy, was no stranger to this evolution. However, the reform, whose aim was to essentially alter the structure – reorganizing the governing body, redefining the role and purposes of the *comité national de la recherche* – did not touch on the core problem. The CNRS retained the double heritage it had at its beginnings: carrying out research in all sectors (particularly those not covered by the universities), financing university research and, as far as other research centers accepted it, leading French research at least by default.

2.1.3. *From the "Assises de la recherche" of 1981–1982 to the 2000s*

In 1981, following François Mitterrand's election to the French presidency, the *Assises de la recherche* (national conferences on the research situation) were organized, being held in 1981–1982, leading to the "*Loi d'orientation et de programmation de la Recherche*" (Research Guideline Law). The CNRS was no longer under the control of the Ministry of National Education, but instead under that of the ministries combining research and industry. It became an *Etablissement public à caractère scientifique et technique* (national public scientific and technical establishment) in principle validating the center's independence and its missions. Besides those pertaining to research itself, these missions again included the analysis of the national and international situation for strategic and programmatic goals. At the highest level of the State, the CNRS' responsibility in national and innovation processes was reaffirmed – a principle which had already been present in the 1979 reform, but extended now to all

k By way of example, the minister Alice Saunier-Séïté, a university academic, opposed the integration of the INRIA (*Institut national de la recherche en informatique et en automatique*) in 1978 so as not to expand the CNRS' boundaries. Scientific logic played little part in that decision.

1 Archives, CNRS 940035-3.

research. In addition, the prospective stemmed once more from its missions. Research staff enjoyed a status equivalent to that of higher education staff. This was intended to create real mobility, to open up the CNRS to university lecturers and professors but also doctoral candidates trained in the universities, and conversely, send researchers to university. Thereafter, the history of the CNRS has fairly closely mirrored that of the State which, since the mid-1980s, has had the constant aim to disengage with public issues. However, the State has great difficulty accepting change whatever the sector in question (research, teaching, fiscal matters, etc.). Thus, in 1986 there was a heated debate concerning the CNRS: Minister Alain Devaquet opposing the proposal of Yves Durand and Jean Foyer, who wanted to dismantle the CNRS in order to reform the teaching/research system.

To respond to the criticisms and to compete with the national and international issues, the CNRS developed a "strategic approach". It was based on a scientific policy, an evaluation of research, a development of partnerships in particular with industrialists, a strengthening of the regional hubs and increased involvement in the construction of a European research effort. Nevertheless, there were numerous criticisms because the performance indicators in terms of research and innovation were unfavorable for France in comparison to the results obtained by similar world powers. Thus, between 1998 and the mid-2000s, there was a succession of reform plans. The State maintained its uncertain relations with the CNRS, oscillating between interfering, as shown by the rapid turnover of directors general in the top office, all aware of the urgency of the situation, and respecting the institution's autonomy. In 2000, a new decree established the Board of Trustees – which had, in fact, existed prior to 1979 – directed by a president with an increased power and autonomy. From then on, it was the Board which was to take on the responsibilities and follow the instructions decided upon by the administrative council, but the Director General retained his/her prerogatives. The State could not decide between administration and entrepreneurial-type government, which some deemed to be more responsive and therefore more appropriate for dealing with new scientific and technological issues. These hesitations reflected the government's vacillating scientific policy, which led to a significant increase in the size of the administrative apparatus. Managing the CNRS in a robotic, mechanical manner, this body became the State's most effective tool, applying decrees and other official texts, sometimes to the detriment of the scientific logic itself.

In 2002, a multi-year action agreement was signed for the first time. In the wake of the signing, Bernard Larrouturou, the DG, attempted to implement his own project for change, whilst the State, embodied by the minister in charge, was doing its utmost to establish a line which would serve as a reference point in terms of national scientific policy in a difficult European context. From 1998 until the mid-2000s, there was a succession of think tanks aiming to reform the organization, which was still one of the major players in French research. Although this was not explicitly called for, these think tanks operated with a relative degree of continuity, with certain people having participated in the different change exercises. *A priori*, the various reports constituted a reasonably coherent whole in the analysis of the problems, although the groups focused on different objectives. Their conclusions pointed out that over the past two decades, the State's commitments had been unreliable; the CNRS, as an institution, as yet had a fairly uninspiring identity; researchers identified more closely with their own laboratories or with their host institutions (universities or *Grandes écoles*). In terms of budget, the CNRS' identity as the main holder of the purse strings was very real; however, the strategy seemed to be an empty dressing, with no real objective or content; Europe was perceived as a distant entity, and researchers were not particularly interested in constructing a European research area. These were the problems the center was suffering at the dawn of the 21st Century.

The *Institut de chimie des substances naturelles* (ICSN) whose creation and management were entrusted to two directors (see discussion below), was a noteworthy player in this broad sketch of the CNRS' history. As the first dedicated natural substances chemistry institute – whilst it was, from the word "Go!", a laboratory belonging to the CNRS itself – the Ministry for Research often took a direct interest in its activities.

2.2. Chemistry at the CNRS[m]

State interference in scientific policy, both at the global (macro) and local (micro) levels, is not a new phenomenon, and often irregular[41], so the continuity of that involvement in the structuring and organization of scientific activities is not easy to decrypt[33]. Chemistry offers an excellent illustration of this[7,8]. Benefiting from the State's decisions to act, such as those of provincial authorities, there was a small network of institutions concerned with teaching and research. Chemistry was taught at university, in engineering schools and technical colleges – both national and municipal[42] – whilst public and private, academic and industrial research centers had, for quite a while, been in existence[43]. Far from being negligible, this set of institutions was highly disparate. The most innovative teaching did not come from the universities. Proof of this lies in the fact that it was industrial actors who financed the chair in mineral chemistry in Paris in 1924[43]. Furthermore, the research carried out in mineral or organic chemistry included very few modern theories, which were developed in English-speaking universities. Thus, industrialists were heavily involved in the development of chemistry schools both in Paris and outside of it, and therefore in applied research.

On the eve of the Second World War, the three main university cities in France where fundamental chemistry research was being done were Paris (the ENS, the *Collège de France*, the *Laboratoire de Chimie Physique* at the *Faculté des Sciences*, the *Institut du radium* founded in 1909 by Marie Curie, with the help of the *Faculté des Sciences* and the *Institut Pasteur*), Nancy and Strasbourg (including, amongst others, the Charles Sadron laboratory)[44]. Biological

m Besides the archives consulted, this section is based on the work carried out by historians for the 50th anniversary of the CNRS, particularly the interviews and those of the Committee on the history of the CNRS. In addition, thanks go to Virginie Durand, researching engineer at SIRICE, for collating the archives of the AN in Fontainebleau and Gif-sur-Yvette, contributing to *Histoire documentaire du CNRS*, 3 t., Paris, CNRS éditions 2005–2009.

chemistry, for its part, was only taught in Paris and Lyon (2 chairs)[21], while the most wide-reaching research was being conducted at the *Institut de biologie physico-chimique* (IBPC) [Institute of Physico-chemical Biology] in Paris, financed by the Rothschild Foundation from 1928 onwards, and led by Georges Urbain (a chemist), Jean Perrin (a physicist) and André Mayer (a biologist)[45]. University research in the domain of natural substances was done in departments whose primary concerns were not the study of natural substances. The *Faculté de Pharmacie*, in Paris, was one of the rare places where they could be studied, particularly thanks to the work of Professor Marcel Delépine (1871–1965)[n]. Thus, the domain of interest to us was rather disadvantaged; this observation led Edgar Lederer (who was one of the first two directors of the ICSN, researcher at the IBPC at that time – see below) to say that France was poorly endowed in this area. In line with the situation in the 19th Century, there were precious few significant academic research centers in chemistry before the Second World War, although some of those few were performing very high-level research. There was a major gap between the quality of fundamental research, which was innovative, and university teaching, which was usually rather conservative[o].

In 1939, the new CNRS had absorbed the *Caisse Nationale de la Recherche Scientifique* (set up in 1935) and the *Conseil Supérieur de la Recherche Scientifique*, with Jean Perrin at its head[p]. The CNRS

n Pharmacist, Professor at the *École supérieure de pharmacie*, he was elected Professor at the *Collège de France*, where he held the chair in organic chemistry from 1930 to 1941, and at the *Académie des sciences* in 1930. He received the CNRS' gold medal in 1962. He supervised the thesis of M.-M. Janot: one of the first directors of the ICSN.

o Dominique Pestre, in *Physique et physiciens en France (1918–1940)*, Paris, 1985, made the same observation for that discipline.

p The forefather of the *Comité national de la recherche scientifique*, divided into 14 discipline-specific sections, helped the university professors to choose scholarship candidates, their promotions and the distribution of credits between the laboratories; it would have had to coordinate all research bodies in France. Archives G 940035-23 Gif-sur-Yvette, PV of the CA of the CNRS, 1940–2000.

was structured into two sections: the CNRSA (set up in 1938) under the leadership of Henri Longchambon became the "Applied Research" section of the new organization, and the "Fundamental/Pure Research" section, headed by Henri Laugier. Thus, the CNRS covered the whole spectrum of research activity. What became of chemistry under the auspices of the new organization?

From the start of the Second World War to 1944, the archives mention different centers with an obvious applied-research orientation. These were the *Laboratoire des traitements chimiques* (chemical treatment laboratory) in Thiais, the *Laboratoire des peintures et vernis* (paint and varnish research laboratory) headed by M. Vila, the *Laboratoire des très basses temperatures* (very low temperature research unit) under the leadership of A. Cotton, and M. Lainé's *Station du froid* (cold station) on the Bellevue estate in Meudon. In 1941, in Marseille, the *Centre de recherches scientifiques, industrielles et maritimes* (center for scientific, industrial and maritime research) was set up[q]. In 1944, the *Laboratoire des ultra-réfractaires* (ultra-refractory laboratory) – under the auspices of the *Comité d'organisation de la verrerie* (glassmaking organization committee), the *Laboratoire des ultra-hautes pressions* (ultra-high-pressure laboratory), the *Laboratoire du feu* (fire laboratory) and the *Laboratoire des corps gras* (fatty substances laboratory) operated as best they could[r]. In 1945, the CNRS set up the *Centre de recherche de physique et de chimie nucléaires appliqué* (research center for physics and nuclear chemistry applied to biology) in Strasbourg.

Besides the consequences of the Second World War for the country, it is worth bearing in mind the complexity of the landscape of science in France at the end of the war, with certain ministries having developed their own research center (see above). Looking at the whole of the period of interest to us, and applying the definition, which is certainly recent (1980), of chemistry given by Jean-Marie Lehn – "chemistry tells people about matter and its transformations, how to

q Archives G 940035-23 Gif-sur-Yvette.
r PV of the CA, 12 October 1943.

act on it, modify it and invent new manifestations of it…"[46] – we can understand that in spite of the indigence of the resources for the whole of French research in the wake of the Second World War, the successive leaders of the CNRS lent their support to that discipline, which promised to contribute first to the country's reconstruction, and then to its development, in spite of the oversights of the Plan's first commissioners.

Between 1944 and November 1945, under the headship of Frédéric Joliot-Curie[s], the CNRS established an organization to deploy a strategy to conduct its agenda of reorganizing research in France. The Steering committee, composed of over 400 members, became the *comité national de la recherche scientifique*. It included 65 chemists out of the 280 representatives of the exact sciences[t]. It was organized into 29 sections, four of which were devoted to chemistry: physical, mineral, organic and biological chemistry. Fifteen members of the *comité national de la recherche* – including four chemists: Georges Dupont[u,47], Eugène Aubel[v], Georges Champetier[w]

s A partisan of engaged research in cooperation with industry, he wanted to turn the CNRS into a research commission.

t *Rapport d'acitivité*, 1944–1945. .

u 1884–1958, a student of the *Ecole Normale Supérieure*, awarded a doctorate of sciences in 1912, lecturer and then Professor at Bordeaux University in 1925, chemistry Professor at the ENS. Physico-chemist, head of the fundamental research laboratories, he set up and also directed applied-research centers.

v 1884–1975, a chemical engineer from the city of Paris, awarded a doctorate of sciences in 1922. He was handed the headship of the physico-chemical biology department at the IBPC in 1928; in 1934 he became lecturer and then, in 1946, became Professor of biological chemistry at the Sorbonne. His research focused on anaerobic bacteria and on amino and fatty acids. A member of the *Parti communiste français* (PCF) he was also a member of the national council of the peace movement.

w 1905–1980, a chemical engineer having graduated from the *Ecole supérieure de physique chimie industrielle* (ESPCI) in Paris, specializing in macromolecules both in academia and in the industrial domain. Following his early research at the Sorbonne, in 1928 he became assistant to Georges Urbain at the IBPC. Introducing macromolecular chemistry in France, he was the first holder of the chair in macromolecular chemistry created in France at the Sorbonne, in 1953. He was deputy director general of the CNRS, and head of chemistry from 1951 to 1956. Besides the ICSN, under his guidance and that of Charles Sadron, the *Strasbourg Centre de recherche sur les macromolécules* was set up. He created and, from 1956 to 1973, ran the *Laboratoire de chimie macromoléculaire* (macromolecular chemistry laboratory)

and Marcel Mathieu[x,48] – made up the CNRS board of directors; in November 1945, there were still three chemists[y]. The head of the CNRS, Joliot-Curie, the president of the board of directors, was assisted by a deputy director: first the chemist Charles Dupont, then replaced by the biologist Georges Teissier[z,34]. G. Dupont and G. Champetier[47] had worked together under the Occupation, whilst E. Aubel and M. Mathieu were members of the PCF like F. Joliot-Curie. In addition, G. Champetier, E. Aubel and M. Mathieu had worked at the IBPC[49]. It is worth noting the wise balance that prevailed, both from a political and a disciplinary point of view, between two conceptions: those of the partisans of an engaged science, cooperating with industry, and those of the advocates of a pure science, with the CNRS supporting disciplines which were not well represented at university. However, the opposition F. Joliot-Curie encountered resulted mainly from university staff, irritated by being kept at arm's length in the management of the CNRS and adversaries of his pragmatic management based on cooperation between science and industry: "If

at the *Faculté des Sciences* in Paris, associated with the CNRS. Trained at an engineering school, he supported the development of relations between universities and industry, contributing to the operation of structures such as the *Institut textile de France*, the *Institut des corps gras* and the *Fondation française pour la nutrition*. He headed the concerted action committee on "Macromolecular Chemistry" at the DGRST from 1963 to 1972. Elected as a member of the *Académie des sciences* in 1960, he became the first President of the *Groupe français d'études et d'applications des polymères* in 1970.

x 18??–19??, Head of the service at the *Laboratoire des services chimiques de l'État*, a former student of Georges Urbain, member of the general chemistry laboratory at the Sorbonne, close to F. Joliot. He was also secretary of *Jeune Science* (an association for the promotion of science), one of the heads of the *Union nationale des ingénieurs et des techniciens* (UNITEC, a union) and a member of the PCF.

y Order no. 45-2632, 2 November 1945, *Journal Officiel*, 3 December 1945.

z 1900–1972, a zoologist and biologist, an *École Normale Supérieure* student awarded a doctorate in science in 1931, he was, in turn, a "*agrégé préparateur*", at the ENS (1924–1928), work supervisor, lecturer and Professor at the *Faculté des Sciences* in Paris. He was also head of the *Station Biologique* in Roscoff and then the *Laboratoire de génétique évolutive* (evolutionary genetics laboratory) at the CNRS in Gif-sur-Yvette. From 1946 to 1950, he was DG of CNRS. He was a member of the PCF, and was opposed to any cooperation with industrialists.

our laboratories are impoverished, it is because they do not have a close enough relation with industry", he said[aa,50]. Chemistry at the CNRS was, in a manner of speaking, representative of Liberated France, where political oppositions corresponded to the various strategies to control the country's reconstruction. The tension between "pro- and anti-applicable research" represented a dividing line which, in certain cases, would constitute a demarcation line in some departments of the CNRS. This heritage had an impact in the genesis of the ICSN. This balance or tension, as the case may be, in "conceiving" the future of research, served as a backdrop for the evolution of the ICSN, at least up until the 1980s.

Continuing to look at the involvement of the CNRS in the carrying out of research, this desire to support new or marginal scientific fields first manifested itself in the scientific boards of the *comité national de la recherche scientifique* which, in chemistry, placed two neighboring subdisciplines on a level: physical chemistry and biological chemistry, which both had poor representation at the universities. These boards were helped in terms of the direction they took and in terms of their choices by the work of individual study commissions, brought together to achieve a specific objective. Out of the thirty-odd commissions existing in 1945, ten were dedicated to chemistry. Their work led to the majority of the creations of *laboratoires propres* (intramural laboratories, fully funded and managed by the CNRS, others are joint laboratories funded and managed in partnership with universities, research organizations and/ or industries). Unfortunately, this organization never evolved again until 1966. Without going into detail, what seemed promising in 1945 actually turned out not to be very dynamic after that[49]. The lack of young men, the competition between the leading players for the headship of the new laboratories, added to the slow progress of industrial chemistry, undoubtedly account for the discipline's lackluster position within the academic landscape[49].

aa Archives AN 80-284, l. 114, cited by J.F. Picard, in "La longue marche vers le CNRS", *op. cit.*

Furthermore, the happenings at the CNRS mirrored the events in the universities, where few new chairs were created, and few lecturers were promoted to professorships[bb]. A certain tension reigned between two constraints which, in the eyes of some at the time, became antagonistic: to run the chemistry laboratories at the CNRS, managers were looking mainly for men with links to industry, whilst others essentially wanted to promote "pure" research. G. Teissier, a communist belonging to the latter circle of people, was opposed to links with industry[51]. However, the Cold War added further tension, and the general atmosphere became even more divided. Chemists, some of whom belonging to the new disciplines and being partisans of cooperative science, were ill received in court, especially if they were also adherents to or members of the PCF. These questions of political loyalties became very significant, as G. Teissier, the communist, was replaced by Gaston Dupouy[cc] as head of the CNRS. In actual fact, two worlds collided: the "old" world, of the university as the heart of the classic disciplines, operating in a clerical fashion, and the "modern" world, of research centers, borderline disciplines, more flexible and pragmatic in terms of its operation.

From the very beginning, the new DG paid particular attention to disciplines which were poorly represented in the universities. Thus, intramural laboratories were set up to work on physical chemistry and biological chemistry between 1950 and 1966, whilst the reports from the period[dd] complained of "the lack of people capable of properly running the laboratories" in French biochemistry[34, 49]. G. Champetier played a particular role as head of chemistry at the CNRS during those years, working with politicians from the research commission for the 2nd Modernization and Equipment Plan, of which he was a member

bb This could account for E. Lederer's appointment of Professor without a chair… see below.

cc A physicist, and Director of the CNRS from 1950 to 1957 – see bibliographical note by Gaston Dupouy, *Comité pour l'histoire du CNRS*: http://www.cnrs.fr/ComiHistoCNRS/spip.php?article15.

dd Archives G 990001-64 Gif-sur-Yvette. CNRS archives, MRT, bundle 102, cited by Micheline Charpentier-Morize.

(1953), aiming to bring university and industry closer together. His desire to support this type of research indubitably spearheaded the ICSN's creation and destiny. His commitment should also be stressed as the DGRST seemingly paid little attention, from then on, to natural substances chemistry – at least in the 3rd and 4th Plans. Was it then considered that with the ICSN, the State would fulfill the contract? Without a doubt.

In 1961, the CNRS had 19 intramural chemistry laboratories – two thirds of which had been set up in Île-de-France; that number would rise to 25. From 1966, they were overseen by 6 sections of the *Comité national de la recherche*. The same year, the creation of the status of associate laboratory changed the face of research in France; these new university laboratories enjoyed the support of the CNRS in terms of staff and financing, and further expanded the reach of the discipline, helping to develop sub-disciplines in the universities. Natural substances chemistry was not to be outdone, with the ICSN training a number of chemists who joined the science faculties of the developing universities[52]. In addition, 1966 marked the start of the "sectorialization" of scientific policy[53] which, through the 1979 decrees[ee] reorganizing the CNRS, led to the creation of scientific departments. From that point on, the work of the DG was assisted by directors skilled in their own disciplinary field, thus leading to the emergence of sub-disciplines. This creation of the department, which became the *Institut de chimie* (INC) [Institute of Chemistry] on 1 January 2009, was considered by some to be a transitional step in the State's scientific policies, whilst others viewed it as an attempt to organize the scientific community.

In 1971, the CNRS had 23 intramural laboratories for chemistry and 31 associate CNRS/university laboratories; in 1996, there were 22 *unités propres de recherche* (UPRs) [intramural research units] and

ee Decrees no. 79-778, no. 79-779, no. 79–780. The CNRS is now led by a Director General, assisted by a Secretary General, scientific directors and scientific advisors.

33 *unités mixtes de recherche* (UMRs) [joint research units]. In 2001, the chemical sciences department had 16 UPRs, 13 of which had been running for over 15 years, and 185 UMRs. In 2002, the chemical sciences department employed around 3,500 people – of all different statuses – including 1,973 researchers.

From the Liberation of occupied France until the 2000s, the CNRS provided chemistry with a structure – the department having become an institute – whose form of organization was only determined over the course of time, with priority having been given to the development of fundamental research structures, with or without the aim of applicability, in the form of intramural or joint laboratories, which helped the spread of new sub-disciplines or borderline disciplines. By facilitating/supporting partnerships with industry, almost from the get-go, the CNRS built a bridge between "its" academic chemistry and the economic and social world, in accordance with the wishes of the heads of the CNRS when the center was deployed after the Second World War. Through the development of such collaborations with all the universities, the science produced by the CNRS actually invigorated the whole of the education system. It is now time to recount the ICSN's part in this story.

2.3 The ICSN: a place for discovery (from 1955 to the 2000s)

Throughout this period, chemistry at the CNRS was therefore practiced at two main types of unit: intramural and joint laboratories; the *Institut de chimie des substances naturelles* belongs to the first category. The French system of higher education and research is difficult to comprehend for an observer on the outside looking in, particularly when we also include the *actions programmées* (planned actions) in the equation. The question which springs to mind is: why was that institute not set up as part of a university? Whilst this is a legitimate question, it is a theoretical one, because to ask it, one has to ignore the political, social and academic context which led to its founding. The general conditions were difficult from a material point of view – the country's reconstruction was not yet complete – and an intellectual one – in addition to the scientific retardation due to the war, there were political rivalries caused by it as well. Thus, the history of chemistry at the CNRS and, *a fortiori*, that of the ICSN, beyond the history of the structures and their organizations which can be gleaned from consulting the archives, necessitates an analysis of the role played by each of the actors, which is the only way to gain an understanding of the genesis and evolution of the institutions[ff,49].

Thus, for the first heads of chemistry at the CNRS, there was no question about the purpose or applicability of the majority of the work being done – the very nature of the lists of CNRS laboratories mentioned above speaks for itself. However, in the view of certain scientists, including G. Teissier – DG of the CNRS from 1946 to 1950 – it was crucial to define areas where science alone – pure science, science for the sake of science – reigned, keeping it apart from applications and therefore from the world of industry. For others, such as G. Champetier, to distinguish between science and its applications could damage "the development of French science"[gg]. In the eyes of this latter group, in accordance with the country's five-year plan, it was important to organize collaborative relationships. It is difficult to explain this dichotomous tension, which, at times, was almost a "brother against brother" conflict. One possible hypothesis is that the scientists, having experienced difficult professional conditions until the CNRS' creation in 1939, viewed the center as their own – as a space for unconstrained research, without any material boundaries, and above all, free of any finalized, applicable objectives. The

ff The testimony gathered by Micheline Charpentier-Morize during the work conducted in 1989 for the CNRS' 50th anniversary is all the more important since the archive had not been systematically maintained. See her article, n° 49 in this book's bibliography.

gg Georges Champetier, L'État et la science, la recherche et l'enseignement scientifique en France, report to UNESCO on 14 August 1952.

creations of specialized, purpose-specific research centers during the Second World War seemed to be attempts to exploit research both for political and financial purposes. Succinctly put, there were already enough places to practice research with specific goals; thus, targeted research would no longer have been perceived as a priority by the community of researchers who were still, at that time, recipients of grants from the CNRS. That researcher status, which had to be renewed each year, undoubtedly contributed to their desire for independence, as it would have been felt that their days (in their positions) were numbered.

Next, the structuring of the communities around political positions of opposition to "big capital" could offer another explanation. In his autobiography, E. Lederer recalls the disagreement that he had with G. Teissier on this point, regarding his assistant Daniel Mercier who, in addition to his status as a technician at the CNRS, had contracts with industry[51,21]. The DG of the CNRS, G. Tessier, obtained the resignation of the technician, who rejoined the CNRS in 1960. E. Lederer, who also had contracts with industry, reports that G. Teissier told him "You are a communist; you should never have had connections with industry"; following this incident, his promotion was blocked and he received a reprimand. After G. Teissier's departure, these sanctions were reversed by G. Champetier, with the agreement of G. Dupouy, the new DG. To gain an idea of the extent of that tension, in addition to the national problems mentioned above, we need to take account of the impact of the Hiroshima and Nagasaki bombings on the different scientific communities. Thus, in 1950, F. Joliot-Curie, as a member of the World Peace Council, along with others, launched the Stockholm Appeal, calling for an absolute ban on all nuclear weapons; this sentiment was echoed by the Pugwash movement from 1957 onwards. Scientists – particularly physicists and chemists – became extremely distrustful in terms of the applicability of their results and the real-world exploitation of their work, whilst others suffered a sort of opprobrium, as was the case in the DuPont de Nemours conglomerate based in the United States[54]. The applicability of science, its real-world utility, divided the scientific community, complicating the legacy left by the Occupation, without any seeming correlation between the various commitments or positions of principle.

Whilst we may dispute the validity of these hypotheses, it can be seen that this state of mind, where the proponents of "pure", dispassionate science were at odds with the partisans of fundamental but "useful" science, created a particular atmosphere that endured up until the early 1980s, if not even longer[hh]. However, at the same time, the definition of the domains of fundamental science and applied science was blurred by the evolution of the circulation of knowledge, as fundamental science was ultimately mobilized on all fronts. This phenomenon, which is sometime known as "big science", led physicist Yves Farge[ii] to say that "there is as much science in a drinks can as there is in an airbus or a medication", pointing out that in his view, that had been the case since at least the 1950s[jj]. Thus, Science Studies facilitated a new understanding of the processes, by advancing the idea of "techno-sciences". The exhaustive approach to the circulation of knowledge, people and practices engendered by that idea accounted for the breakdown of the boundaries between pure and applied sciences, between academic and industrial research[55,56,57]. Although the idea of pure and fundamental science was not undermined, the disciplines within it melded into a broader ensemble, where the boundaries between pure science and applied science had disappeared in favor of mutual complementarity. The expression of

hh Thus, the chemist Jacqueline Belloni, *directrice de recherche émérite* (emeritus senior researcher) at the CNRS, *Laboratoire de chimie physique* (Physical Chemistry Laboratory), Université de Paris-Sud Orsay, began her career in 1957 as a research intern at the CNRS, and defended her State Doctorate in 1961. Since then, she has regularly worked with Kodak and Fuji, in view of her discoveries. However, when she retired, one of the heads of the CNRS told her that she had not had as illustrious an academic career as she would have been expected to have, simply because of her regular scientific relations with industrialists. Interview with Jacqueline Belloni – Muriel Le Roux, 27 May 2005 in Paris.

ii Physicist, founder and director of the LURE in Orsay, he was the head of R&D at Pechiney before returning to the CNRS as an adviser (1998–2000) to the DG Catherine Bréchignac, and becoming Vice-President of the *Académie des technologies*.

jj Interview with Yves Farge – Muriel Le Roux, 27 May 2005.

that tension between pure and applicable science, between academic research and industrial research, and the emergence of these new disciplines set the pace of life at the ICSN, from its opening right up to the present date. In this context, the history of the ICSN would serve as an exemplary case study in more than one area.

For reasons of control of scientific and management policy, by law, the intramural laboratories were directly dependent on the directorate general of the CNRS and on the board of directors; thus, there was a "natural proximity" which existed between those proprietary laboratories and the leaders of the center, but also between the heads of those laboratories and the world of politics. Hence, G. Champetier – who, as we have seen, was head of chemistry at the CNRS in the 1950s – left the legacy of very personal direction[49]. However, as a supporter of usable research, in connection with the country's needs and industry, he expressed regret at the fact that such relations were "often clandestine" in France[kk].

As the sections of the national committee played no part in matters of this type, it was at G. Champetier's urging, with the support of the DG of the CNRS Gaston Dupouy, who shared his desire for the CNRS to support "new disciplines which do not fall within the conventional curriculum at universities"[ll], that the creation of the ICSN was tabled in December 1953[mm]. It was not until 1955, though, that in line with these two men's suggestion the CNRS board of directors finally decided to set up the ICSN. Edgar Lederer had, in fact, expressed the same necessity a year earlier[58, nn].

kk *Réunion de la 6e sous-commission* (meeting of the 6th sub-commission), "Développement et efficacité", 7 April 1954, MRT archives, CNRS, bundle 103, cited by M. Charpentier-Morize.

ll Biographical notice by Gaston Dupouy, *Comité pour l'histoire du CNRS*, http://www.cnrs.fr/ComiHistoCNRS/spip.php?article15.

mm *Réunion du directoire* (meeting of the directorate), 1 December 1953, archives G850003 DG2 Gif-sur-Yvette; *ibid.*

nn The documents cited by Pierre Potier were in his office at Gif in 1995, when he wrote his paper for the 21st International Congress on the History of Pharmacy. They were broken up after his death in 2006. E. Lederer's letter is on the ICSN website: http://historique.icsn.cnrs-gif.fr/IMG/pdf/Necessite.pdf.

En communication

INSTITUT DE BIOLOGIE PHYSICO-CHIMIQUE
FONDATION EDMOND DE ROTHSCHILD
13, RUE PIERRE CURIE, PARIS-V°

Paris, le 26/5/1954

Sur l'opportunité de créer en France un Institut de Chimie organique et biologique consacré à la chimie des substances naturelles

Par un développement tout à fait particulier de la chimie organique en France, dont il n'y a pas lieu ici d'analyser les causes, les organiciens français se consacrent en grande majorité à des travaux théoriques ou de synthèse pure, délaissant ainsi l'immense champ de la chimie des substances naturelles où les chimistes des autres pays ont récolté des fruits si magnifiques. Il suffit de rappeler qu'à peu près tous les travaux qui ont conduit à l'isolement de nouvelles vitamines, de nouvelles hormones, de nouveaux antibiotiques, à la détermination de leur structure et finalement à leur synthèse, ont été effectués à l'étranger. (Angleterre, Suisse, USA, Allemagne). Le domaine si important de la chimie des stérols est également déserté par les chimistes français.

Les prix Nobel de Chain, Karrer, Kuhn, Reichstein, Robinson, Ruzicka, soulignent l'importance de ces travaux qui ont largement profité aux industries chimiques et pharmaceutiques de leurs pays respectifs. En France au contraire, l'industrie pharmaceutique doit le plus souvent se contenter d'acheter des licences étrangères.

Voici à titre d'illustration une petite statistique du nombre de travaux consacrés à l'isolement et à l'étude de la structure de substances naturelles, publiés au cours des six derniers mois dans les Bulletins des Sociétés Chimiques de cinq pays: *)

Bull. Soc. Chim. France: 9
Chemische Berichte: 20
Helv. Chimica Acta: 29
Journal of the Chemical Society: 51
Journal of the american Chem. Society: 67

Le retard de la France dans ce domaine est indiscutable; comment peut on y remédier? Il faut former des équipes de chercheurs, et pour cela créer des laboratoires consacrés spécialement à la chimie des substances organiques naturelles.

*) Nous n'avons pas inclu dans ce chiffre les travaux de [illegible], qui sont effectués en Suisse.

Ces laboratoires devraient recevoir tout l'équipement nécessaire, en particulier des installations de microanalyse quantitative, d'analyse spectrale comprenant des spectrographes pour l'ultraviolet et l'infrarouge, ... le tout formant un ensemble cohérent.

E. Lederer
Directeur de Recherches
au C.N.R.S

Figure 2.1. *Letter from Edgar Lederer*[oo]

On 20 May 1955, a decree opened up authorizations for programs at the CNRS, which, in the context of the equipment plan, decided to

oo "A vast majority of French organic chemists devote themselves to theoretical or pure synthesis work, leaving untouched the immense field of natural substances chemistry where chemists from other countries have gathered such marvellous fruit (…) France's shortfall in this domain is indisputable. How can it be remedied? We need to train teams of researchers, and in order to do so, we must set up laboratories devoted especially to natural product chemistry."

set up the ICSN in Gif-sur-Yvette. The directors of the CNRS had gained ground. The position held by E. Lederer was extremely well known and confirmed by different enquiries conducted nationally, notably by P. Mendès-France's supporters; all information confirmed the calamitous state of natural substances chemistry in France at the time. To pursue a serious career in natural substances chemistry, one needed either to emigrate – as did the first two directors of the ICSN, M.-M. Janot and E. Lederer – or practice covertly under the cover of another discipline, or be financed by a foundation. Along that line, the reports from the officers from the Rockefeller Foundation regularly visiting France leave no room for doubt[pp,45,59].

The foundation sought to involve itself in the creation of an institute in France which would be dedicated to natural substances chemistry, with a view to developing teaching and research in that discipline. Penicillin had recently been discovered[4]. Louis Rapkine[qq,60]

pp We would like to very warmly thank Pierre Verschueren, a doctoral candidate at IHMC, who, when in New York conducting his doctoral research, entitled: "Le savant, le patron, le chercheur. La fabrique du scientifique et le métier de physicien et de chimiste en France de 1945 à 1968", took the time to open up the 1954, 1955 and 1956 boxes, as well the files pertaining to E. Lederer, and to correspond with us to refine the analysis presented here.

qq A French biochemist of Russian origin (1904–1948), graduating in science from McGill University (Canada) in 1924, he came to the *Faculté des Sciences* in Paris in the fall to take the embryology and zoology classes. He worked at the *Collège de France*. He was taken on, in 1927, at the IBPC as an assistant, and became joint head of department in 1936. He undertook secondments in Cambridge and New York. In July 1936, Rapkine created the *Comité français pour l'accueil et l'organisation du travail des savants étrangers* (French Committee for hosting and organizing the work of foreign scholars). A year later, Henri Laugier, the head of the CNRS, entrusted him with an information mission in Britain on issues of biochemistry. In August 1940, he returned to New York, with H. Laugier, to enact a plan to rescue the French scientific elite, in collaboration with the Rockefeller Foundation. In December 1941, in the delegation from Free France to the UN in New York, he spearheaded a scientific bureau to obtain the participation of French scientists to the Allies' war effort. In August 1944, he brought together exiled French scientists in a French scientific mission in Great Britain, which he led. This mission was the first step towards their return to France and their active participation in reconstruction. In September 1945, he returned to the United States to negotiate with the Rockefeller Foundation on the attribution of funds for the CNRS. He obtained two allocations for a period of three years: one for laboratory equipment ($250,000), and the other for the organization of international conferences ($100,000). In 1946, the cellular chemistry service at the

should undoubtedly have been offered the opportunity to head up such a center. His premature demise in 1948 appears to have delayed that creation.[49] Thus, the associate director of the natural science division of the Rockefeller Foundation, Gerard R. Pommerat (holder of a doctorate in cytology, Harvard, 1940), based in New York, made annual trips to Europe between 1946 and 1962, always passing through Paris, and was interested by E. Lederer's work. He is cited as the French scientist with international influence in this domain, notably because, besides his work, he was supported by Claude Fromageot[rr], himself a "Rockefeller Foundation fellow". Whilst E. Lederer's closeness to the PCF may have made him *persona non grata* in the United States (to where he was banned from traveling), he was recognized for the quality of his work and his membership of a renowned international scientific network, making him absolutely indispensable for the development of biochemistry in France, particularly in the eyes of the American foundation.[ss,21] Why was he not named as the sole director at the head of the ICSN? There is no single answer to this question; there are, however, multiple hypotheses.

Institut Pasteur was created for L. Rapkine, where he finally returned to the work that had been interrupted so many times.

rr A French chemist (1899–1958), a member of the higher research council, of the *caisse nationale de la recherché scientifique*, holder of the chair in chemistry and head of the organic chemistry laboratory in Lyon, until in 1946, he was appointed to the *Faculté des Sciences*, holding the chair of biological chemistry and heading the biochemistry laboratory. Three times, he received a grant from the Rockefeller Foundation for secondments in Germany and the United States between 1928 and 1949. On the list of French scientists to be protected in 1940, he remained in France and hosted E. Lederer in Lyon, allowing him to work in spite of the laws prohibiting the employment of Jews, notably requesting an exemption in 1943. In addition, because the researchers at the CNRS were grantees, C. Fromageot wrote the reports so that, each year, E. Lederer's grants would be renewed. Their careers remained intertwined: E. Lederer followed him to Paris after the war. C. Fromageot hosted him in the fall of 1946 in his laboratory in Paris, when his protégé was also rejoining the IBPC. C. Fromageot was a genuine academic support for E. Lederer who, owing to the former's premature death, became his successor. Archives of the CNRS – CAC Fontainebleau, personal file of E. Lederer, consultable by dispensation. See French grantees, Rockefeller Fellowships, 1917–1970, List compiled by Ludovic Tournès. http://webext.pasteur.fr/archives/b-rockf.html.

ss Rockefeller Archives Center, Rockefeller Foundation Archives, Record group 12, Boxes 386–387.

Pierre Potier, in his text[58], mentions the nomination letters sent by Gaston Dupouy to Edgar Lederer and Maurice-Marie Janot (1903–1978)[tt], on 22 July 1955 without saying anything about this double nomination, which was fairly surprising in comparison to the norm for the CNRS' other intramural laboratories, whatever the discipline in question[uu]. From the archives in New York, it is plain to see that American patronage played a not-insignificant role in the setting up of the CNRS' intramural laboratories.

Thus, Boris Ephrussi[vv] personally enjoyed large subsidies from the Rockefeller Foundation, whilst the CNRS received funds for the creation of an institute of genetics on the new campus in Gif-sur-Yvette, which pre-dated that of the ICSN by several years. E. Lederer, rather than M.-M. Janot, is cited in these reports, but G. Dupouy, who was infuriated by the direction which the negotiations on the work to set up the institute of genetics had taken[61], was also very well acquainted personally with the American foundation, having benefitted from its support in the acquisition of a microscope when he was still at Toulouse. This obviously raises the question of how great an influence the American network had, not in terms of the appointments of French scientists to the leadership of innovative research centers, but in the vision held by the directors of the CNRS. G. Dupouy and G. Champetier were partisans of open science, of "science *à l'Americaine*", in an atmosphere where contrary aspirations clashed.

tt *Caisse nationale de la recherche scientifique* grantee between 1932 and 1937. Pharmacology graduate in 1926, receiver of a State doctorate in natural sciences in 1932 after having done a doctoral stay in Switzerland in Ruzicka future Nobel prize laboratory, a doctorate in medicine in 1950, after having been an assistant in 1926, and then lecturer in 1937, he became a professor, holding the chair in galenic pharmacy at the *Faculté de Pharmacie* in Paris from 1942 until 1974. Director of the ICSN with E. Lederer from 1955 to 1973, he was elected to the *Académie des sciences* in 1967. His work and that of his students, including Robert Goutarel and Pierre Potier, pertained mainly to the isolation, structural analysis, synthesis and study of the biological properties of plant-based natural products. The raw materials studied included several botanical families, such as the Apocynaceae, Loganiaceae, Rubiaceae, Cruciferae and Lamiaceae, usually harvested overseas.

uu On the question M. Le Roux asked many times, P. Potier always remained evasive, while the interviews and published memoires of E. Lederer are not always as accurate as they might appear: *op. cit.*

vv A French geneticist (1901–1979), who also began his career in France at the IBPC.

G. Dupouy and G. Champetier noted a lack and an urgent need in this sector, but the State's finances were limited. Lederer was the scientist who seemed the obvious choice. In his favor were the facts that he was a biochemist who was *au fait* with "the science being done today", conducting research on a topic which was barely treated in France, pragmatic by necessity – an Austrian Jew, he became a naturalized French citizen in 1939[21] – who had regularly worked for and with industry. He had all the prerequisites to benefit from the Rockefeller Foundation's support, particularly in terms of buying equipment, simply by virtue of the acclaim of his work; this was not insignificant for the patrons of the CNRS: while he was politically committed, E. Lederer's personal credibility was damaged in the United States. These positive criteria, which were recognized both in France and on the other side of the Atlantic, obviously did not make up for the shortcomings in his *curriculum vitae*. Against him, he had the fact that he did not come from a largely conservative academic circle in France, such as that of pharmacy or medicine. However, it was the *Faculté de Pharmacie* which took greatest interest in natural substances before the war. In addition, as a biochemist, he belonged to none of the scientific disciplines held in high regard in France[51], such as mathematics and physics taught in the *grandes écoles*. In a sub-discipline of chemistry (which, itself, was less prestigious than other fields), this biochemist had been able to forge a career from himself, like other specialists in "new" disciplines who came to France during that period, precisely because he was a biochemist. The milieu of chemistry – a hybrid between the academic and the industrial – was more open and, as yet, not heavily dominated by elite culture[ww]. However, to ensure the new center's future, its legitimacy, it was important to win the good graces of the "traditional" university world without upsetting what was already in place and working (Fromageot's chair, for example). Thus, the choice was limited. However, M.-M. Janot, a pharmacologist and doctor, holder of the chair in galenic pharmacy at the *Faculté de Pharmacie* in Paris,

ww G. Champetier offers a perfect illustration of this: his second-level studies were completed at the Lavoisier College. He took the entrance exam for the *École supérieure de physique et chimie industrielles de la Ville de Paris*, where he was received in 1922. He graduated from there in 1925, as a chemical engineer, before undertaking doctoral research at the Sorbonne.

practised this brand of chemistry. Weighing in his favor was the fact that he represented both the most academic and the most conservative circles of the time: the *Faculté de Pharmacie* and, thereby, the world of medicine.

This joint appointment of E. Lederer and M.-M. Janot to lead the ICSN was indubitably the result of reflections and compromises, and confirms G. Dupouy and G. Champetier's great vision and pragmatism. The principle of dual direction or codirection[xx] of the ICSN, which was to last until 1990, helped them circumvent the political antagonisms, the rivalries between the men, the social hierarchies generated by the older disciplines. They supported the emerging disciplinary fields and organized gateways between chemistry and biology, whilst allowing relations between the CNRS and industries to be woven. If economies of scale and the need to develop synergies between bordering fields were probably very important arguments, combining the university and research, maintaining the direction that the CNRS heads had set themselves by moving past the logics of opposition of the field of politics and that of academia accounts for the nomination of two so utterly different personalities as E. Lederer and M.-M. Janot. After all, was not the idea behind the ICSN to have an arena in which to make up France's lost ground in this area and send chemists to Stockholm[yy]? The naming of two directors brought together the best possible skills, a scientific reputation which could scarcely be disputed, and sufficient youth to have the time to develop and establish the new institute in the field of natural substances chemistry.

However, whilst it is apparent that the CNRS needed American support, it should by no means be forgotten that this limited the CNRS directors' power to act when a scientist received that support. For example, B. Ephrussi, who received huge sums from the Americans

xx E. Lederer, in his oral testimony, points out that there were two directors, while in his autobiography he uses the word "codirection", which is also the word found in the archives. The two men were on an equal footing. This needs to be taken into account, because it was not truly the case when D. Barton was named head of the ICSN. Potier compared his codirection with the Nobel Prize winner to the relation between an enzyme and its coenzyme – see below.

yy Interview PP – MLR, Maison de la chimie, Paris, 13 March 2001.

for the *Institut de Gif* (genetics institute) understood that he should be allowed to spend the money as he wished. That created tensions between the sage scientist and the heads of the CNRS, who affirmed their right to consult as to how those funds should be used. We can see that G. Dupouy seized upon the intervention of Paul Lebeau[zz] (aged 87 at the time) in favor of M.-M. Janot as a pretext to limit the institutional autonomy of the future director of the ICSN – E. Lederer, who was reputed to be difficult to approach[21]. Finally, according to his testimony in 1989[51], which differs slightly from that of 2007[21], E. Lederer recalls that G. Teissier wanted to appoint him as head of the future institute, but that he was profoundly hostile to the idea of any cooperation with private industry, and refused. G. Dupouy, for his part, wanted to make the Gif campus into "a city of science" of international renown, whilst keeping his hand in with, and particularly without being dismissive of, his predecessor, who was now back in his own laboratory on the Gif campus.

At the same time, the need to set up the ICSN was urgent, and not just academic. The opportunity to harness political support could not be missed. However, unless yet another new organization were founded, the CNRS was the only existing research center which could easily accommodate a large-scale institute. In addition, the ICSN was conceived and then designed as the largest chemistry laboratory at the CNRS, and it remained so for a long time. The need to keep both sides – i.e. the university and the world of research – happy, on the one hand, and to move past the dichotomy between pure science and applied science by cooperating with industry, on the other, whilst maintaining the American patrons' goodwill, also accounts for this twin appointment to the headship of the ICSN. Was this a strength or a weakness? It is difficult to say. However, the variety of skills collected by these two men and brought together at the ICSN made it a melting pot that was ideal for combining bordering and then leading disciplines.

zz (1868–1959), Professor of chemical pharmacy from 1918 to 1939, at the *Faculté de Médecine* in Paris.

With this question of the appointment resolved, and the scientific agenda drawn up by the two directors, on 9 May 1956 the head of the CNRS lodged a request for permission to build the new institute of the CNRS campus in Gif-sur-Yvette. Yet the creation of such an institute involved not only the CNRS, but also fitted in with the State's scientific policy, with the CNRS being one of the cogs in that State machinery. Thus, it was unsurprising that, as soon as the decision was enacted, every academic hub in France – some in reconstruction, some in development – applied for the right to host the new institution. It took all the charm and flesh-pressing of both directors, M.-M. Janot and E. Lederer, to ensure the ICSN stayed at Gif. The building permit was finally delivered on 6 January 1958. The building went up in 1959[aaa].

"(…) the buildings are under construction in Gif, and will be completed around June 1960. This institute's mission will be the isolation of new natural substances, the determination of their structure, and their synthesis. There will be two sections, each led by a director: the alkaloids and antibiotics section; and the microbial, vegetable or animal-based substances section."[bbb,62] The construction project was completed, and opened to the first teams of researchers, at the start of the new university year, in October 1960. The ICSN was the only significant laboratory built in Île-de-France, whilst the rest of the CNRS' fundamental chemistry research, in domains that were poorly represented at university, was carried out in Strasbourg at the *centre de recherche sur les macromolécules* (CRM, macromolecular research center), in Lyon with the *institut de la catalyse* (catalysis institute) and Bordeaux with the *centre de magnétochimie* (magnetochemistry center).

Without exception, the management of the ICSN, as a intramural laboratory, depended directly on the DG of the CNRS, and as such, was delegated to the authority of a board of directors appointed by the directorate of the CNRS and responsible to that board (see above). Besides the two directors of the institute, who were statutory

aaa Archives G 990001-64, Gif-sur-Yvette, activity report 1958–59.

bbb Archives G 850003-DG, Gif-sur-Yvette, PV of the CA in CNRS from 23 December 1959.

members, the first board, led by G. Champetier, was made up of Pierre Desnuelle[ccc], Alain Horeau[ddd], Marc Julia[eee], Jacques Monod[fff], Henri Normant[ggg] and Guy Ourisson[hhh], who represented the top names in chemistry at the time[47]. The first meeting took place on 20 January 1961 to precisely define the scientific projects and the way in which they were to be organized, because: "the ICSN [had] to become the

---

ccc (1911–1986), a chemical engineer, and doctor of physical sciences (Lyon, 1935). Director of the *institut de chimie biologique* (biological chemistry institute) at the *Faculté des Sciences* and the *centre de biologie moléculaire du CNRS* (CNRS' molecular biology center), in Marseille. He was elected a member of the *Académie des sciences* in 1977.

ddd (1909–1992), a chemical engineer (Nancy), pharmacist (Paris,1941), doctor of science, Paris 1951, Professor at *Collège de France*, holder of the chair in hormonal organic chemistry between 1956 and 1980, and he was elected a member of the *Académie des sciences* in 1977.

eee (1922–1992), former student at the ENS, *agrégé-préparateur* in 1946, gaining a doctorate at Imperial College in 1948, and a doctorate in science in Paris, in 1949. He taught at the *École polytechnique*; he was lecturer and Professor at the *Faculté des Sciences* in Paris in 1963, a researcher at the Institut Pasteur (1957–1970) and head of chemistry laboratory at the ENS in 1970. He was elected as a member of the *Académie des sciences* in 1977 and received the CNRS' gold medal in 1989.

fff (1910–1976), assistant at the *Faculté des Sciences* at Paris University in 1934, he was a Rockefeller grantee in genetics at the California Institute of Technology, in 1936, gaining a doctorate in natural sciences from Paris in 1941, he was in the *Résistance* until 1945. He was laboratory head at the Institut Pasteur (1945–1953), set up and headed the cellular biochemistry department at the Institut Pasteur in 1954, was appointed Professor at the *Faculté des Sciences* in Paris (chair in metabolic chemistry, becoming the chair in molecular biology), in 1959. He received the Nobel Prize in Physiology or Medicine, jointly with François Jacob and André Lwoff in 1965, and was appointed Professor at the *Collège de France* (chair in molecular biology) in 1967.

ggg (1907–1997), *agrégé* in physical sciences in 1931, becoming a doctor in science in 1942, *chef de travaux*, he was appointed as lecturer at the *Faculté des Sciences* in Caen in 1945–1948, professor at the *Faculté des Sciences* in Lille in 1949–1950, lecturer in 1953, and then Professor in chemistry – organic synthesis (1963) at the faculty of science in Paris, the ENSC in Paris and the ENS in Saint-Cloud.

hhh (1926–2006), an organic chemist, former student at the ENS from 1946 to 1950, defended his doctoral thesis at Harvard in 1952, and earned a doctorate in physical science in 1954 from the Sorbonne. Appointed as lecturer in 1955, and then Professor at the University of Strasbourg in 1958, a co-founder of the *Université Louis Pasteur* in Strasbourg and its first president (1971–1976), he performed the functions of director general of higher education in the Ministry of National Education, from 1981 to 1982. He was head of the ICSN from 1985 to 1989, Vice-President of the *Académie des sciences* 1998–1999, and then President in 2000–2001 and the President of Rhône-Poulenc science council.

driving force behind natural substances in France"[iii]. Thus, the institute was deliberately structured into two sections: that led by M.-M. Janot (alkaloids and antibiotics) and that headed by E. Lederer (microbial, vegetable or animal-based substances), which were, in turn, organized into different teams. Gathered together under one roof, then, were different but mutually complementary scientific ambitions. M.-M. Janot, a pharmaco-chemist, had the aim of producing knowledge which would lead to the creation of new medicines; E. Lederer, a biochemist, very much aware of the international scientific competition, also had a long history of collaboration with industry (Firmenich and Ciba)[jjj]. The directors were seconded by Robert Goutarel[kkk] and Judith Polonski (one of the rare female directors of research at the CNRS at the time)[lll]. These four scientists all had their own research teams, whilst the ICSN also hosted external teams in dedicated laboratories specific for that purpose in each wing of the building. This organization was filled with horizontal structures composed of general services, common and available to all researchers.

In 1974, Pierre Potier succeeded M.-M. Janot as head of the section which had become the Department of Therapeutic and Biological Organic Chemistry. Furthermore, in 1977, Derek Barton arrived at the

iii CNRS archives 85001-46, report from the meeting of the board of directors, 20 January 1961.

jjj The former is a Swiss company manufacturing perfumes and synthetic fragrances in Geneva; the latter is a pharmaceutical company in Basel.

kkk A chemist, specializing in alkaloids, who began working with M.-M. Janot in 1935. Even though no building had been built at that time, in a letter on 27 February 1956, he applied for a 3rd-class *maître de recherche* (senior researcher) post at the CNRS and an assignment to the ICSN. In 1958, R. Goutarel requested his renewal "in order to prepare future researchers destined for the institute (...)". CNRS archives, personnel files, partially consultable on dispensation.

lll A biologist, her work pertained to the isolation and structural study of natural products of animal, microbial and plant origin. After working at the IBPC, she joined the CNRS in 1946, became *maître de recherche* (senior research fellow) in 1957, *directrice de recherche* (research director) in 1963. CNRS archives, personnel files, partially consultable on dispensation.

ICSN. He was to succeed E. Lederer, who was heading his biological chemistry department and the ICSN alongside P. Potier. The two departments were fused into a single entity, with the chemist Derek Barton[mmm] becoming the director and P. Potier his co-director. In 1985, Guy Ourisson replaced Barton, rather than P. Potier, who stayed on as co-director. Thus, the pair of directors M.-M. Janot and E. Lederer were succeeded first by the pair of co-directors D. Barton and P. Potier, followed by G. Ourisson and P. Potier. Then, between 1989 and 2000, P. Potier alone headed the ICSN[nnn], as did Jean-Yves Lallemand (1943-) until 2009[ooo], David Crich (1959-) until 2011[ppp], Max Malacria

mmm (1918–1998). After undergraduate work at a technical college, he obtained his doctorate in natural substances chemistry at Imperial College, London, in 1942. Having spent the rest of the war in the service of his country and having worked at a chemical company for a year, he became an assistant, in 1945, teaching physical chemistry and inorganic chemistry, and then a researcher carrying out his postdoctoral research in organic chemistry. After a spell at Harvard, following which he published his article "The Conformation of the Steroid Nucleus" (1950) – research for which he received the Nobel Prize for Chemistry in 1969, he returned to England to take up a position as Professor of organic chemistry at Birkbeck College, University of London. After a Professorship in Glasgow between 1955 and 1957, he returned to Imperial College, where he pursued his career until 1977. He was approached by Jean Cantacuzène, the scientific director for chemistry, with a mandate from the DG of the CNRS, Bernard Gregory and Jean Mathieu, director of external relations of Roussel-Uclaf and a member of the board of directors of the ICSN to replace E. Lederer, who was to take retirement in 1978. Thus, he became the head of the ICSN until 1985, with P. Potier as co-director. Having, himself, reached the legal retirement age in France, he became Professor emeritus at Texas A&M University, in the United States. He also regularly collaborated with industry – notably Schering – for over 40 years. D. Barton's file cannot be published for material reasons (it is archived in a dangerous building at the CAC headquarters in Fontainebleau). P. Potier's personal archives and http://historique.icsn.cnrs-gif.fr/spip.php?article6.

nnn Correspondence between P. Potier and François Kourilsky, and decree naming P. Potier as director of the ICSN, effective as of 1 October 1989. Potier's personal archives – ICSN.

ooo Director of the ISCN, from 2000 to 2009. A student at the *Ecole polytechnique*, he authored a doctorate in chemical science, under the supervision of Marc Julia at the ENS. After a postdoctoral study period at the California Institute of Technology, in 1973 he joined the ENS' chemistry laboratory. In 1981, he set up a new research group in nuclear magnetic resonance at the ICSN, whilst working as a lecturer at the *Ecole polytechnique*, and then as a professor. In addition to his election to the *Académie des sciences* (corresponding member in 1996, member in 1997), he received the CNRS' silver medal in 1984.

(1949-) until 2014[qqq] and Angela Marinetti. It is worth taking the time to consider these collective or individual strategies, which highlight the uniqueness of the ICSN on the French academic scene, and also the impressive flexibility of the CNRS.

Without broad access to the archives, though, it is difficult to fathom all the motivations in the minds of the members of the CNRS board of directors and the minister in charge. The minister participated in the appointment of scientists at this level, and was therefore a stakeholder in maintaining this two-person team of directors. It is reasonable to think that, once again, pragmatism was behind these decisions. As D. Barton, a Nobel laureate for chemistry, was free of all commitments, having taken compulsory retirement at age 65 from his university in England, the directors, represented by Jean Cantacuzène (scientific director for chemistry from 1973 to 1977) felt that for the CNRS and the ICSN to have such a personality among their ranks would bring prestige. The research being done at the ICSN converged with D. Barton's, and he was offered the headship of the institute. Once again, E. Lederer's testimony reflects how the decision to appoint a director for the ICSN was taken at the highest levels of the French academic community. E. Lederer hoped to attract D.

---

ppp Director of the ICSN from 2009 to 2011. Having graduated from the University of Surrey (UK), he came to the ICSN to work on his doctoral thesis, supervised by D. Barton and defended at *Université Paris XI-Orsay*, where he remained for his postdoctoral research from 1984 to 1985, under the stewardship of D. Barton and P. Potier. After teaching at University College London from 1985 to 1990, he taught in the United States at the University of Illinois at Chicago from 1994 to 2007, first as a lecturer and then as a distinguished chemistry Professor; then between 2007 and 2009 he worked as chemistry Professor at Wayne State University in Detroit, to where he returned as Professor in 2011.

qqq Director of the ICSN from 2011 to 2014. Holder of a State doctorate from 1974, from *Université d'Aix-Marseille III*, under M. Bertrand's supervision, he became an assistant lecturer in 1974 and then lecturer in 1978 in Lyon in Professor Jacques Goré's laboratory. After spending two years as a post-doctoral NATO grantee at the University of California, Berkeley, he was named *maître de conference* (lecturer) at the *Université de Lyon* I in 1983; then, in 1985, he became Professor of organic chemistry at *Université Pierre et Marie Curie* (UPMC) Paris. He was director of the *Laboratoire de chimie organique* (Organic Chemistry Laboratory) between 1995 and 2011. He held the chair in organic chemistry at the *Institut universitaire de France* (IUF) and, besides numerous prizes, he received the CNRS' silver medal in 2001.

Barton as a foreign member of the board of directors, and had written to him but never received a reply. It was through Jean Mathieu at the pharmaceutical company Roussel-Uclaf that E. Lederer and P. Potier[rrr] – who had replaced M.-M. Janot – learned of D. Barton's appointment as director of the ICSN. Without waiting for E. Lederer to retire and for his position to become vacant, D. Barton had been appointed head of the ICSN. The Nobel laureate required a "full" position in order to make the move to France, which is why the two departments of the ICSN were merged. However, P. Potier could not be moved aside, as he represented the generation of promising, innovative natural-substance chemists. A scheme was hit upon whereby D. Barton and P. Potier were co-directors[sss]. The Briton gave the Institute a great boost[2], definitively bringing it into a very high-level international network.

Looking closely at the association between G. Ourisson and P. Potier, which followed the Barton–Potier collaboration, we can see that it too was created with the same pragmatic goal in mind. P. Potier was well placed to become director when D. Barton left, but, at the request of the DG of the CNRS Pierre Papon and of the President of the pharmaceutical company Roussel-Uclaf, Edouard Sakiz, he decided to embark upon a foray into industry, assuming the leadership of a joint laboratory combining the CNRS and Roussel-Uclaf. Out of friendship for P. Potier, but also because he was a tactician in the field of French scientific policy, G. Ourisson, who was in a job in Strasbourg he had no desire to leave, accepted the headship of the ICSN, so that the experiment of an associated CNRS–industry laboratory would be tried, whilst allowing P. Potier to co-direct the ICSN. This was imperative because, at that time, he was conducting important research[ttt].

rrr Interview with PP – MLR, Maison de la chimie, Paris, 13 March 2001.

sss Correspondence between Pierre Potier and Pierre Papon, 14 March 1983, following D. Barton's appointment for 4 years at the head of the ICSN and the publication of Decree 82-993 of 24 November 1983. Potier's personal archives – ICSN.

ttt *Idem* and Potier's personal archives, ICSN, correspondence between Ourisson – Potier, correspondence between P. Potier and the scientific board of the chemistry department and DG of the CNRS.

Thus, as we can see, we are dealing with an institute of the CNRS which, at the time, and of course later on when navelbine and taxotere were discovered, was receiving the full attention of the directorate general of the CNRS and the minister in charge. The direction and management of the ICSN did not really follow the common principles of the running of CNRS laboratories, up until 1990. For significantly different reasons, the organization and management were adapted to the requirements and constraints of the people within the framework of unchanged structures, but did the CNRS not allow for this kind of practice?

Up until the end of the 1990s, we see a regular increase in the number of chemists recruited to the CNRS; there were 712 in 1958, and, 1,973 by 2002. Designed to dynamize bio-organic chemistry, the ICSN was one of the most important intramural laboratories at the CNRS, and as such had significant resources at its disposal from the moment it opened – issues which were closely monitored by the two directors. There were 114 researchers and technicians in the fall of 1960 (out of a total of 858 chemists – CNRS), 134 (out of a total of 907)[uuu] the following year, to which must be added the general service staff. In 1986, at the start of G. Ourisson's tenure as director, the 285 members making up the staff of the ICSN were distributed as follows: 100 researchers from the CNRS and Inserm, 95 *ingénieurs, techniciens* and *personnels administratifs* (ITA, engineers, technicians and administratives), 90 students, post-docs and interns; that staff included 60 non-French nationals, of 25 different nationalities, attesting to how far the reach of the institute had spread[vvv]. Over time, the total number of staff ranged between 250 and 320 people. The number of researchers, which was high even to begin with, reached a peak at the end of the 1960s, before gradually decreasing, whilst the curve for the number of students obeyed the opposite evolution, with the two curves crossing at the end of the 1980s. The number of engineers and

---

uuu Lionel Dufaux, *La chimie au CNRS*, research report for the *Comité pour l'histoire du CNRS*, Paris, 2005.

vvv Speech written by P. Potier and G. Ourisson for the DG of the CNRS Serge Feneuille in honor of D. Barton, 6 7 October 1986. Potier's archives, ICSN.

research technicians was roughly parallel to that of the researchers. A number of facts account for these trajectories. Firstly, the distinction between researchers and students was in place from 1966, and then the modification of the thesis regime in 1984 did away with the *doctorat d'Etat* (State doctorate); however, these people were considered to be researchers, holding the title of research attaché, which also disappeared at that time. After that, the "new regime" doctorate, closer to British or American doctorates, once it was created in 1984, became the prerequisite to enter the CNRS as a researcher. The distinction between researchers and students became clear. From that point on, a student was a doctoral candidate, and a researcher was at least a doctor. Add to this the fact that E. Lederer, but many others after him (e.g. Yves Langlois, one of the inventors of navelbine) were also teachers or professors at the nearby Université d'Orsay[www]. For aspiring chemists interested in natural substances and wanting to undertake doctoral research at a prestigious institution, the ICSN was the ideal place either to write a thesis under the co-direction of a university faculty member and a "*Giffois*", or to conduct postdoctoral research which was becoming more widespread at that time for people wishing to pursue a career in academia. Whilst students became the majority at the start of 1990s, almost at the end of our story, we can say that, over the first 30 years, personnel were, *grosso modo*, divided into three thirds: researchers, students and engineering/technical/administrative staff. Out of these chemists, researchers, associate professors, post-docs and doctoral candidates, a portion came from abroad, and almost 80 nations were represented by this panel. This international recruitment of researchers and doctoral candidates for the ICSN is due to the very nature of the chemistry practised there, which focused on natural products irrespective of the country from which they came. Thus, developing contacts to help the supply of materials also created links which evolved into scientific networks. However, this is also explained by the impulsion given by the directors who, because of their personal profiles or their own careers, had very international connections from the very start, all

www Set up in 1958, this university hub, very near to the city of Gif, became independent of the Université de Paris ten years later.

having conducted a portion of their research abroad. In total, over the period of interest to us, there were between 25 and 30 research teams composed of 2 to 4 researchers, in addition to the students and the ITAs. There were significant disparities between these teams. The work of phytochemistry and semisynthesis which led to the discovery of navelbine was done by the team including P. Potier, Nicole and Yves Langlois, and the doctoral students Philippe Rasoanaivo, Françoise Guéritte, Pierre Mangeney and Ratremaniaina Zo Andriamialisoa. The work leading to taxotere's discovery was done in the team composed of P. Potier, Daniel Guénard, Françoise Picot, Gérard Chauvière, F. Guéritte and students reading for a *diplôme d'études avancées* (advanced diploma or 1st year of a doctorate), Brigitte Bourdillat and Véronique Sénilh, not forgetting the collaboration provided by Rhône-Poulenc in the person of Michel Colin[xxx] who joined them in Gif (see Chapter 4).

The building, which was vast to begin with, was extended in 1969, reaching over 7,000 m^2. In 1966, a 550 m^2 extraction and fermentation laboratory, known as "the factory" by the staff, was added. In addition, from 1968, the ICSN financed the work of Thierry Sévenet[yyy] who, in cooperation with the *office de la recherche scientifique et technique outre-mer* (Orstom, today IRD), with funds

xxx A Rhône-Poulenc engineer, attached to the ICSN, he worked in P. Potier's laboratory, with a number of different teams: those led by Christiane Poupat and Alain Ahond during the 1980s, working on girolline – an antitumoral substance extracted from a New-Caledonian sponge; that of D. Guénard from 1981 to 1989, where he was also highly involved in isolating taxol analogs from the yew *Taxus baccata*, and in the large-scale semisynthesis of taxotere.

yyy A pharmacist, after military service in New Caledonia, aided by G. Mathé and P. Potier, he entered the ICSN as a research assistant in 1968. The same year, he returned to Nouméa. Having written his thesis under Claude Thal's supervision, a researcher and a senior researcher (*directeur de recherche*), he was in charge of the natural substances branch of the ICSN. It was during this period that he and P. Potier managed to develop what would become the medicinal plant laboratory of the CNRS in Nouméa. ICNS archives, ICSN activity reports and Titres et Travaux de P. Potier, 1956–1982.

from the Territory of New Caledonia and dependencies, collected and transformed local plants. In 1972, that structure became the "*Laboratoire des plantes médicinales du CNRS à Nouméa*" (CNRS Medicinal Plant Laboratory, Nouméa). The agreements with Orstom/IRD were regularly renewed thereafter. This Antipodean laboratory, which was said to be "the window to Australia, New Zealand, Japan, South-East Asia…" under cover of agreements with the New Caledonian authorities, has, since then, been supplying plants endemic to the country's dense, humid forest and mining grounds, thus providing the ICSN with natural plant substances. From the very beginning, the ICSN was equipped with the very latest physico-chemical measuring devices (mass spectrometers, NMR machines – nuclear magnetic resonance); it was truly remarkable for the time. The quality and performance of the equipment has since been a constant source of worry for the directors. Note that royalties on the exploitation of the patents for Navelbine® and Taxotere® have greatly contributed to this necessary upkeep.

Led by researchers of international stature, E. Lederer and M.-M. Janot, having brought with them qualified researchers who themselves were leaders of their own teams and supervisors of students, these chemists, in a pleasant environment and in well-equipped laboratories, developed the field which had, thitherto, remained fallow in France: natural substances chemistry. In addition to the grueling hours at the laboratory bench, and to the work of research, there were internal seminars, participation in university seminars, and organization of both national and international conferences. In the space of 15 years, the first two directors had kept their word and achieved their mission: to make up the lost ground in this domain of chemistry and develop a shining research hub which would serve the academic needs by training the research-teaching staff needed for the rise of the universities, both in France and in developing countries, but also training chemists for industry in France or abroad. With that mission accomplished, the presence of D. Barton meant the ICSN was able to incorporate the international standards of high-level research. It was in this dynamic environment, open and rich in different possibilities, that Pierre Potier operated, leading the teams who would discover navelbine and taxotere.

2.4. "Science is a social and political act": Pierre Potier (1934–2006)

If science is a social and political act, as P. Potier so liked to point out, the discovery of navelbine and taxotere definitely was one. After all, it was said of him that he was "the Frenchman who managed to launch two molecules on the American market". This shared adventure involved a very great many people, and it is impossible to mention all of them, whether in terms of the story of the academic work or that of the industrial development of these drugs. We have already pointed out the difficulty of gaining access to the sources needed to tell such a story. Whilst the scientific archives of Pierre Potier, Françoise Guéritte and some of Daniel Guénard's papers at the ICSN[zzz] have been largely exploited for constructing the narrative of the scientific facts (see Chapter 3 and 4), Pierre Potier's archives constitute the main source, supplemented by Françoise Guéritte's own, to put these scientific facts into their historical context. This limitation, in the attempt to render the telling of the story objective, is compensated by the use of oral testimonies and the critical analyses of the various actors asked and recorded by the authors; however, had the authors had access to the archives still kept by other players, the telling may have been rather different. The authors have tried everything, or almost everything, to limit any distortion in the analysis of the discovery process and restore it to its rightful place, to "tell the truth" regardless of the subject, as P. Potier always strove to do[1,63].

It was undoubtedly the synergies between the people themselves, and between those people and the institutions, which facilitated the discovery and its transformation into innovation. A bias imposed by the archival sources, but assumed by the authors as well, is that the

zzz The archives of Pierre Mangeney (see Chapter 3) tracked it to Jussieu. They disappeared when the building was cleared to remove the asbestos. Yves and Nicole Langlois refused to grant access to their archives.

events are mainly seen through the eyes of Pierre Potier, team leader and leader of men, in charge of the teams who, under his guidance, invented navelbine and taxotere. P. Potier was the "product" or, better put, the "synthesis of the culture, scientific practices and possibles of his time". He used them and pushed the opportunities offered him to the extreme – scientific, industrial and political opportunities alike.

2.4.1. *Learning from research*

Pierre Potier (1934–2006)[1], after a propaedeutic year in 1952 in SPCN (*sciences physiques, chimiques et naturelles* – physical, chemical and natural sciences) at the Sorbonne, and having been admitted to the veterinary school, enrolled in the *Faculté de Pharmacie*, not to have a dispensary and "sell pills, but to take the courses there which interested [him]"[aaaa]. Received for the entrance exam in October 1953, he began his studies in pharmacy with a year-long internship in a dispensary. As a grantee, he was able to make replacements during holiday periods, but, working from 17:00 to 24:00, he managed to take classes in the *Faculté des Sciences*, even though this was prohibited because he was already enrolled in the *Faculté de Pharmacie*. Graduating in sciences in the fall of 1955, he enrolled to write a thesis whilst continuing his pharmaceutical studies.

A student at the *Faculté de Pharmacie*, interested in botany, he sought information from the assistants working with Professor M.-M. Janot, the holder of the chair in galenic pharmacy, within that faculty. M.-M. Janot also headed one of France's only research teams with a reputation on the international stage: "he was the only one in the

aaaa Interview with PP – MLR, 29 January 2001, Maison de la Chimie Paris. Archives ICSN – CNRS 910025 DPAA and Potier's personal archives. Unless otherwise stated, all quotes come from the same interview and the same archival source.

Faculté de Pharmacie who was comparable to E. Lederer". His assistant, Jean Le Men[bbbb], whom P. Potier had met at the *Faculté des Sciences* meeting, suggested that he choose an original, groundbreaking topic for his thesis. After having introduced P. Potier to his boss M.-M. Janot, J. Le Men, who was older and therefore further along in his research, agreed to supervise his thesis, entitled: "Étude chimique de la Lunarine, alcaloïde du *Lunaria biennis* Moench".

At the end of the 1955–1956 academic year, thanks to Professor Raymond Paul, P. Potier undertook a summer internship (as he would do regularly) at Rhône-Poulenc, in the analytical chemistry research laboratory in Vitry, to "earn money and gain some idea of how that company worked". Unenchanted by this type of research, nonetheless he met a number of people there with whom he stayed in touch, and who would later be affected by his work. In 1957, he became a pharmacist, and was able to focus entirely on his thesis, and presented an application to join the CNRS at the recommendation of M.-M. Janot. He was recruited as a full-time intern[cccc] and assigned to the ICSN from 1 October, in M.-M. Janot's laboratory, at the *Faculté de Pharmacie* until it moved to the Gif site at the start of the 1960–61 university year. Under the leadership of M.-M. Janot and J. Le Men,

bbbb (1923–1978), an engineer by training, he had to study for diplomas in chemistry and botany in order to enrol to write his thesis. Awarded a doctorate of science from the Faculty of Paris, working in M.-M. Janot's laboratory, specializing in pharmacy, sent to Reims in 1955 to the School of Medicine and Pharmacy, he contributed to the setting up of Reims University, where he became a professor, dean of the *Faculté de Pharmacie* and then administrator and president (1976–1977) of the university. A researcher at the CNRS, he was one of the first to be assigned to the ICSN (off the main site), in M.-M. Janot's laboratory complex, 4 Avenue de l'Observatoire, Paris 6.

cccc P. Potier was an intern for two years at the ICSN-CNRS, and then from 1959, full-time junior researcher (*attaché de recherche*) for a further two years. Having obtained his doctorate, called up in the service in the armed forces, he pressed for and won a promotion to researcher 1st class without salary, and then deferred the position 2nd class until he returned from military service. He was quickly brought up to speed, and was promoted with deferral to researcher 3rd class in July 1963, with deferral to 4th class in March 1964, became *maître de recherche* (senior researcher) in 1967 and *directeur de recherché* (higher senior researcher) on 1 January 1972, after changing section for the evaluations of the *comité national de la recherche*.

and being proposed by Charles Mentzer (1911–1967), holder of the chair in biological chemistry at the *Faculté des Sciences* in Lyon, P. Potier carried out his doctoral research in the most favorable possible conditions.

Having discovered spermidine in Lunaria, he identified teams also working on alkaloids in Scotland and Switzerland, who possessed equipment that would enable him to confirm his initial discoveries. Supported by M.-M. Janot[dddd] with the aim of supplementing his research, Potier left for Glasgow, with Professor P. Bladon, to carry out what he derisively called his "pre-doctoral internship", as he was unable to obtain an extension of his deferment to carry out a "post-doc".

Besides the intellectual exchanges, P. Bladon gave him access to equipment that simply did not exist in France – namely a mass spectrometer – and also allowed him to send his samples to the laboratory of the Californian firm Varian in Palo Alto, which made NMR spectrographs. After this, P. Potier returned to France. However, before submitting his thesis, thanks to an introduction made by M.-M. Janot, he departed for a further two months in Zurich to verify his results, because the laboratory at the *École polytechnique fédérale* had just acquired the first routine nuclear magnetic resonance spectrograph. Finally, he handed in his thesis, which was the first in France to include NMR spectra. While waiting for his viva, he studied the structure of an antibiotic on behalf of Marc Julia at the Institut Pasteur, in a laboratory which cooperated with the army health services. He had begun publishing work with J. Le Men, and later with J. Le Men and M.-M. Janot. Before departing to fulfill his military service obligations, he defended his *thèse de doctorat d'Etat* (see Figure 2.2) on 22 December 1960, before a panel of adjudicators composed of M.-M. Janot, J. Le Men, M. Julia, Henri Normant (1907–1997) and Charles Prévost (1899–1983).

dddd Rare between the two World Wars, he departed for Zurich, to the *Ecole polytechnique fédérale*, in Léopold Ruzicka's laboratory (Ruzicka won the Nobel Prize for Chemistry in 1939).

At the same time, at the *Faculté de Pharmacie*, he had met Marie-France, whom he married in 1958. She became a pharmacist. They had three children.

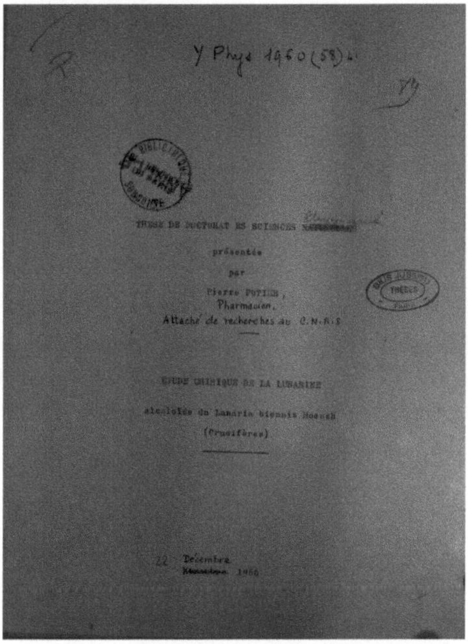

Translation:

DOCTORAL THESIS IN PHYSICAL SCIENCES

submitted by

Pierre Potier
Pharmacologist, and research attaché to the CNRS

CHEMICAL STUDY OF LUNARINE

Alkaloid of Lunaria biennis Moench (Cruciferae)

22 December 1960

Figure 2.2. *Cover page of P. Potier's doctoral thesis - photo: P. Verschueren*

By this point, all the attributes characteristic of P. Potier's career were in place: his quest for truth, his noted taste for solving questions and problems, his independent spirit, critical analysis of the norms and rules, and the ability to mobilize different networks.

Upon his return to civilian life, he rejoined the ICSN, in the "Janot wing". There he stayed for almost 45 years, serving in all positions both within the ICSN and outside of it[eeee].

eeee To recap, he was the director of the ICSN from 1974 to 1977 with E. Lederer, co-director from 1978 to 1989 with D. Barton and G. Ourisson, director from 1989 to

2.4.2. *Research is a resource*

The ICSN had all the necessary personnel and equipment to become the flagship for natural substances chemistry: the personality of the directors, of their students, their guests and of the researchers contributed to this, creating a highly stimulating academic, intellectual environment, in which originality and daring were never discouraged, but instead actively encouraged. Besides their area of specialty, the common denominator linking the two directors together was their ability to achieve results: they did everything within their power to create the necessary conditions for the researchers to succeed. The researchers were allowed the freedom to invent any techniques or resources, and to follow whatever path they wished. In comparison to other research organizations – particularly American ones, which were often cited as a yardstick – the CNRS, and hence the ICSN, appeared to be places of very significant freedom and autonomy, especially during the period of interest to us here[64].

When P. Potier finally rejoined the ICSN, as we know, the institute was divided into two sections, which were to become departments. These sections themselves each hosted a number of different teams of researchers. Before becoming team leader in 1967, P. Potier joined the team led by J. Le Men, made up of Christiane Kan, René Beugelmans and Henri-Philippe Husson. Whilst there was genuine competition and rivalry between the teams making up the ICSN, which occasionally marred the atmosphere in the institute[65], this was not all there was; in

2000, an elected member in the different sections and commissions of the national committee for scientific research of the CNRS. He set up and led the joint laboratory CNRS-industrie Roussel-Uclaf, between 1984 and 1989, he was director of the Pirmed (*programme interdisciplinaire de recherche sur le médicament* – interdisciplinary medical research program) from 1977 to 1984, scientific adviser to the DG of the CNRS until 1978, DG for Research and Technology at the *Ministère de l'Éducation nationale de l'Enseignement supérieur et de la Recherche* from 1994 to 1996, and then adviser to Minister François Bayrou. He was a tenured professor with the chair in chemistry, at the *Muséum national d'histoire naturelle* (1990–91), Professor at the University of Strathclyde (UK) (1984–1990), a member of the *Académie nationale de pharmacie* (1983), a member (1986) of the *Comité des applications de l'Académie des sciences* (Cadas) which, in 2000, became the *Académie des technologies*, member of the *Institut (Académie des sciences)* (since 1988), president of the *Fondation de la Maison de la chimie* (1995–2006).

actual fact, both formal and informal collaborations between teams, between the two branches, or between the ICSN and the other research centers on the Gif campus were quite real. The activity reports prove this, and P. Potier, organizer, then team leader, then director, made abundant use of collaborations, with no negative impact on the function of the ICSN.

As soon as he arrived at the ICSN, P. Potier resumed his work, first publishing papers with P. Bladon, and then with the members of his research team, duly focusing on different alkaloids. Then, he went on to study and make adjustments to the Polonovski reaction (discovered in Paris in 1926) in 1965; the results were published in *Tetrahedron* in 1967. The modification of that reaction played an important role in the genesis of navelbine (see Chapter 3). However, drama in his personal life was to shape his career. Accompanying his wife to undergo treatment for a cancer which ultimately took her life at 35, he became aware of the significant distance between the research effort, the doctors, the pharmaceutical industry and the patients suffering from that disease. His dual education as a pharmacist and a chemist gave him the investigative tools to remedy that situation, and his status as a researcher the means to act; the ICSN was an appropriate place at which to conduct the research, as it did not prohibit its researchers from working with industrial partners. Also, expressing his desire to reorientate his research to find "molecules which could target diseased cells", in 1969, he turned down an offer from Rhône-Poulenc to take the headship of a research center, as he wished to maintain his independence in terms of choosing the directions his work took. Having worked in the industrial sphere, he knew that it was not in industry that he would be able to succeed, given the lack of creative freedom. "It was by remaining at the CNRS, but working in collaboration with industry when necessary, that we could make progress, because it is important to remain the master of your own kitchen; chemistry is cookery", he said.

In the start of the 1960s, massive collection campaigns were launched by America's National Cancer Institute, to sample plants from temperate and then from tropical regions. The researchers funded by this program provided the scientific community with a vast mass of important data, and published a great many articles in all journals even remotely interested in cancer research, which was a "national cause" in the United States. The state of knowledge and the different ways of treating cancer in the 1960s – surgery and radiotherapy – still left a lot of room for chemotherapy[66]. In this context, given that over half the available medications were extracted or derived from natural products (plants, mainly), it was essential to analyze them and determine their structure[22]. When P. Potier decided, after the tragic death of his wife, to work with his collaborators more specifically on natural substances with antitumoral properties, because he was already an international specialist on alkaloids, he also knew "where to cast the line".

In this context, P. Potier knew that the Madagascan periwinkle had been being used in pharmacopeia for a very long time. He read the work of the Canadians R. Noble and C. Beer, who had isolated vinblastine, an alkaloid, from the periwinkle in 1958, whilst in 1964, a symposium of the American Society of Pharmacognosy entitled "*Chemistry and Biological Activity of Catharantus, Vinca and Related Indole Alkaloids*" had taken place in Pittsburg, focusing on the properties of vinblastine and vincristine – two compounds found in the Madagascan periwinkle. Again, in the United States, the firm Eli Lilly was working on the same issues[ffff]: collaboration between American and Canadian scientists had produced two extremely costly medications, available in France in 1969. P. Potier studied those medications. Drawing on his personal skills and his network of contacts, he defined a strategy, at that time, which he would regularly use later on to gain time: identifying what already exists, going back to the study of the active ingredients either to understand why the substance was toxic or to try to find a way to synthesize it, or indeed put forward a biomimetic process by which to obtain it. P. Potier and the teams under his direction launched themselves into this international academic and industrial race to synthesize compounds with complex chemical formulas[gggg].

ffff Rhône-Poulenc Cy and Laboratoires Servier in France, Richter Gedeon in Hungary and Omnichem in Belgium also studied these molecules. Potier's archives.
gggg Potier's archives.

2.4.3. *Intuition and daring in service of a cause: the discoveries of Navelbine® and Taxotere®*

2.4.3.1. *Navelbine®*

At the beginning of the research program which led to the synthesis of Navelbine®, P. Potier had almost entirely ceased to work in the laboratory, unlike the members of the different teams he directed or with whom he collaborated.

On the other hand, as co-director and then director of the ICSN, he had – not without opposition[65] – put in place a means of managing the circulation of results and information within the ICSN, which ought to operate first and foremost like a bubble. By giving priority to collaborations which were propitious in view of the results of the research done by the members of the different teams in the ICSN, in the researchers' immediate interests – in accordance with the directors with whom he was associated – he hoped to achieve his goal more quickly[hhhh,2]. Mobilizing the human resources, technology and knowledge available at the ICSN, and those of his industrial contacts in service of his commitment in the fight against cancer, he was vigilant and eager for progress.

It was in 1968 that he began to focus his research more specifically on plants from New Caledonia and Madagascar and, in 1969, he published his initial results, with Nicole Langlois, one of the co-discoverers of navelbine, although he had already filed patents on a number of other alkaloids. This collaboration with the Langlois (Nicole and Yves) gained momentum with the study of *Catharantus* (see Chapter 3), notably from 1972 onwards. This initial trio – P. Potier, N. and Y. Langlois – were joined, from 1974 onwards, by, amongst others, the doctoral candidates Françoise Guéritte, Pierre Mangeney[iiii] and Ratremaniaina Zo Andraimialisoa[jjjj], whose names

hhhh Potier's archives.

iiii A researching student from 1974, pursuing a DEA (diploma of advanced studies) in Orsay and Gif, he then undertook a 3rd-level thesis on the Polonovski reaction, before moving on to a higher-level State thesis: "*Application de la réaction de Polonovski modifiée à l'hémisynthèse de la Vinblastine*" (Application of the modified Polonovski reaction to semisynthesis of Vinblastine), supervised by Y. Langlois and appear on the various patents, in accordance with Potier's wishes. This way of working led him to say that he was "only physically" away from the laboratory bench. This allowed him to reflect, to formulate hypotheses and to lead the research efforts in novel directions, enriching them with the accumulated knowledge. He researched using the minds and hands of the other researchers as his tools, firstly because chemistry lends itself to this approach, but also because as a student of M.-M. Janot, who had introduced him to it, he was utterly convinced that the complementarity of teamwork helps achieve goals, because "each individual has specific skills and a specific approach". Antitumoral compounds were highly active, being exploited by the US firm Eli Lilly. However, it was not yet possible to synthesize these natural substances, which were extracted from the Madagascan periwinkle. Potier based his research on these substances.

We have stressed that he had also worked on the modification of the Polonovski reaction – whose importance we shall see later on – with Adrien Cavé, Christiane Kan, J. Le Men and Alain Ahond, whilst maintaining an active interest in the studies of quinquina alkaloids, never failing to turn his attention to other plants or living species as soon as any antitumoral activity was indicated[kkkk].

In this quest, it was crucial to be able to monitor the activity of the molecules isolated or obtained. On the campus, not far from the ICSN, was the Institute of Enzymology, hosting the biologist Dominique Pantaloni, who was studying the biological structure of tubulin. He

---

P. Potier, which he defended in 1979. He joined the CNRS in 1981. In 1984, he joined Jean Normant's laboratory at UPMC, where he became senior researcher in 1994. Interview with Pierre Mangeney – Muriel Le Roux, 25 April 2012, Conflans Sainte-Honorine.

jjjj He arrived from Madagascar in October 1974 to prepare a DEA, followed by a thesis, defended in 1978, at the ICSN, which pertained to a chemical study and semisyntheses of alkaloids of *Catharanthus ovalis Mgf.*, a Madagascan periwinkle containing antitumoral bisindolic alkaloids of the type of vinblastine. He very soon entered the CNRS. Thanks to the experience he had acquired in this domain, he played a very important role in the discovery of navelbine, and developed the semisynthesis method used in the medicine's industrial manufacture. See http://historique.icsn.cnrs-gif.fr/spip.php?article272.

kkkk P. Potier, *Synthèse des titres et travaux scientifiques*, 1956–1982, Potier's archives – ICSN.

told P. Potier that mescaline (a substance found in a Mexican hallucinogenic mushroom) had an impact on tubulin. However, mescaline has a small part in its structure similar to the alkaloids found in the periwinkle. P. Potier had read an article by the American Michael Shelanski[67], describing tubulin and explaining how to monitor its activity *in vitro*. P. Potier asked one of the young researchers at the ICSN, Daniel Guénard[llll], to study how tubulin worked, which led to the development of the tubulin test (see Chapter 3). Now, the French had a reliable way of testing the potential antitumoral activity of the natural substances on which they were working. By 1976, the tubulin test was reliable as a "screening" test for antitumoral agents (see Chapters 3 and 4).

The idea underlying this way of working was for P. Potier to use the specific resources (freedom, peace, informal and formal cooperations, etc.) of fundamental academic research to synthesize these substances, which would, in the long term, facilitate their industrialization. In fact, fairly early on, in 1974, P. Potier expressed the hypothesis that there should be a biomimetic way of obtaining vinblastine-type compounds from other compounds in the plant. After the checks performed by N. and Y. Langlois, he was convinced that they "had a good product". Thus, in order to protect this discovery, on Monday 14 October 1974, P. Potier, N. and Y. Langlois filed the *pli cacheté* no. 15634 (sealed report, a form of proof of work, prior to the filing of a patent) at the *Académie des sciences*.

llll Co-finder of taxotere, chemical engineer from 1966 to 1969 in Strasbourg, on the advice of G. Ourisson, he transferred to the ICSN in 1969 to write a 3rd-level thesis, under the supervision of René Beugelmans: "*Réactions de fragmentation photochimique. Formation d'oxétanne en série stéroïde*" (Photochemical fragmentation reactions. Formation of oxetane in a steroid series), defended in 1971. Then, he returned to research for a higher-level State thesis entitled Réactivité photochimique d'alcools allyliques et homoallyliques en série stéroïdique (Photochemical reactivity of allylic and homoallylic alcohols in a steroid series), defended in 1974. He was recruited to the CNRS in 1972. After a post-doctoral secondment at the Institut Pasteur from 1974 to 1976, he began working on tubuline on his return to the ICSN, in 1976, spending six months in D. Pantaloni's laboratory. He was promoted to *directeur de recherche* (senior researcher) in 1988. Interview with Daniel Guénard – Muriel Le Roux, 23 May 2012, ENS, Paris.

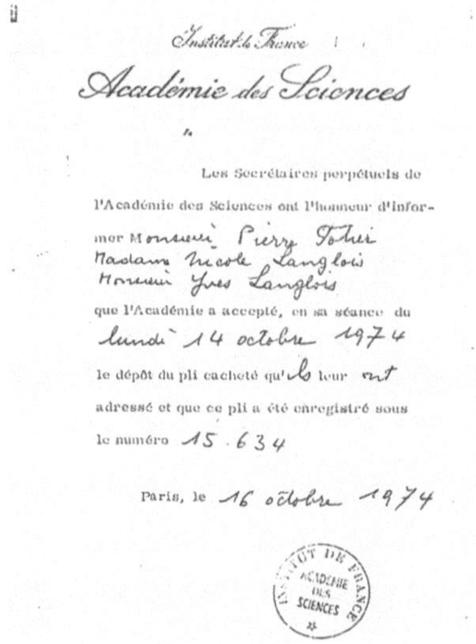

Institut de France

Académie des Sciences

Les Secrétaires perpétuels de l'Académie des Sciences ont l'honneur d'informer Monsieur Pierre Potier
Madame Nicole Langlois
Monsieur Yves Langlois
que l'Académie a accepté, en sa séance du lundi 14 octobre 1974
le dépôt du pli cacheté qu'ils leur ont adressé et que ce pli a été enregistré sous le numéro 15 634

Paris, le 16 octobre 1974

Translation:

The permanent secretaries of the Académie des Sciences have the pleasure of informing:

- Mr. Pierre Potier,
- Mrs. Nicole Langlois, and
- Mr. Yves Langlois

that, at its session on:
Monday, 14 October 1974,
the Académie accepted the sealed report submitted by the aforenamed, and that the said sealed report has been registered with number 15 634.

Paris, 16 October 1974

Figure 2.3. *Pli cacheté (sealed report) no. 15634: P. Potier's archives*

In the hospital-university world, research to combat cancer was hard to beat. Professor Mathé[mmmm], whom P. Potier knew personally for obvious reasons, had in 1964 founded the *Institut de cancérologie and d'immunogénétique* (Oncology and Immunogenetics Institute), combining the Inserm research unit 50, "Oncology and immunogenetics", and CNRS associate laboratory 189 at the Paul-Brousse Hospital, in Villejuif. There, alongside Dr. René Maral from Rhône-Poulenc, he conducted clinical trials with vindesine – a close relative of vincristine – to study its antitumoral effect. P. Potier persuaded him to help evaluate the quality of the substances produced at the ICSN. Together, they compiled a dossier of the medical properties of various substances, eventually presenting it to pharmaceutical firms. The project took around three years.

mmmm Cancerologist. Head of hematology department, Institut Gustave-Roussy, Villejuif (up until 1990).

P. Potier "naturally" offered the results of this research to Rhône-Poulenc. However, the same firm which had been involved in P. Potier's early research on alkaloids was distrustful of public research. At the time, the company directors were fending off fiery opposition from unions of researchers, opposed to the preparation of the general framework agreement between the CNRS, represented by its DG Bernard Grégory, and that company, represented by André Pacoud. Also, given that, at the time, Professor J. Kutney from Vancouver, a competitor of the French academic team, was scheduled to visit in January 1975, P. Potier, N. and Y. Langlois, with the help of J. Pilard from Rhône-Poulenc's patent department, drafted an initial patent, which was filed by Anvar[nnnn] on 30 December 1974[oooo,68]. This was an urgent matter because, during his visit to Gif, J. Kutney, who was doubtful about the French team's discovery, led P. Potier, secure in the knowledge that the patent had been filed, to disclose some of the information. As soon as he returned to Canada, J. Kutney and his team published without even acknowledging that the work of the French had come first (see Chapter 3). This led to the establishment of the first transatlantic judicial dispute[pppp]. This first semisynthesis using the Polonovski-Potier reaction, confirming P. Potier's hypothesis, resolved questions that scientists the world over had been unable to solve. This discovery was at the heart of the first semisynthesis of vinblastine and the discovery of navelbine (see Chapter 3).

These other explored avenues were also patented by Anvar, because whilst, in 1975, the framework agreement had finally been signed between the CNRS and the chemical company Rhône Poulenc,

---

nnnn Anvar, created by Law no. 67–7, was an industrial and commercial public undertaking, placed under the auspices of the CNRS, but with financial autonomy. Its purpose was to "compete to market the results of scientific and technical research (...), it prospects for inventions, ensures their protection on a national and international level, notably by filing the corresponding patents, respecting inventor's rights and acting in accordance with those rights. It performs all the necessary operations to prepare to market the inventions, apart from the exploitation operations themselves". *JO* on 5 January 1967, p. 131.

oooo Potier's archives.

pppp They were to last for 14 years. Potier's archives, correspondence between P. Potier and the DG of the CNRS. The second pertain to taxol.

there was still a very high level of tension. François Guinot[qqqq] pointed out that the violence of the reactions to this agreement resulted from a miscalculation committed by both parties, in their desire to draft the agreement in the greatest of secrecy. The press, at the time, reported that the State had allowed Rhône-Poulenc to misappropriate public-domain research. Nonetheless, this agreement rubber-stamped practices which were already in place. P. Potier, as we all know, followed in the footsteps of his predecessors. In addition, the statutes of the CNRS stipulated, remember, that the organization must be mindful of the socio-economic impacts and benefits of its research and discoveries. It is understandable that the chemists at the company, affected by the reactions of the CNRS researchers, should not have supported the development of the discoveries made by the ICSN in spite of P. Potier's conviction. However, Rhône-Poulenc, who were studying a similar product with G. Mathé and R. Maral, had even dispatched a technician to work at the ICSN[rrrr]. In 1975, though, there was an upset in the chemical industry in France; Rhône-Poulenc did not escape the trouble, and restructured its organization; the research department and the development department did not serve the same governing body, which undoubtedly complicated the company's exchanges with the ICSN. When the company was threatened with nationalization, it refused to accept the dossier on navelbine, and even ceased its collaborations with the institute, for a time[ssss].

However, this rejection did not temper P. Potier's determination. He submitted the dossier to Laboratoires Servier, which also refused, doubtless because the large enterprise Rhône-Poulenc had refused it. He put on his pilgrim cap and offered his "product" to the American firm Eli Lilly, who also declined the offer, as they also produced two anti-cancer medications derived from Madagascan periwinkle: Velbe®

---

qqqq He represented the enterprise in the negotiations. He became President of Rhône-Poulenc Santé, at the time of the research into Taxotere (see Chapter 4). Interview François Guinot – Muriel Le Roux, Académie des technologies, Paris, 14 June 2007.

rrrr Interview with PP – MLR, 12 June 2001, Paris, Maison de la chimie and Potier's archives, correspondence.

ssss Interview with FG – MLR, Académie des technologies, Paris, 14 June 2007 and interview with PP – MLR, 12 June 2001, Paris, maison de la Chimie and Potier's archives,

(vinblastine) and Oncovin® (vincristine). In spite of these failures, over the course of the next three years, P. Potier continued to encourage his team who, for their part, made additional discoveries leading to navelbine, helped by Professor G. Mathé and Dr. R. Maral – who had joined the department in Villejuif in 1977[tttt] – carrying out further tests in a hospital environment[uuuu]. He refused to be beaten, and personally contacted Maurice Ponte, then the head of Anvar, to help him find other industrial partners; Pierre Potier successfully convinced him. Thus, Pierre Fabre, the founder and head of his eponymous laboratories, met with P. Potier in Gif, in November 1981. The two men, pharmacists, studying natural substances, had fairly similar visions of the purposes of their actions. After a period of reflection (very short, according to P. Potier), P. Fabre agreed to produce Navelbine®. A partnership linking the Anvar, the CNRS, the ICSN, P. Potier and his collaborators and the firm Laboratoires Pierre Fabre was signed in July 1982. The time for development had come.

For Laboratoires Pierre Fabre, the risk was a calculated one, as Anvar was to finance the patent applications, but nonetheless it was a bold move. It represented a radical change of direction for that SME, which decided to develop in a sector at a time when the large pharmaceutical groups were not greatly involved in the production of natural-substance-based antitumoral therapeutic agents. From that point on, everything happened very quickly, because the Potier-Mathé team had already done the bulk of the work[vvvv]. Two members of the ICSN, one from the Paul Brousse Hospital and three members of Laboratoires Pierre Fabre made up the technical committee in charge of monitoring the development of the molecule[69]. After research development with the participation of Annie Pouilhès from the ICSN (see Chapter 3), fabrication in galenic form and establishment of the appropriate dosages, the industrial process was completed at the end of summer 1988. Pierre Fabre, at the moment of the building of the factory which was to produce Navelbine® in Pau, decided to apply, to that production process, the standards of the American Food and Drug

tttt Interview with François Lavelle - Muriel Le Roux, 21 June 2012, ENS, Paris.
uuuu Potier's archives, correspondence and lists of his publications and patents.
vvvv Interview PP-MLR, 12 June 2001, Paris, Maison de la chimie and P. Potier's archives, correspondence.

Administration, which were far more stringent than the French standards at the time, in order to place the product *de facto* on the same level as those of the "big pharmas" in terms of quality[wwww]. That strategic choice was crucially important for the company, which set up Pierre Fabre Oncologie in 1988.

The clinical trials conducted at Paul Brousse Hospital demonstrated the effectiveness of the new medicine in comparison to existing treatments, so market authorization for the drug was granted in April 1989, and it was officially launched in November the same year. The FDA, for its part, granted market authorization in 1994. Navelbine® became the first French cancer medication to be sold in the United States. In 2001, its oral form, developed by Laboratoires Pierre Fabre, also received market authorization.

Although the attempts to make synthetic products imitating the active principles in the Madagascan periwinkle had failed 15 years before, from 1974, P. Potier's team managed, in the space of three years, to invent a new molecule: 7'-Nor-anhydrovinblastine, yielding Navelbine®; P. Mangeney had performed the first semisynthesis of navelbine in 1977. It took all of P. Potier's tenacity and determination to see the process through to completion. Thus, in spite of the support of the directors of the ICSN, he had been soundly reproached, notably in the 1970s, for working with Rhône-Poulenc. Then, he was ridiculed because the companies had refused his product. Thus, when Navelbine® received market authorization in France, and then throughout the world, he humorously pointed out that he had been "right too early, and in the face of ill omens", notably when people began to point to the success of the ICSN as an example. By virtue of the agreements signed, the CNRS, the ICSN and all the researchers involved in that research received royalties. In spite of this, the researchers of the ICSN, having delegated the questions of commercialization of their results to P. Potier, began, under his leadership, to study taxanes because, according to "an unfurling plan" to which he held the secret, he still had a project in the pipeline.

wwww Interview Yves Ledieu – Muriel Le Roux, 10 May 2011, at the Laboratoires Pierre Fabre Paris head office.

However, a 1979 publication had set the direction in the international competition.

2.4.3.1 *Taxotere®*

As Professor Martine Piccart remarked[xxxx], in the late 1970s, oncologists were limited in the choice of chemotherapy treatments to care for their patients. Thus, the arrival of taxanes sparked great hope in the hearts of everyone – patients and doctors alike. This expectation on the part of cancer sufferers in the most advanced countries, whose associations were beginning to make themselves heard, rendered the competition all the more lively, as the pharmaceutical companies too were highly desirous for new molecules. The 1980s and 1990s saw the rollout of strategies of mergers/acquisitions/absorptions of the pharmaceutical firms, transforming into multinational health conglomerates. In this context, any new molecule with the potential to become a "blockbuster" – i.e. a high-added-value product – became an important element in their strategies. At the same time, we see the rise to power of financiers to the detriment of pharmacists and chemists on the boards of directors of those firms, accentuating a culture of "return on investment" around medication, transforming a "health product" into a capitalist "business product". This twofold change characterizes the landscape in which these new molecules surrounding taxanes emerged.

After systematic testing, during collection campaigns by the National Cancer Institute to sample plants from temperate regions, it was discovered that an extract of yew bark destroyed tumoral cells. Taxol was isolated by M. Wani in 1971. In 1979, the American, S. Horwitz, explained how taxol was able to defeat cancerous cells (see Chapter 4). This publication in *Nature* rekindled the competition at a time when other avenues had failed and the challenge set 10 years earlier by Nixon, to defeat cancer, had not been met. As the Americans had published the first results on the structure of taxol and

xxxx Professor Martine Piccart, Professor of oncology at the Université Libre de Bruxelles and director of the medicine department of the Institut Jules Bordet, the center of the fight against cancer in Belgium, in the film made by Jean-Luc Bouvret: *L'if, aux frontières de la vie* (The Yew, on the Boundaries of Life), 2010, *Le Miroir*, ARTE France, CNRS Images and *Muséum national d'Histoire naturelle.*

its antitumoral properties, a patent could no longer be filed on that specific point. This fact was to influence the way of seeking to communicate – in short, to direct P. Potier's research[yyyy].

However, the future of taxol was limited by the conditions of its production, which would lead to a major ecological crisis. It would have taken eight tons of yew bark – yews being wild trees that grow extremely slowly, requiring 100 years to reach maturity – to make 1.3 kg of taxol; but the Americans alone needed 25 kg of the product per year. The reaction of American ecologists to the risk to yew forests hundreds of years old, which were also home to protected animals on the west coast, was very powerful. However, it was to be hoped that synthesis chemistry could replace extraction chemistry. To deal with the pressure from suffers associations, between 1983 and 1993, but particularly because all the data had been published, at least 30 teams tried to synthesize taxol. The French also launched themselves into that competition (see Chapter 4).

This was all the easier because, while the navelbine program was on the point of completion, the team began by felling one yew, and then, at the request of the *direction départementale de l'equipement* (DDE, county public work department), a number of the other yews on the campus in Gif-sur-Yvette where the ICSN was situated. However, as we shall see, unlike the prevailing practice in the United States, the researchers at the ICSN had very easy access to these plants without any administration saying anything against it or rendering access complicated[64]. At the time, P. Potier had a program in the pipeline to study the activity of thuja. Drawing upon the acquisitions from that work and the American publications on taxol, he formed another team around Daniel Guénard and Françoise Guéritte, and set the objective of achieving synthesis of taxol as quickly as possible… In fact, it would be a question of semisynthesis (see Chapter 4). D. Guénard began studying all parts of the yew, rather than only the bark, and used the tubulin test to evaluate the activity of all molecules whose chemical structure was reasonably similar to that of taxol. Hence, in 1980, 10-deacetylbaccatin III was

yyyy Interview with PP-MLR, 12 June 2001 and 24 September 2003, at his home in Paris.

isolated from the leaves of the European yew, *Taxus baccata*. The chemical studies conducted on 10-deacetylbaccatin III and the use of a Sharpless hydroxyamination reaction led to a non-natural compound which was more active on tubulin, taxotere, and then to taxol. The environmental issues were resolved. Unlike the predominant practice at the CNRS, before even beginning to think about filing a patent or publishing, P. Potier waited to have proof of the molecule's activity not *in vitro*, but *in vivo*. Thanks to the tubulin test, the team also showed that the presence of a lateral chain was crucial for the molecules' biological activity. 10-deacetylbaccatin III, which had no lateral chain, was actually inactive, whereas taxol and taxotere, with a lateral chain, were biologically active. Therefore, P. Potier, who was then director of Pirmed[zzzz], commissioned one of his collaborators – a pharmacologist – to find, in France (preferably in a public-domain organization), someone capable of helping them to synthesize that lateral chain. Pirmed was able to rapidly finance this type of research. Thus, Andrew Greene, senior researcher at the CNRS at Joseph Fourier University in Grenoble, successfully solved this issue. In this story, it was "the French and not the Americans who discovered the inexhaustible source of Taxol"[aaaaa]. The team at the ICSN isolated 10-deacetylbaccatin III from the leaves of the European yew in 1982, whilst the Americans isolated taxol from the bark of the pacific yew. The semisynthesis of taxol became possible, and was performed (see Chapter 4). Without the involvement of Anvar this time, the French firm Rhône-Poulenc, which had renewed contact with P. Potier in 1981, filed patents in 1986, on several procedures for the semisynthesis of taxotere and taxol, in association with the researchers at the ICSN and CNRS on the one hand, and with the researchers in Grenoble on the other[bbbbb]. Dozens of laboratories throughout the world tried, in vain, to find a better solution.

---

zzzz Interdisciplinary research program on the scientific bases of the medication set up by P. Potier on demand from the director general of the CNRS, which he led from 1978 to 1984. Poitier's archives, *dossier d'informations préalables à la demande de la Légion d'honneur*. Pirmed was aiming for the finalization and ultimate release of the research on the market, in the interests of public health.
See http://www.annales.org/ri/1998/ri02-98/claverie.pdf.

aaaaa Interview with PP-MLR, 12 June 2001.

bbbbb Interview with Jean-Louis Fabre – Muriel Le Roux, 6 May 2015, ENS, Paris.

P. Potier and François Lavelle, a biologist and head of the department of research in experimental oncology at Rhône-Poulenc, had met at the request of the company during 1980, to discuss taxol as presented by the American publication from 1979. Rhône-Poulenc was demanding, and P. Potier knew that he could no longer conduct the same kinds of collaborations as had taken place with navelbine. The times were changing, and so too were practices. The development research which led to Taxotere® was quickly done because, on the one hand, Rhône-Poulenc was interested in the American research on taxol and, on the other hand, P. Potier's and him team's credibility was notably enhanced thanks to the initial successes of Navelbine®. The company, which had commissioned F. Lavelle to evaluate the feasibility of research on this topic, gave him complete freedom to organize scientific collaborations with the Gif researchers[ccccc]. It was the start of a cooperation where understanding and rapport were of prime importance, the complementarity of the knowledge and skills being crucial, and the research conditions were the very best[ddddd]. The work of research took place in collaboration between chemists, pharmacologists, toxicologists, doctors and industrialists: "our collaboration was perfectly clear", recalls F. Lavelle. "The chemists from Gif worked on the fundamental study; the industrialists took care of the delivery in pharmaceutical form, and the doctors the clinical testing."[eeeee]

However, because the company had severed its contracts with him, P. Potier ensured that each step of the research was contractually agreed upon between the ICSN, the CNRS and Rhône-Poulenc. An initial contract was signed, therefore, in 1981[fffff], based on the framework agreements from 1975, for studies on the thuja and the yew; but it was amended on his request and in accordance with his desires every time it was necessary when revised annually. That contract was then supplemented and amended by other, more specific

ccccc Interview with François Lavelle – Muriel Le Roux, 21 June 2012, ENS, Paris.
ddddd The interviews with Françoise Guéritte, Daniel Guénard, François Lavelle, Jean-Louis Fabre, Pierre Etienne Bost and Pierre Potier are unanimous on this point.
eeeee Interview FL– MLR, *op. cit.*
fffff Agreement signed on 19 October 1981, with validity from 10/10/81 to 9/10/82, renewed each year; the contract called for RP to employ a technician or engineer on a full-time basis. ICSN archives, Potier's archives.

ones[ggggg], because P. Potier had become a strategist in innovation, researching, developing and managing his team's discoveries as an industrial outfit would have done[hhhhh]. He wanted to keep a handle on the results found by the researchers at the ICSN without sacrificing the possibilities afforded by such collaboration. At the same time, it had to be noted that the agenda was constrained, because no public-domain laboratory could afford the cost of research to develop a medication which, in addition to the years of fundamental research, could last between 8 and 12 years, costing hundreds of millions of dollars. The huge increase in the cost of this developmental research resulted from new standards required to obtain market authorization, also leading to a higher number of clinical trials required. The human resources, equipment and financing provided by Rhône-Poulenc alone helped get through these steps and obtain the patents – 1986 and 1988 for Taxol as a natural molecule, and 1988 for Taxotere, as a synthetic molecule based on a natural substance. The issue was equal to the international scientific competition which lasted for over 20 years. In 1990, the molecule was being synthesized in large quantities and, in 1995, Rhône-Poulenc obtained the market authorization for Europe[iiiii] and the United States. It was the pharmacologists and doctors at Rhône-Poulenc who assumed responsibility for monitoring the clinical trials conducted by Professor Michel Marty's team at the Saint-Louis hospital in Paris. Taxotere® was first administered to a patient in 1990[jjjjj].

P. Potier pointed out that this evolution "[necessitated] collaboration between academic research and industrial research, although there were those sitting on 'nothing committees' who represented public organizations and industrials; some people said that 'it is not up to public-sector researchers to try to find medications'..." He denounced this type of discourse which, in his view, was also exploited by industrialists. By playing down the contribution made by academic research, they were able to use ("plunder", said P. Potier),

ggggg Interview JLF– MLR, *op. cit.*

hhhhh Interview FG – MLR, *op.cit.*

iiiii The European patent had been created, simplifying the MA for EU countries. Taxotere® was the first medication to benefit from that new legislation.

jjjjj Interview JLF– MLR, *op. cit.*

the results of public research at a lower cost, acting so that work would remain free to access. In fact, this practice diminished, in France, after the research committee meetings in 1981–1982, which reaffirmed that in certain cases and certain conditions, that cooperation was justified. P. Potier defended his way of cooperating with industry, which enabled the researchers in the two spheres to "work on an equal footing"[kkkkk]. He added that it was important to "always seize an opportunity when it presents itself, and thus collaborate with industry but on condition that we remain in control of our own research choices". He jealously defended his independence and refused to suffer the dictates of the investment/time/return on investment ratio used in industry.

We have already stressed the degree to which P. Potier was attached to the written word, to the conservation of documents and to communication[2]. P. Potier had an intuitive awareness of the possibilities offered by his work as a researcher. He read, observed and commentated on all work within his area of expertise and of which he was aware. All hypotheses were likely to be of use one day. In that sense, P. Potier fits in with the long tradition of the naturalists who went before him. Doubtless, a greater awareness than others of the pressing nature of the economic competition which – like it or not – drives research, explains the care Potier took to preserve the documents, control the communication[2] and the attention and energy he invested in protecting the results of the research, exploiting them and obtaining the recognition and the fruits of the labor, even if it meant pleading, which he also did. However, having laid out the general framework of the intrigue, it is now time to dive into the "science in action"….

kkkkk Correspondence between P. Potier and the President of the Board of Directors of Aventis Pharma, December 2002, Potier's archives.

3

From *Catharanthus roseus* Alkaloids to the Discovery of Vinorelbine (Navelbine®)

In 1989, the anti-cancer drug Navelbine®, whose International Nonproprietary Name (INN) is vinorelbine, was commercialized by Laboratoires Pierre Fabre, ten years after its discovery by Potier's team at the ICSN in Gif-sur-Yvette. The name "navelbine", given at the start by the researchers of that team, comes from the contraction of nor-anhydrovinblastine, whose structure resembles that of vinblastine – a natural antitumoral compound isolated from *Catharanthus roseus*, and commercialized under the name of Velbe® in 1961 by Eli Lilly.

If we compare the structure of vinorelbine to that of vinblastine (Figure 3.1), the difference lies in the absence of a water molecule (H_2O, highlighted in red in the figure), and the loss of a methylene group (CH_2, highlighted in blue) – hence the name nor-anhydrovinblastine, the prefix "nor" indicating the loss of a carbon atom.

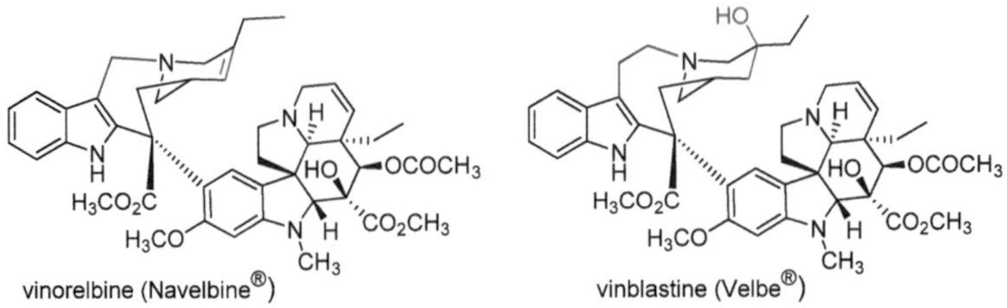

Figure 3.1. *Structures of vinorelbine and vinblastine. For a color version of the figure, please see www.iste.co.uk/leroux/navelbine.zip*

The discovery of vinorelbine – a semisynthetic compound which has never been isolated from natural sources – was the result of various fundamental research projects and other, more applied, research efforts.

A plant (*Catharanthus roseus*), a reaction (the Polonovski-Potier reaction), an *in vitro* test (the tubulin test), a group of people (P. Potier and his collaborators, an industrial and commercial public undertaking, placed under the auspices of the CNRS (Anvar, see Chapter 2) and a pharmaceutical firm (Laboratoires Pierre Fabre) contributed to the discovery and subsequent development of Navelbine® – a medication used in anti-cancer chemotherapy – notably in treating metastatic breast cancer and non-small-cell lung cancer.

3.1. *Catharanthus roseus*: botany, herbaria, empirical medicine

We cannot tell the story of the discovery of vinorelbine without recapping some essential elements pertaining to the preliminary studies conducted on the genus *Catharanthus*, whose species *roseus* was the starting point for this scientific adventure.

The genus *Catharanthus* belongs to the Apocynaceae family and includes eight species, seven of which are endemic to Madagascar: *C. lanceus* (Bojer ex A. DC) Pichon, *C. coriaceus* Markgr., *C. ovalis* Markgr., *C. longifolius* (Pichon) Pichon, *C. scitulus* (Pichon) Pichon, *C. trichophyllus* (Baker) Pichon, *C. roseus* (L.) G. Don. One species is native to India and Sri Lanka: *Catharanthus pusillus* (Murray)

G. Don. Of these eight species, *C. roseus* has been most thoroughly studied from the chemical and pharmacological point of view.

In 1976, Friedrich Markgraf, with the contribution of Pierre Boiteau, published the "*Flore de Madagascar et des Comores*" (Flora of Madagascar and the Comoros)[70], which provides a detailed description of the different species of *Catharanthus*. The Madagascan periwinkle, *Catharanthus roseus* (Figure 3.2) is presented thus:

> Vivacious herb or subshrub, 15–75 cm tall. Pivoting root, fairly weak. Vigorous stems, downy in immature state. Oblong-obovate leaves, sometimes elliptical, obtuse at the top, much shorter at the base, smooth or downy, (1-) 2.5–6.5 × (0.6-) 1–2 cm. Petiole 1–5 mm long. Flowers generally appearing in pairs. Pedicels 1–2 mm long. Sepals (2.5-) 5 mm long. Pink-violet corolla with a darker, or white, core….

Figure 3.2. *Catharanthus roseus.*
Photos by Bruno David

3.1.1. *Creation of the genus* Catharanthus

Catharanthus roseus (L.) G. Don[a] is known as the Madagascan periwinkle or the tropical periwinkle. The botanical nomenclature

a In botanical nomenclature, plants are named by the name of their genus (here *Catharanthus*), followed by the species name (*roseus*), and then the abbreviation of the name of the botanist who originally described the species (L. for Carl von Linné), and if need be, that of the botanist who changed the name of the species (G. Don for George Don).

C. roseus, determined by the Scottish botanist George Don, has been the subject of numerous questions and polemic debates about its denomination. This species, the first of its genus, had been described in 1759, under the name *Vinca rosea*, by Carl von Linné, a Swedish naturalist who developed the nomenclature for plants and animals in the form of a binomial[71]. Then, in 1828, the German botanist Heinrich Gottlieb Ludwig Reichenbach proposed the genus name *Lochnera*, mentioning the taxonomic disparities existing between the species *Vinca rosea* and the other species in the same genus (notably *Vinca minor* and *Vinca major*), but he did not give a detailed characterization for the genus *Lochnera*[72]. The species was renamed *Lochnera rosea* by an 1838 publication of the Austrian botanist, Stephan Ladislaus Endlicher[73]. Yet at the same time, Don, also distinguishing the species *Vinca minor* and *Vinca major* from the species *Vinca rosea*, attributed by Linné, created the genus *Catharanthus* (from the Greek *katharos* (pure) and *anthos* (flower)), precisely detailing the plant's taxonomy[74], then naming the Madagascan periwinkle *Catharanthus roseus*. As comparative analysis of the dates of the publications of Don and Endlicher shows that Don's appeared a few months earlier, the genus name *Catharanthus* is given priority. In 1966, William Stearn confirmed the botanical name *Catharanthus roseus* as the correct appellation of the Madagascan periwinkle[75]. In addition, Stearn points out in his chapter "Synopsis of the Genus *Catharanthus*" that the genus name *Lochnera* is not valid because it is too close to the name of another genus, *Lochneria*, published in 1777 by the naturalist Giovanni Antonio Scopoli[76].

3.1.2. *The earliest samples and herbaria of* C. roseus

A century before Linné, Étienne de Flacourt, a French colonial administrator posted in Madagascar from 1648 to 1655, described *C. roseus* by the name *Tongue*, in his book *Histoire de la grande isle de Madagascar* (History of the Great Island of Madagascar), and brought or sent a specimen of the plant back to the Museum of Paris[77]. Pierre Boiteau, an eminent botanist and connoisseur of Madagascan flora, tells us in his publication, *Sur la première mention imprimée et le premier échantillon de Catharanthus roseus* (L.) G. Don[78], why the first sample of *C. roseus*, inserted in 1715 into the herbarium of the French doctor and botanist Sébastien Vaillant, can only be attributed to E. de Flacourt. Still kept in the *Muséum National d'Histoire Naturelle* in Paris, this sample represents the oldest herbarium of a tropical plant (Figure 3.3).

Figure 3.3. *Book and herbarium plate for* Catharanthus roseus *by Sieur de Flacourt (photos by Lucile Allorge)*

As pointed out by P. Boiteau and W.T. Stearn, other herbaria of the plant were compiled in the 18th Century, notably by Michel Adanson, a Scottish-born French naturalist[78], and by Philip Miller, an English botanist[76], from cultures of *C. roseus*. These herbaria are respectively kept at the *Muséum* in Paris and the British Museum. Pierre Boiteau highlights that:

> *C. roseus* thus had spread far beyond Madagascar from this second half of the 18th Century[78].

Stearn[76] and van der Heijden[79] also relate in their article how this plant had spread through Europe. In the 19th Century, various other specimens of herbarium of *C. roseus* were made, including those from several countries in South America, Asia and Oceania, which are kept at the National Herbarium of the Netherlands, in Leiden.[79]

3.1.3. *From the use of* C. roseus *in popular medicine for its antidiabetic properties to the discovery of cytotoxic properties*

As previously mentioned, *C. roseus* is endemic to Madagascar. It was probably introduced into the tropical regions when it was transported by sailors, who used it as an appetite suppressant during their lengthy journeys at sea. The plant's leaves and roots were used to treat numerous diseases, not only in Madagascar but also in other countries in Africa, in Asia and Oceania. Researchers in different countries throughout the world working on extracts have reported – amongst other things – hypotensive, antimalarial, antibacterial, antidiabetic and purgative properties. Of the numerous publications mentioning the medicinal uses of this plant, we could cite, in particular, that of René Paris and Hélène Moyse, from 1958[80], and the more recent one from Junaid Aslam *et al.* (2010)[81]. In the majority of cases, it is aqueous extracts of the leaves or of the whole plant, which were taken orally, as an infusion or decoction. While some of these uses have been the subject of scientific validation tests by *in vivo* or *in vitro* experiments[81], the Madagascan periwinkle is perhaps best known because of the tests to validate its hypoglycemic and antidiabetic properties, which began in the 1920s.

3.1.3.1. C. roseus*: an antidiabetic plant?*

The numerous works devoted to the study of the plant's hypoglycemic properties, still being conducted even today, have often yielded conflicting results. Thus, a short news item, published on 11 April 1924, in the New Zealand newspaper *Mount Ida Chronicle*, mentioned that, following the curing of Mr. Ernest Whyte's diabetes with Vinca leaves, the plant might come to be a rival for insulin (Figure 3.4)[b].

b https://paperspast.natlib.govt.nz/newspapers/MIC19240411.2.23, consulted on 2 October 2014.

VINCA MAY BE A RIVAL TO INSULIN.

Properties of a Natal plant called vinca, as a specific for diabetes, have just been made public by a man living in Durban, who declares he ridded himself of the malady two years ago, and has had no return of it. He has since sent its leaves to many other sufferers. Some of them are shortly being sent to England for a scientific test.

The man is Ernest Whyte, a native registration officer at Greyville. For him the vinca treatment was prescribed in 1921 by a medical man who refuses to make his name public.

Mr Whyte is convinced that the two years which have elapsed since he ridded himself of diabetes are sufficient time for the malady to return if it were going to do so. He now cultivates the plant on his own property.

At present experiments are being made with a view to discovering whether the leaves can be dried and an extract made from them without impairing their properties.

The treatment, if followed as Mr Whyte himself followed it, lasts about eight months, and for the first half of that period there is stated to be little apparent improvement. After that time, however, the improvement is marked and rapid.

If vinca is what Mr Whyte thinks it is, it may be a rival to insulin—and very cheap, too.

Figure 3.4. *Extract from the Mount Ida Chronicle (Volume XLV, page 3), 1924*

A year later, in 1925, the Australian botanist Cyril Tenison White revisited this discovery and published an article in *The Queenslander*, entitled "Vinca Rosea – A reputed cure for diabetes"[82], describing how to use the leaves of the plant to treat diabetes. The same year, that article was translated into French and published in the *Revue de botanique appliquée et d'agriculture coloniale*, under a slightly different title: *Le Vinca rosea ou Pervenche de Madagascar employé dans le traitement du diabète*[83]. It mentions that:

> In South Africa, Mr E.E. Whyte, the discover of the value of Vinca in diabetes, has just put up a proprietary medicine termed "Convinca", for which it is aimed that eight out of every ten cases of sugar diabetes will find the use of insulin and strict dieting unnecessary. [Sic]

Similarly, a preparation made of the plant's leaves, commercialized in Britain as "Vin-q-Lin" or "Vinculin", was used to treat diabetes (Figure 3.5)[84].

Figure 3.5. *A Vinculin vial sold on eBay* [c]

As soon as this use was brought to public attention, many pharmacologists attempted to confirm that anti-diabetic activity by way of experimentation on animals, but did not obtain the desired results. Thus, in 1926, David Epstein, a pharmacologist at the University of Cape Town, published the preparation of Vinca leaves, called *Covinca*, studying its hypoglycemic effect on rabbits.[85] He concluded:

> "Covinca" or vinca, has no effect (a) in reducing the normal or fasting blood sugar of rabbits, nor has it any effect on (b) the experimental hyperglycemia produced in rabbits by adrenalin.

In Australia, similar experiments conducted on rabbits confirmed this result[86], whilst two clinical studies performed on diabetics using preparations of the leaves of the plant, as a tincture or an infusion, produced no improvement in their blood sugar levels[87].

Later on, in the 1950s, Paris and Moyse, from the *Faculté de Pharmacie* in Paris, also intrigued by the contradictory results obtained since this program of research began, conducted tests on the normal blood sugar level of the rabbit or rat and studied the influence of tincture, fresh flowers and total alkaloids[d] of the plant on rats made diabetic by the injection of alloxan[80]. In their 1958 publication, they noted in conclusion for the fresh tips of the plant:

> In view of our own experiments, we believe there is little hypoglycemic effect in the case of alloxanic diabetes in

c www.ebay.co.uk/itm/SUPER-AMBER-VINCULIN-DIABETES-CURE-MEDICINE-/231061421074, consulted on 21 April 2014

d Alkaloids are naturally-occurring basic nitrogenous molecules usually with high levels of biological activity. Total alkaloids are the complete set of alkaloids isolated from an organism.

> rats and normal blood sugar in rabbits. On the other hand, we see an obvious effect in rabbits in glucose-induced experimental hyperglycemia. In this case, then, at least, the experimental study has partly confirmed the use of vinca in popular medicine.

Still in the 1950s, similar studies researching the plant's antidiabetic effect were conducted in Canada, by a team at the University of Western Ontario. Those studies demonstrated not hypoglycemic activity, but highly cytotoxic activity – potentially antitumoral. These properties were, independently and at the same time, also discovered by a team at the American pharmaceutical firm Eli Lilly.

3.1.3.2. *From antidiabetic properties to antitumoral activities*

The tests to confirm the plant's antidiabetic properties were conducted by Robert Laing Noble, in the laboratory run by James Bertram Collip, a biochemist and the co-discoverer of insulin, at the University of Western Ontario, Canada. His work began because of his brother, E. Clark Noble, who, in the early 1920s, participated in research on insulin in the laboratory of Frederick Banting, who received the Nobel Prize in 1923 with John MacLeod, for the discovery of insulin, sharing the prize money with Charles Best and James Collip[e]. C. Noble continued working on insulin, and took care of many patients with diabetes. Thus, one of his patients from Toronto, Miss Farquharson, on a trip to Jamaica, in 1952, sent him leaves from the Madagascan periwinkle, which were used in traditional medicine in the form of a tea, to treat diabetes in that country. C. Noble forwarded that precious package to Dr. Collip's laboratory, where his brother, R. L. Noble, worked, so the latter could examine the effect of the plant on diabetic animals. No antidiabetic activity was found for an aqueous extract of the plant administered orally. On the contrary, administrated as an intraperitoneal injection, the response was astonishing… in rats, who died following a dramatic

e A contentious relationship occurred between the four researchers (http://clinchem.aaccjnls.org/content/48/12/2270). And, the "forgotten" participation of E. Clark Noble in the discovery of insulin and vinblastine has been related in numerous articles, including that of James R. Wright, Jr: "Almost famous: E. Clark Noble, the common thread in the discovery of insulin and vinblastine" *Canadian Medical Association Journal*, *167* (12), 1391–1396, 2002.

drop in the number of white blood cells and the destruction of the bone marrow. This observation, with no connection at all to the sought antidiabetic activity, led R. Noble and his colleagues to study the plant's chemical composition, their objective being to isolate the compound or compounds responsible for this astounding toxic effect. Thus, the Canadian researchers isolated one alkaloid, in crystalline form, that was highly active which they named vincaleukoblastine[f]. These results were published in 1958, with the title: *Role of Chance Observations in Chemotherapy: Vinca rosea* (see Figure 3.6)[88].

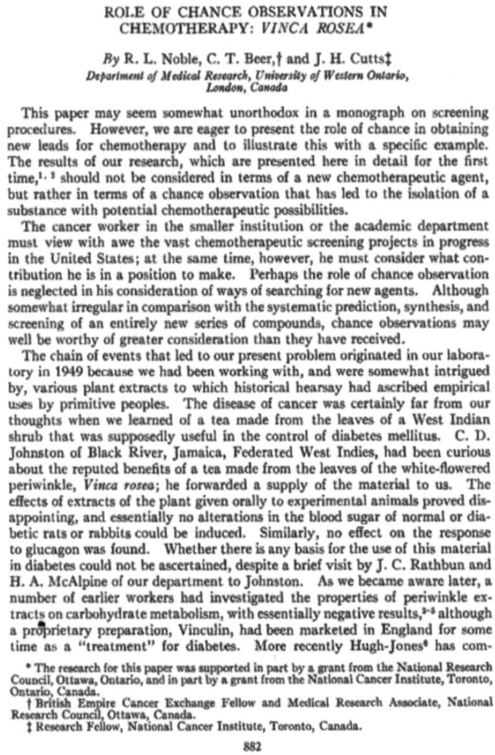

ROLE OF CHANCE OBSERVATIONS IN CHEMOTHERAPY: *VINCA ROSEA**

By R. L. Noble, C. T. Beer,† and J. H. Cutts‡
Department of Medical Research, University of Western Ontario, London, Canada

This paper may seem somewhat unorthodox in a monograph on screening procedures. However, we are eager to present the role of chance in obtaining new leads for chemotherapy and to illustrate this with a specific example. The results of our research, which are presented here in detail for the first time,[1, 2] should not be considered in terms of a new chemotherapeutic agent, but rather in terms of a chance observation that has led to the isolation of a substance with potential chemotherapeutic possibilities.

The cancer worker in the smaller institution or the academic department must view with awe the vast chemotherapeutic screening projects in progress in the United States; at the same time, however, he must consider what contribution he is in a position to make. Perhaps the role of chance observation is neglected in his consideration of ways of searching for new agents. Although somewhat irregular in comparison with the systematic prediction, synthesis, and screening of an entirely new series of compounds, chance observations may well be worthy of greater consideration than they have received.

The chain of events that led to our present problem originated in our laboratory in 1949 because we had been working with, and were somewhat intrigued by, various plant extracts to which historical hearsay had ascribed empirical uses by primitive peoples. The disease of cancer was certainly far from our thoughts when we learned of a tea made from the leaves of a West Indian shrub that was supposedly useful in the control of diabetes mellitus. C. D. Johnston of Black River, Jamaica, Federated West Indies, had been curious about the reputed benefits of a tea made from the leaves of the white-flowered periwinkle, *Vinca rosea*; he forwarded a supply of the material to us. The effects of extracts of the plant given orally to experimental animals proved disappointing, and essentially no alterations in the blood sugar of normal or diabetic rats or rabbits could be induced. Similarly, no effect on the response to glucagon was found. Whether there is any basis for the use of this material in diabetes could not be ascertained, despite a brief visit by J. C. Rathbun and H. A. McAlpine of our department to Johnston. As we became aware later, a number of earlier workers had investigated the properties of periwinkle extracts on carbohydrate metabolism, with essentially negative results,[3-5] although a proprietary preparation, Vinculin, had been marketed in England for some time as a "treatment" for diabetes. More recently Hugh-Jones[6] has com-

* The research for this paper was supported in part by a grant from the National Research Council, Ottawa, Ontario, and in part by a grant from the National Cancer Institute, Toronto, Ontario, Canada.
† British Empire Cancer Exchange Fellow and Medical Research Associate, National Research Council, Ottawa, Canada.
‡ Research Fellow, National Cancer Institute, Toronto, Canada.

882

Figure 3.6. *First page of R.L. Noble* et al.*'s publication*

f The name vincaleukoblastine (VLB) was chosen in reference to the plant (vinca) and because the alkaloid isolated, administered to rats, led to a drastic decrease in the number of leukocytes (leukopenia). The name "vincaleukoblastine" was later shortened to "vinblastine".

At the same time, researchers at the pharmaceutical firm Eli Lilly demonstrated a beneficial activity of alkaloidic fractions of the plant on mice with implanted P-1534 leukemia[89]. Several active alkaloids, whose structures are similar to that of vinblastine, were isolated by Gordon Svoboda: leurosine[90], leurosidine and leurocristine (also known as vincristine)[91]. The team at the Canadian university and the researchers at the American pharmaceutical company, both involved in that work, had a chance meeting in 1958, at a conference organized by the New York Academy of Sciences, during which R. Noble presented his results[92]. Finally, the activity of various alkaloids isolated was confirmed in animals by both teams[93], and the results of the clinical trials in humans were published in 1960 with vinblastine[94], 1962 with vincristine[95] and 1963 with leurosine[96].

A highly interesting, in-depth study on the relations existing at the time between the small team of Canadian researchers and the American pharmaceutical group Eli Lilly was published by historian Jacalyn Duffin, from Queens University in Kingston, Ontario[97]. In that publication, Duffin also analyzes the role actually played by "chance" or "luck", mentioned by the Canadian researchers in the discovery of vincaleukoblastine (Figure 3.6). She summarizes it thus in her abstract:

> In 1995, Canadian scientists Robert Noble and Charles Beer were inducted into the Canadian Medical Hall of Fame for their 1950s "discovery" of Vinblastine. Their "chance" finding of an anticancer drug in the leaves of the periwinkle plant (Vinca rosea, Linn.) is used to explore the historical issue of discovery, accidental discovery, and priority. The elements of the discovery are reconstructed through the oral testimony of key players and their published and unpublished records. Several "unsung heroes" played key roles in this project and reasons for their relative invisibility will be presented. Special attention is paid to the relationship between the small Canadian academic group working at UWO and the large pharmaceutical company (Eli Lilly) engaged in similar research at the same time.

3.2. Bisindolic alkaloids of *Catharanthus roseus* (1950s–60s)

3.2.1. *From the first chemical studies to the structural characterization of vinblastine and vincristine*

As we shall see later on, vinblastine, vincristine, leurosidine and leurosine – cytotoxic alkaloids isolated from extracts of *C. roseus* – have a structure composed on two indole subunits; hence the name "bisindolic alkaloids". The first phytochemical studies on *C. roseus* (or *V. rosea*), leading to the discovery of indolic alkaloids, were conducted in France, in the early 1950s, by Professors René Paris and Hélène Moyse, at the *Faculté de Pharmacie* in Paris. The samples of *C. roseus* on which the work was done had been received through the *Office de la Recherche scientifique et technique outre-mer* (Orstom – Overseas Scientific Research Bureau)[g], where certain researchers were attempting to compile an inventory of the medicinal plants found in Madagascar. From the roots of the plant, then, R. Paris and H. Moyse isolated the first alkaloid in a crystallized state, which they called vinceine[98]. At that time, some publications had previously spoken of the presence of alkaloids in the plant: those of M. Greshoff (1890),[99] W. G. Boorsma (1899)[100] and that of R.C. Cowley and F.C Bennett (1928)[101]. Other work was pursued in the 1950s, conducted notably by M.-M. Janot and J. Le Men[102], by Robert Pernet and his collaborators,[103] and by the teams of Carl Djerassi in America[104] and Asima Chatterjee in India[105]. Amongst other alkaloids, ajmalicine had been isolated by M.-M. Janot, J. Le Men and C. Djerassi, and vincaine by A. Chatterjee. In fact, it has been proven that ajmalicine, vincaine and vinceine are merely one and the same product. That product, which is also known as raubasine because it was also obtained from the roots of species of the genus Rauvolfia[106], has been commercialized for its antihypertensive effect. Also in the 1950s, other alkaloids, such as yohimbine, serpentine and tetrahydroalstonine were isolated from *C. roseus* by Japanese[107] and Indian[108] teams.

g In 1998, Orstom became the *Institut de Recherche pour le Développement* (IRD).

Then, at the start of the 1960s, work on the isolation and structural determination of alkaloids from *C. roseus* intensified following the pharmacological results, cited above, found by R. Noble, C. Beer and J. Cutts[88,109], and those found by Eli Lilly[89]. At the time, the structure of a small number of alkaloids had been determined, including catharanthine[110] and vindoline[111] (Figure 3.7) – compounds present in large quantities in the leaves of *C. roseus*, but with no cytotoxic properties. The absolute configuration[h] of the two molecules would be elucidated later[112]. These two compounds belong to the series of indolic alkaloids[i].

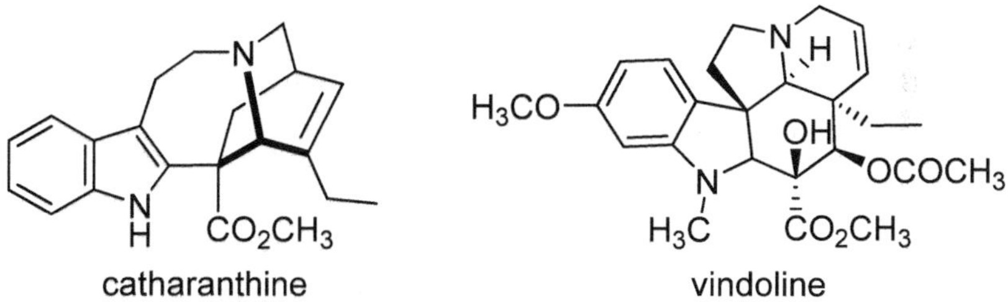

Figure 3.7. *Structures of catharanthine and vindoline*

By comparing the infrared (IR) and nuclear magnetic resonance (NMR) spectra of catharantine and vindoline against those of bisindolic alkaloids, an initial structure for vinblastine was suggested as being the combination of an indolic part: hydroxycatharanthine and a dihydroindolic part: vindoline (Figure 3.8). The chemical degradation, in an acidic environment, of the bisindolic alkaloids vinblastine, vincristine, leurosine and leurosidine yielding a derivative of vindoline and an indolic compound seemed to bear out that suggestion[84,113].

h The absolute configuration of a molecule is the spatial arrangement of each atom attached to stereocenters.

i Indolic alkaloids are characterized by the presence of an indole ring in their structure. Catharanthine has an indole ring, and vindoline, a dihydroindole ring.

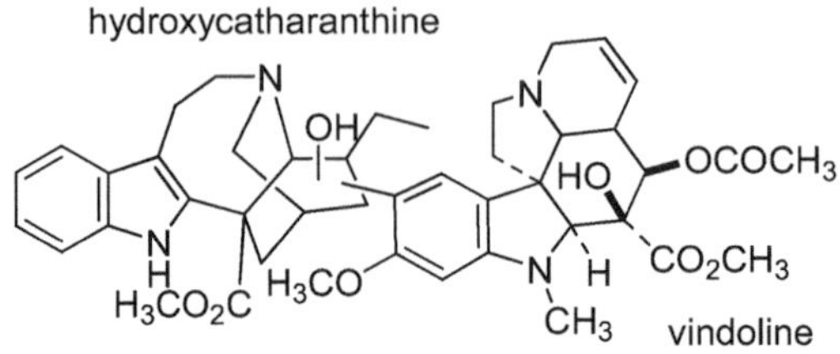

Figure 3.8. *First structure put forward for vinblastine*

Finally, the exact structure and configuration of vinblastine and vincristine were determined and published in 1965 and 1966, thanks to the X-ray diffraction spectrum of vincristine in the form of iodomethylate[112a,114]. Vinblastine and vincristine are bisindolic alkaloids, which have an indolic part in the form of cleavamine[j] rather than hydroxycatharanthine, and a dihydroindolic part, which does indeed correspond to vindoline. The structure of those two antitumoral compounds is distinguished by the substituant attached to the nitrogen atom in the dihydroindole, with vinblastine carrying an N-methyl group and vincristine having an N-formyl functional group (Figure 3.9).

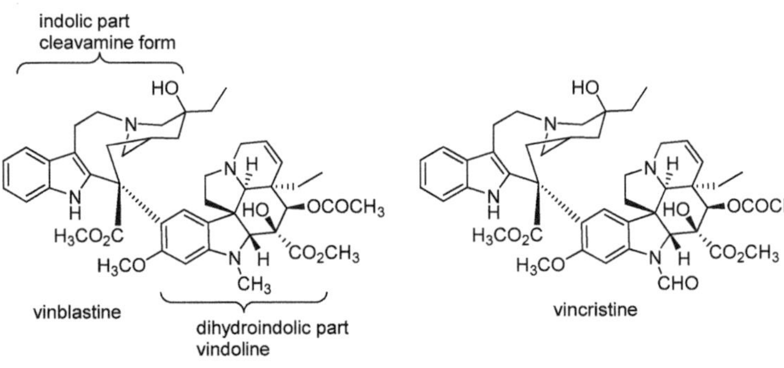

Figure 3.9. *Structures of vinblastine and vincristine*

A few years later, the structures of leurosine[115] and leurosidine[115b] were brought to light, notably thanks to NMR studies of carbon 13,

j Cleavamine is the product of rearrangement of catharanthine in an acidic environment (see Scheme 3.7).

mass spectrometry and chemical degradation, and confirmed by synthesis projects, conducted in Canada, by James Kutney for leurosine[116], and in France by Pierre Potier and Nicole Langlois for leurosidine[117]. Leurosine has an epoxide functional group on the indolic part, and leurosidine is an epimer of vinblastine at the carbon carrying the hydroxyl on the indolic part (Figure 3.10)[k].

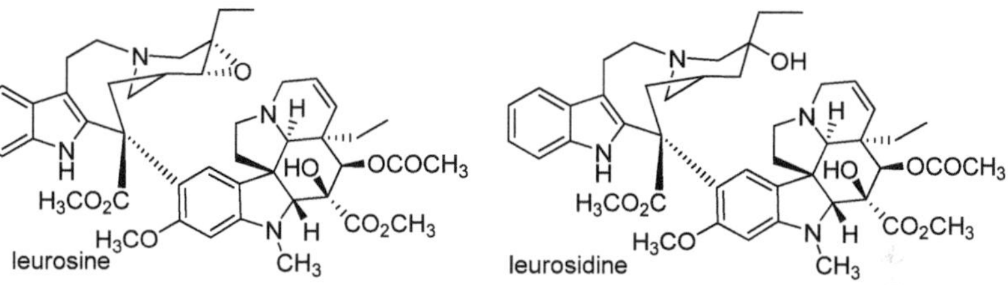

Figure 3.10. *Structures of leurosine and leurosidine*

3.2.2. *Vinblastine and vincristine: the first plant-based anti-cancer medications*

Out of the four bisindolic alkaloids mentioned above, vinblastine and vincristine were the subject of extensive biological and clinical trials in the late 1950s. Of the studies conducted *in vivo*, we could cite the work of Noble's team at the University of Western Ontario[93a], and of the researchers at Eli Lilly[93b], who, in 1960, published the beneficial effects of vinblastine in mice implanted with leukemia cell lines. The same year, the first clinical trials conducted with vinblastine, in the form of sulfate, were published[94,118]; those for vincristine would be published in 1962[119] and 1963[120]. The pharmacological validation and detailed description of the clinical trials for vinblastine and vincristine were published by the Canadian[92] and American teams[84,121], in the wake of their discovery.

Finally, and very quickly after these studies, the United States Food and Drug Administration (FDA) granted market authorization for the first natural-based cancer medications: vincristine under the trade name Oncovin®, in 1963, and vinblastine as Velban®, in 1965.

k Two epimers are two similar molecules which differ only by the absolute configuration of a stereocenter.

At that time, vincristine was recommended primarily for the treatment of acute leukemias in children, and vinblastine for Hodgkin lymphoma. Today, the indications for the use of vinblastine had been extended to, amongst other things, treating non-Hodgkin lymphomas, testicular and breast cancers, and vincristine for bronchopulmonary cancers.

Following the demonstration of the anti-cancerous properties of these two molecules, many laboratories began or continued researching with a view to discovering new antitumoral medications of natural origin. Thus, at the ICSN, research studies began on plants of the genus *Catharanthus* and on the synthesis of their bisindolic alkaloids.

In the 1960s, the structures of vinblastine, vincristine and other antitumoral bisindolic alkaloids having been established, the FDA granted market authorization for vincristine and vinblastine in 1963 and 1965, for treating various types of cancers.

3.3. Studies conducted at the ICSN: modified Polonovski reaction and chemical studies of *Catharanthus* (1960s–1970s)

At the ICSN, as seen in Chapter 2, the preferred research of M.-M. Janot was devoted to natural product chemistry – particularly to the chemistry of alkaloids. The main projects pertained not only to certain chemical reactions, but also to extraction of plants from Africa and Madagascar thanks to the links created, notably with Orstom, to the isolation of new molecules by chromatography and crystallization, and to the elucidation of the structure of these often-complex natural substances – that elucidation becoming easier gradually, with the improvement of mass spectrometry and NMR spectroscopy. If we trace the steps of the subjects studied by Janot's group, and then by P. Potier's, who worked with M.-M. Janot and succeeded him in 1974, we see that the discovery of vinorelbine was the result of various studies conducted at the ICSN, each of which was of capital importance. Some of these projects began with the study of a modification of the Polonovski reaction, and with the chemical analysis of different species of *Catharanthus*.

3.3.1. *The modified Polonovski reaction or Polonovski-Potier reaction*

Before going into detail about the modification of this reaction, it is crucial to highlight the importance of the work of Max and Michel Polonovski, published in 1927, with the title: "*Sur les aminoxydes des alcaloïdes. III. Action des anhydrides et chlorures d'acides organiques. Préparation des bases nor*" (On alkaloid aminoxides. III. Influence of organic acid anhydrides and chlorides. Preparation of nor bases)[122]. Contrary to what is sometimes portrayed in the literature, Max and Michel Polonovski were not brothers; they were father and son. Max Polonovski, a renowned chemist, studied, amongst other subjects, alkaloids from the Calabar bean (*Physostigma venenosum*). His son, Michel, Professor of organic chemistry in Lille and later Professor of biological chemistry at the *Faculté de Médecine de Paris*, was at the same time an organic chemist like his father, an analyst and a biochemist. Father and son collaborated in their research and published together. They studied the chemistry and the therapeutic potential of eserine (physostigmine) and geneserine – both molecules isolated from *Physostigma venenosum*. Their publication, cited above, on alkaloid aminoxides, reports the formation of different analogs of N-demethylated acetyl tropane, from the corresponding N-oxides, in the presence of acetic anhydride. Thus, tropidine N-oxide yields nortropidine via its N-acetyl derivative (Figure 3.11).

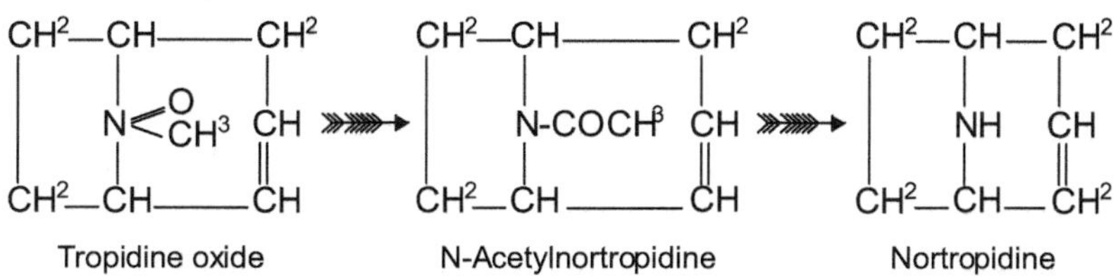

Figure 3.11. *Formation of nortropidine (extract from Max and Michel Polonovski's publication)*[122]

This rearrangement facilitates the N-demethylation of alkaloids in less drastic conditions than those required for the Von Braun method using cyanogen bromide[123]. Generally speaking, the Polonovski reaction can be presented as follows (Scheme 3.1):

Scheme 3.1. *Polonovski reaction*

Amine oxide (amine N-oxide) reacts with acetic anhydride to yield N-acetyl derivative for the most part, and an aldehyde. Somewhat forgotten after its discovery, the Polonovski reaction was the subject of more in-depth studies from the 1950s, notably by Ernest Wenkert, during his study of the role of oxidation in the biogenesis of alkaloids[124], and by Rolf Huisgen who studied the mechanism by which it takes place[125]. In the 1960s, Adrien Cavé and Robert Michelot, doctoral candidates in Janot's and Lederer's groups respectively, focused on the Polonovski reaction but for different reasons. A. Cavé, under P. Potier's supervision, studied the oxidation and demethylation of certain steroid alkaloids belonging to the paravallarine family, isolated from an Apocynacea from Southeast Asia, *Kibatalia gitingensis*[126], whilst R. Michelot, working under the direction of Bianca Tchoubar, on the mechanism of biogenetic C-methylation, examined the mechanism of the Polonovski reaction[127]. A. Cavé and R. Michelot respectively defended their doctoral theses in 1968 and 1969[126a,127b]. Through these different research projects, it was shown that the mechanism of the reaction differs depending on the anhydride used. Thus, N-oxide of

5α–dihydro N-methyl paravallarine leads, for the most part, in the presence of acetic anhydride, to the expected N-acetyl derivative, whilst the use of trifluoroacetic anhydride, after hydrolysis, mainly yields the ketonic derivative and the N-demethyl derivative (Scheme 3.2)[126b].

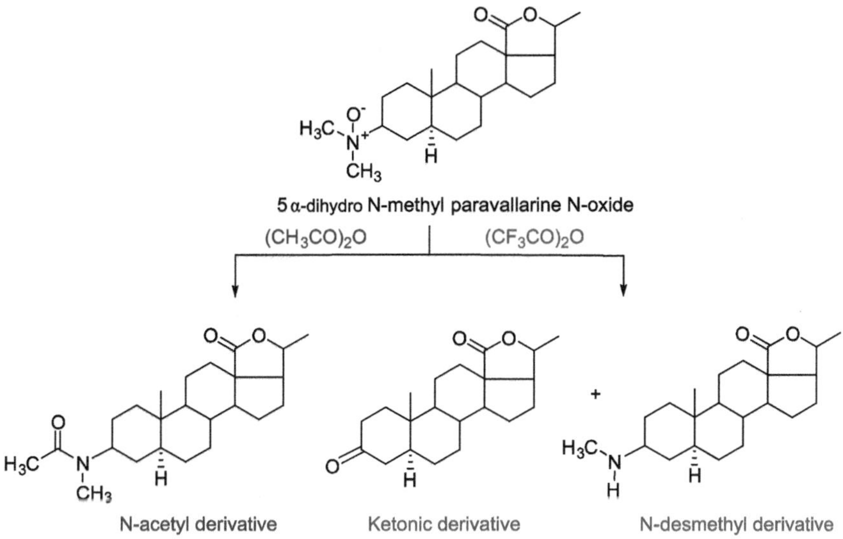

Scheme 3.2. *Action of acetic anhydride and trifluoroacetic anhydride on 5α-dihydro N-methyl paravallarine N-oxide. For a color version of the figure, please see www.iste.co.uk/leroux/navelbine.zip*

A. Cavé and R. Michelot compared the action of acetic anhydride and trifluoroacetic anhydride on different N-oxides of tertiary amines, and used NMR to study the reaction mixtures, to determine the intermediate species which could explain the mechanism of the two reactions[128]. This modification of the Polonovski reaction (replacement of acetic anhydride with trifluoroacetic anhydride), first called the “modified Polonovski reaction”, and later the “Polonovski-Potier reaction”, led to new and exciting research at the ICSN, and proved to be of considerable interest in synthesis. Indeed, this simple modification enabled researchers not only to easily produce the deaminated ketonic derivatives of steroid amines (Scheme 3.2)[126b], but also, thanks to Alain Ahond's thesis work[129], to obtain a new Mannich reagent[130], and find remarkable rearrangements for nitrogenous molecules, by breaking carbon–carbon bonds, helping to explain the biogenesis of certain alkaloids[131].

To summarize the essence of these results, simply, let us take the example of the treatment of tropane N-oxide by acetic anhydride (Scheme 3.3) and of N,N-dimethyltryptamine N-oxide by trifluoroacetic anhydride (Scheme 3.4).

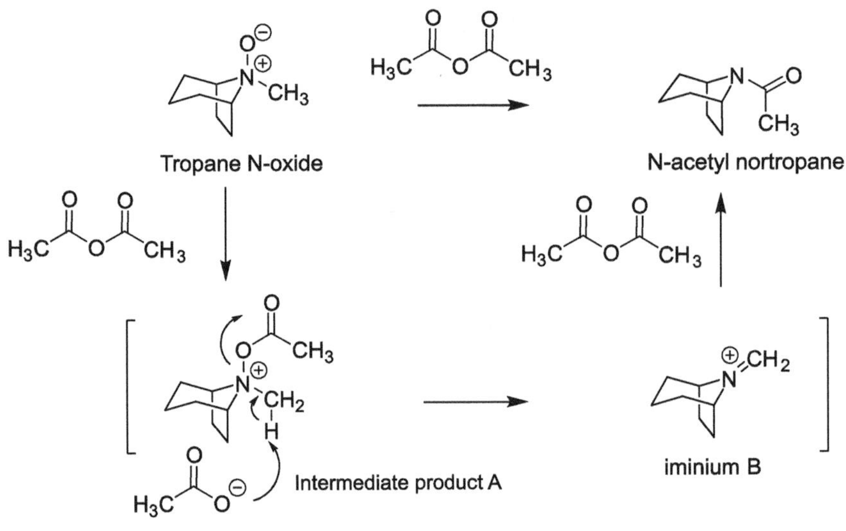

Scheme 3.3. *Action of acetic anhydride on tropane N-oxide*

In the case of tropane N-oxide, a chemical series studied by Max and Michel Polonovski, the action of acetic anhydride leads to the formation of intermediate product A. The basic nature of the acetoxy ion facilitates deprotonation with the elimination of the acetoxy group present on the nitrogen, forming the intermediate product iminium B which, after acetolysis, leads to N-acetyl nortropane (Scheme 3.3).

When trifluoroacetic anhydride acts on derivatives of N, N-dimethyltryptamine N_b-oxide (Scheme 3.4), the intermediate product A is formed first of all. The weak base nature of the trifluoroacetate ion preventing deprotonation and its leaving-group property cause a reaction of fragmentation, producing iminiums B and C. Michael addition of dimethylamine, formed by hydrolysis of iminium C, onto iminium B, thus leads to gramine derivatives[132].

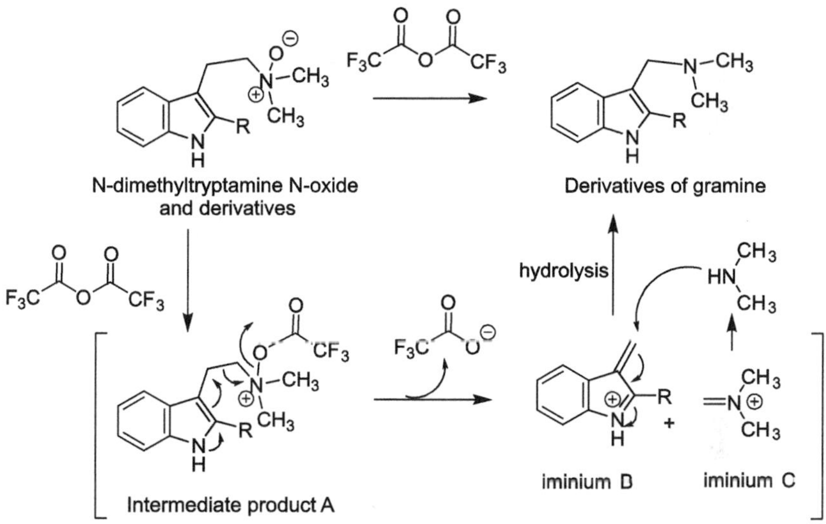

Scheme 3.4. *Mechanism of action of trifluoroacetic anhydride on derivatives of N,N-dimethyltryptamine N-oxide*

To compare the action of acetic anhydride to that of trifluoroacetic anhydride on the same compound, we can cite the work carried out on a model natural-origin molecule: dregamine (Scheme 3.5). These studies were performed in the 1970s, by Pierre Mangeney, carrying out his doctoral research, under Yves Langlois' supervision, in Potier's team[133].

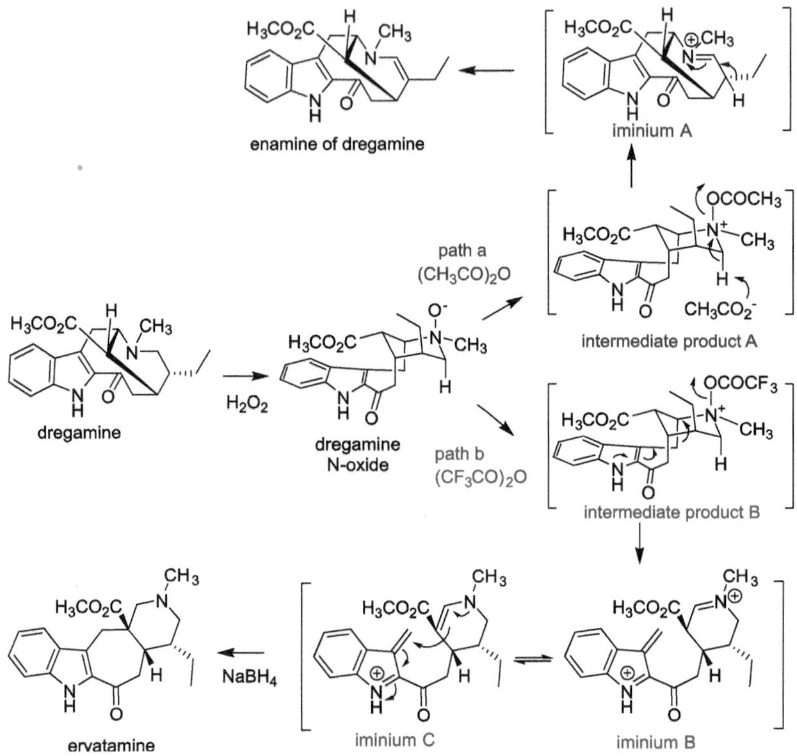

Scheme 3.5. *Action of acetic anhydride (Polonovski) and trifluoroacetic anhydride (Polonovski-Potier) on dregamine. For a color version of the figure, please see www.iste.co.uk/leroux/navelbine.zip*

In this example, we can clearly see the structural difference that exists between the products obtained. In the presence of acetic anhydride (Polonovski reaction, path a), the nucleophilicity of the acetate ion leads to the elimination of the proton in the axial position of the intermediate product A, leading to iminium A and then to the enamine of dregamine. With trifluoroacetic anhydride (Polonovski-Potier reaction, path b), a fragmentation of the carbon–carbon bond in the beta position of the good leaving group trifluoroacetate takes place, which is facilitated by the indolic nitrogen atom intermediate product B), producing iminium B which becomes iminium C to achieve equilibrium. After reduction by sodium borohydride, the compound obtained is ervatamine, whose skeleton is different from that of dregamine.

Thus, the Polonovski-Potier reaction using trifluoroacetic anhydride as a reagent leads to fragmentation of carbon–carbon bonds when applied, notably, to tertiary amine N-oxides. As we shall see in the next section, this reaction was crucially important in the discovery of navelbine. Before detailing the different steps that led to that discovery, it is important to recap the chemical work done on certain species of *Catharanthus*, one of the objectives of which was to seek out new alkaloids with antitumoral properties.

3.3.2. *First chemical studies of Catharanthus species at the ICSN*

It was thanks to Pierre Boiteau, an agronomic engineer, botanist and major expert on Madagascan flora, that many species of *Catharanthus* were collected and studied at the ICSN through missions funded by the CNRS (see Chapter 2). The effective collaboration between botanists from the *Muséum d'Histoire Naturelle* and Orstom on the one hand (Maurice Debray participated, with P. Boiteau, in the various operations of collection and botanical identification), and chemists from the ICSN on the other, was a major asset in the study of the genus *Catharanthus*. Thus, P. Boiteau, along with M.-M. Janot and then P. Potier, studied Madagascan Apocynaceae and their alkaloidic components. He collected different species of *Catharanthus* in Madagascar, which he then gave to P. Potier. During his missions, he had also brought back a sample of the whole plant, *Catharanthus roseus*, collected on the east coast near to Fort-Dauphin – the same place where Étienne de Flacourt, in 1648, had collected the first sample, which is still preserved at the *Muséum d'Histoire Naturelle of Paris*[1]. On her father P. Boiteau's death, in 1980, Lucile Allorge took up the baton of his botanical research on other species of periwinkles and other plants, in Madagascar, in connection with the ICSN.

1 Information from Lucile Allorge, P. Boiteau's daughter, 15 January 2014.

Figure 3.12. *Stamp commemorating Pierre Boiteau*[m]

At the ICSN, the supply of *Catharanthus* species and their botanical determination therefore posed no particular problem. As one of Potier and his team's objectives was to find new bisindolic alkaloids having activities similar to that of vinblastine and vincristine, it was crucial to combine chemical and biological studies. Thus, the different steps consisted of extracting the different parts (leaves, stems, roots) of the plant, and then separating the alkaloids whilst monitoring their antitumoral activity. The alkaloids were extracted in large quantities either by the laboratories of the company Rhône-Poulenc, or at the "factory" of the ICSN[n]. In terms of monitoring the antitumoral activity, the *in vitro* tests conducted on cultures of KB cells, and the *in vivo* trials in mice on grafted tumors and L1210 and AKR leukemias, were carried out by researchers at Rhône-Poulenc's oncology department, with whom P. Potier had been collaborating regularly, for a long time. It should also be noted that the presence, within the ICSN, of excellent mass spectrometry, NMR spectroscopy and crystallography services aided the quick structural determination of the compounds isolated.

In Potier's team, the earliest research on antitumoral alkaloids on the genus *Catharanthus* was conducted by Nicole Langlois, at the end of

m Madagascan stamp from 1982, paying tribute to P. Boiteau.

n Extractive chemistry was developed at the ICSN, in the 1960s, following the creation, by Alexandre Escaut, of a laboratory known as the "factory", where tests for the small-scale extraction and purification of plants conducted by the researchers were transposed to the industrial scale.

the 1960s, on the species *C. ovalis*[134]. In the same team, thanks to the support of P. Boiteau, P. Potier and Jean-Martin Razafintsalama (professor at the Faculty of Sciences in Tananarive), Philippe Rasoanaivo (a Madagascan student) came to France to begin his doctorate studies. Under N. Langlois' supervision, he studied the alkaloidal composition of the species *C. longifolius*[135]. Then, Ratremaniana Zo Andriamialisoa – another Madagascan student – and Luc Diatta, both also working under the supervision of N. Langlois, continued the study of *C. ovalis*[136]. P. Rasoanaivo and R. Z. Andriamialisoa, in their theses respectively defended in December 1974 and June 1978, describe their work isolating alkaloids and characterizing the alkaloids thus isolated[137]. Hence, we can cite the isolation of previously-known bisindolic alkaloids such as vinblastine, vincristine and leurosine, and the characterization of new dimers and the revision of the structures of other bis-indoles, such as vincovaline, the stereoisomer of vinblastine[136b,137b], catharinex[137a,138], and catharinine[137b, 139] (Figure 3.13)[o]. During these first studies conducted on these two species of the genus *Catharanthus* (*C. ovalis* and *C. longifolius*), the pharmacological activity of the different fractions and products obtained during the purification of the raw extracts from the plants was systematically evaluated *in vitro* and *in vivo*.

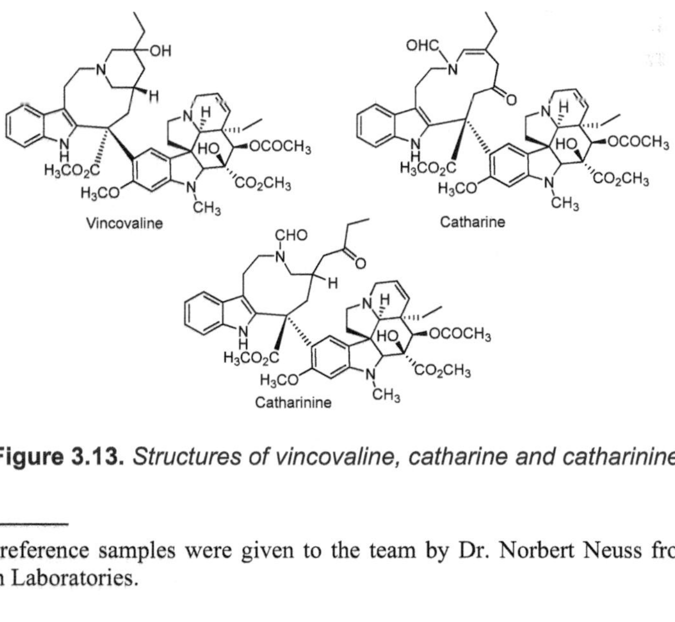

Figure 3.13. *Structures of vincovaline, catharine and catharinine*

o Many reference samples were given to the team by Dr. Norbert Neuss from Lilly Research Laboratories.

3.4. Studies conducted at the ICSN: semisynthesis of alkaloids such as vinblastine – biological activity and biosynthesis (1970s–1980s)

Vinblastine and vincristine are relatively easy to isolate from certain species of *Catharanthus*, but in very small quantities. For example, during the first attempts to isolate vinblastine on a large scale, conducted in the 1960s by Eli Lilly, about 28 grams were obtained from 15 tons of dry leaves of *Catharanthus roseus*[92]. Vincristine, for its part, is isolated in even smaller quantities. The complex structure of these two compounds having been established in 1965[112a], many teams took an interest in their synthesis, and more particularly their semisynthesis[p]. If we take a detailed look at the structures of vinblastine and vincristine, we can see that they are compounds made up of two units: an indolic unit – cleavamine – corresponding to carbomethoxy-velbanamine, and a dihydroindolic unit corresponding to vindoline for vinblastine, and N-demethyl-N-formylvindoline for vincristine. It is essential here to indicate the numbering of the carbon atoms in vinblastine and its analogs or derivatives. Two numbering systems tend to be used: IUPAC (International Union of Pure and Applied Chemistry) numbering, and biogenetic numbering (see Figure 3.14)[q].

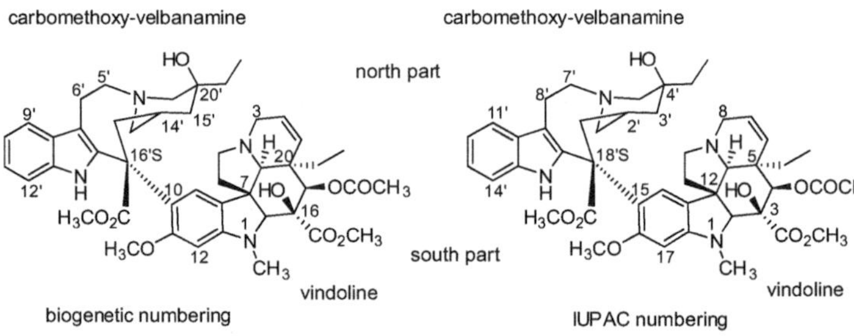

Figure 3.14. *Biogenetic and IUPAC numbering of vinblastine*

---

p Semisynthesis is chemical synthesis performed from natural molecules that can be easily accessed and have simpler structures than the target molecule.

q Biogenetic numbering follows the steps of biogenesis of the compound. IUPAC numbering obeys the rules of IUPAC nomenclature. Throughout the following chapters, we shall use the IUPAC numbering system, as indicated for vinblastine (Figure 3.14).

In the IUPAC nomenclature of vinblastine, carbomethoxyvelbanamine and vindoline, corresponding respectively to the north- and south parts of the molecule, are linked together by a bond between carbons 18' and 15, with a stereochemistry *S* (sinister) of carbon 18'. The derivatives velbanamine and vindoline thus seemed to be precursors all indicated to perform the semisynthesis of bisindolic alkaloids – all the more so given that, in 1962, researchers from Eli Lilly had published the cleavage of vinblastine, in a reducingacidic environment, yielding velbanamine and deacetylvindoline[113a] (Scheme 3.6). Also, the same publication described the production of cleavamine from catharanthine (Scheme 3.7), whose absolute configuration was published in 1963 and 1964[140].

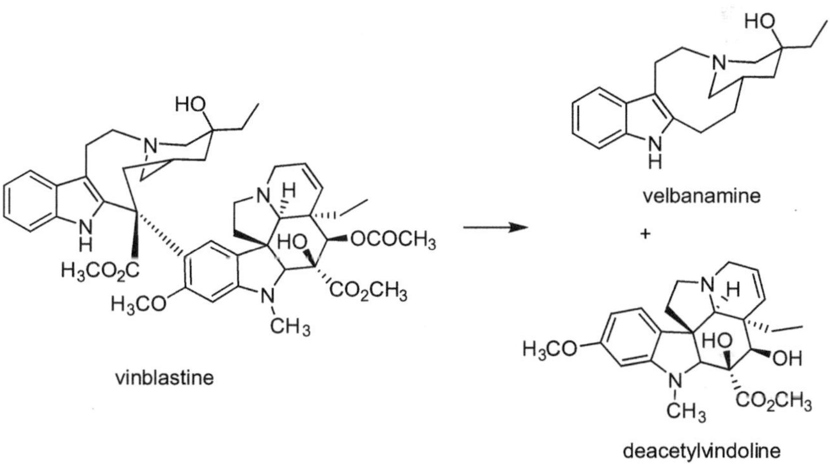

Scheme 3.6. *Cleavage of vinblastine in a reducing acidic environment*

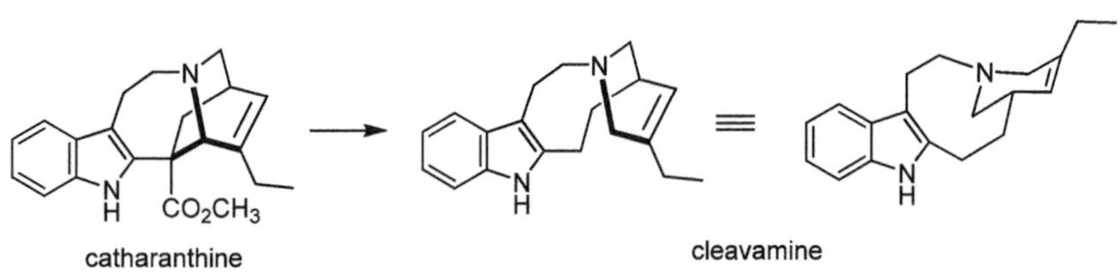

Scheme 3.7. *Cleavage of catharanthine in a reducing acidic environment*

3.4.1. *State of the art: first semisynthesis leading to analogs of vinblastine with "unnatural" 18'R configuration*

The first attempts at semisynthesis of vinblastine were published in 1967, by John Harley-Mason and Atta-ur-Rahman[r], using a derivative of cleavamine hydroxylated at carbon 18. Thus, by treating 18-hydroxidihydrocleavamine and vindoline, in an acidic medium, they obtained a mixture of alkaloids, including demethoxycarbonyldeoxyvinblastine (Scheme 3.8)[141]. If this initial strategy was a definite advance in the synthesis of these complex alkaloids, it was not able to produce the natural configuration (18'*S*), which is crucial for biological activity.

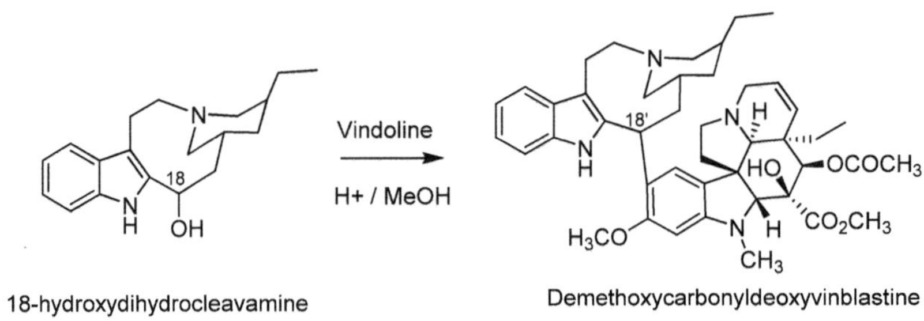

Scheme 3.8. *Semisynthesis from 18-hydroxycleavamine*

A different approach, involving the coupling of vindoline with a cleavamine-type chloroindolenine, was developed simultaneously, in 1968, by Norbert Neuss[142] and James P. Kutney[143], and then by Atta-ur-Rahman, in 1971[144]. The dimers obtained are also inactive, which, at carbon 18', has the unnatural stereochemistry (18'*R*). For example, methoxycarbonyl cleavamine chloroindolenine reacts, in an acidic medium, with vindoline to yield the epimer 18'*R* of anhydrovinblastine (see Scheme 3.9)[144].

r Prof. Dr. Atta-Ur-Rahman, a Pakistani scientist who received a number of honours and awards for his contribution in the field of natural substances chemistry, was at that time working on his PhD at King's College, Cambridge, in Dr. John Harley-Mason's laboratory.

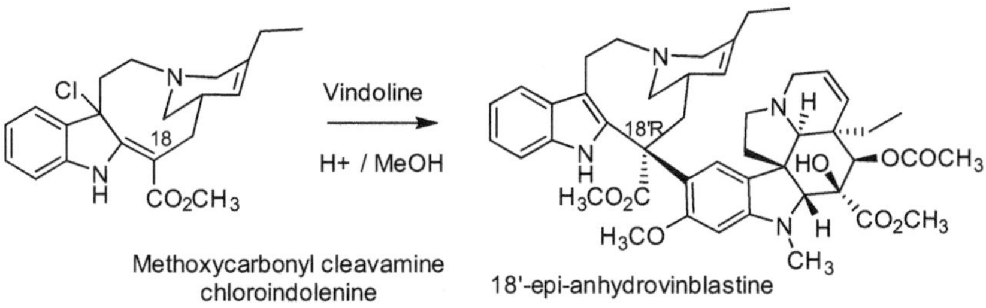

Scheme 3.9. *Semisynthesis from chloroindolenine*

The compounds obtained by these two approaches have proved to be inactive. The major difficulty in vinblastine synthesis, therefore, was to obtain the good stereochemistry *S* at carbon 18', connected to the biological activity.

3.4.2. *First semisynthesis of anhydrovinblastine – an analog of vinblastine with the natural configuration (18'S)*

One of the strategies that can be used to synthesize a natural substance is to try to mimic its biogenesis – that is, to copy the steps performed by the living organism to produce it. In 1954, Ernest Wenkert had described the role of oxidation in the biogenesis of alkaloids, causing rearrangements of their skeletons. He also mentioned that the Polonovski reaction was the most representative chemical reaction likely to perform such rearrangements[124].

Whilst vindoline and catharanthine are two of the most prevalent substances present in the Madagascan periwinkle, velbanamine and cleavamine are not isolated from the plant. In 1971, Atta-ur-Rahman suggested, but not directly demonstrated, that catharanthine could be coupled with vindoline to produce alkaloids such as vinblastine[144]. Then, in 1974, Hutchinson showed, using certain biosynthesis experiments, that vinblastine could be derived from the coupling of vindoline and catharanthine[145]. All of these facts and the demonstration, described above, of the synthetic capabilities of the Polonovski-Potier reaction in the formation of different alkaloids, led P. Potier to imagine a new coupling method using that reaction. He explains it thus in his book, *Le magasin du Bon Dieu* (God's Shop):

> In the case of these dreadfully problematic alkaloids, I suddenly had the idea of using the Polonovski reaction, which I had modified a few years earlier. Remember that this reaction was biomimetic. I was firmly convinced that the plant used the same type of process to make its own metabolites. (p. 96)[22]

In 1974, he submitted his idea to Nicole and Yves Langlois. N. Langlois was therefore the first to obtain the natural configuration (18'*S*) of a new analog of vinblastine: anhydrovinblastine, formed by coupling vindoline with catharanthine N_b-oxide, under Polonovski-Potier reaction conditions. Comparing the structure of anhydrovinblastine with that of vinblastine, the only difference lies in the absence of a water molecule on the $C_{3'}$-$C_{4'}$ bond of anhydrovinblastine (Figure 3.15).

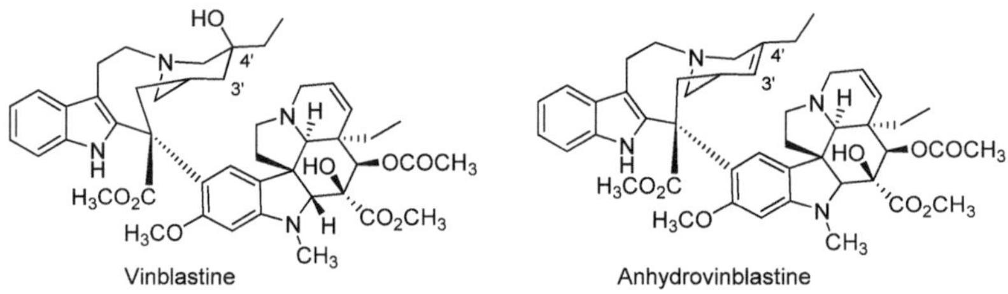

Figure 3.15. *Structural differences between vinblastine and anhydrovinblastine*

In order to prove the originality of this result, a "*pli cacheté*" (sealed envelope) signed by Pierre Potier, Nicole Langlois and Yves Langlois, regarding the preparation of anhydrovinblastine from catharanthine and vindoline, was filed at the *Académie des sciences* on 14 October 1974. That same month, at P. Potier's suggestion, F. Guéritte, a 3rd-cycle doctoral student, joined that team to work on the semisynthesis of anhydrovinblastine and structural analogs.

Some time after the deposition of the *pli cacheté*, a French patent was filed, on 30 December 1974[68], by the *Agence Nationale de Valorisation de la Recherche* (Anvar), and then the results were published in 1975 (Figure 3.16) and 1976[146].

This patenting came not a moment too soon… because J.P. Kutney, using the same process, patented his results on the semisynthesis of anhydrovinblastine, on 30 May 1975, five months after the French team[147]. J.P. Kutney and his collaborators published their results in 1975[148].

670 J.C.S. Chem. Comm., 1975

Partial Synthesis of Vinblastine-type Alkaloids

By Pierre Potier*, Nicole Langlois, Yves Langlois, and Françoise Guéritte
(*Institut de Chimie des Substances Naturelles du C.N.R.S., 91190-Gif s/Yvette, France*)

Summary Application of a modification of Polonovski's reaction facilitates partial synthesis of vinblastine-type alkaloids.

Several antitumour alkaloids have been isolated from *Catharanthus roseus*,[1] two of them, vinblastin (**1**) and vincristine (**2**) being widely used clinically. Attempts[2-8] to synthesize these compounds have not yet been successful;† and although compounds possessing the 'non-natural' configuration at C(16')[3,5,8] have been obtained, they have shown no significant antitumour activity.

All attempts so far have consisted of coupling vindoline (**3**) with a *seco*-16,21-catharanthine derivative, *i.e.* 16-carbomethoxycleavamine (**4**), obtained by reductive cleavage of catharanthine (**5**). However, since in Nature vinblastine-type alkaloids could well be formed through a direct coupling of vindoline (**3**) with a suitable catharanthine (or 20-hydroxycatharanthine) derivative rather than with a *seco*-16,21 compound, we have now devised a new partial synthesis of these dimeric indole alkaloids having a 'natural' configuration at C(16').

Table 1

δ ($CDCl_3$)	(1)	(8a)	(8b)	(9)	(10)
C(12)-H	6·12	6·03	5·92	6·11	6·02
C(9)-H	6·62	6·52	6·85	6·59	6·50
C(18)-H	0·89	0·81	0·60	0·80	0·93

When a derivative of catharanthine such as (**6**), (where X is a convenient leaving group) reacts with vindoline (**3**) an intermediate immonium ion (**7**) is obtained, reduction of which leads to compound (**8**). [(**3**) + (**6**) → (**7**) → (**8**)]. For example, the N_b-oxide of catharanthine undergoes a fragmentation reaction when treated with trifluoroacetic anhydride[9] to give (**6**, X = $OCOCF_3$), and when this reaction is carried out with vindoline (**3**) *in situ*, two dimeric indole alkaloids are obtained after reduction with $NaBH_4$, (**8a**) (30—40%), m.p. 216—218° (decomp.), $[\alpha]_D$ + 19°, ($CHCl_3$) and (**8b**), hydrobromide m.p. >260° (decomp.); $[\alpha]_D$ − 86°, ($CHCl_3$). The yields and relative proportions of these two compounds depend upon experimental conditions; this, and inspection of molecular models

Table 2

c.d.(EtOH)	(1)	(8a)	(8b)	(10)
λ/nm	254	258	258	260
Δ ε	+10·5	+13·3	−13·2	+12·0
λ/nm			280	
Δ ε			+3·2	
λ/nm	302	305	309	304
Δ ε	+4·8	+6·4	+8·0	+4·8

suggest that they are formed by two different mechanisms, either concerted or non-concerted; spectral data are in full agreement with the planar structure (**8**), the nature of the junction between the two monomeric units being established by ^1H n.m.r. spectra[10] [absence of a signal between 4 and 5 p.p.m. eliminates the possibility of a substitution of one of the carbon atoms α to N_b of catharanthine (**5**) by vindoline (**3**)]. Moreover, C(12)-H and C(9)-H appear as singlets in (**8a**) or (**8b**) suggesting that vindoline is itself substituted on C(10). Comparison of δ values of C(9)-H, C(12)-H, and C(18)-H of (**8a**) and (**8b**) with those of the corresponding protons in vinblastine (**1**) and leurosine (**9**) (Table 1) indicates the similarity between these two natural compounds and (**8a**).[5]

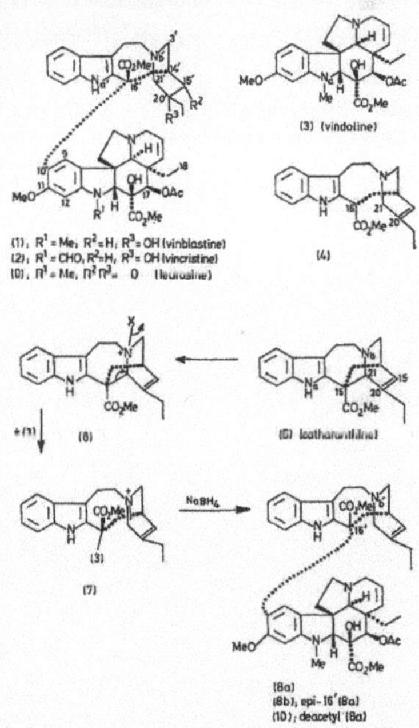

A corresponding similarity is noted between (**8a**) [but not (**8b**)] and vinblastine when the circular dichroism curves are compared (Table 2); this simple spectroscopic method is

† Recently, Prof. J. P. Kutney, University of British Columbia, Vancouver, has kindly informed us of a successful approach to this problem.

Figure 3.16. *Semisynthesis of anhydrovinblastine (first page of the J.C.S Chem. Comm., 1975)[146a]*

3.4.3. *Mechanism of anhydrovinblastine formation*

The idea behind using the Polonovski-Potier reaction was that it could help to activate the nitrogen N_b in catharanthine to weaken the C_5-C_{18} bond, allowing its fragmentation . To do this, catharanthine is first transformed into its N_b-oxide, by the action of an oxidizing agent, such as *p*-nitroperbenzoic acid or *m*-chloroperbenzoic acid. This transformation must be performed at a low temperature to prevent a rearrangement of the skeleton of catharanthine[149]. In the presence of trifluoroacetic anhydride, catharanthine N_b-oxide yields intermediate product A which fragments at the C_5-C_{18} bond. The conformer iminiums B and C formed are attacked by vindoline to give a mixture of two dimer iminiums, epimers at the 18' carbon atom. Those iminiums, after reduction by sodium borohydride, yield anhydrovinblastine and its epimer at C_{18}' (see Scheme 3.10).

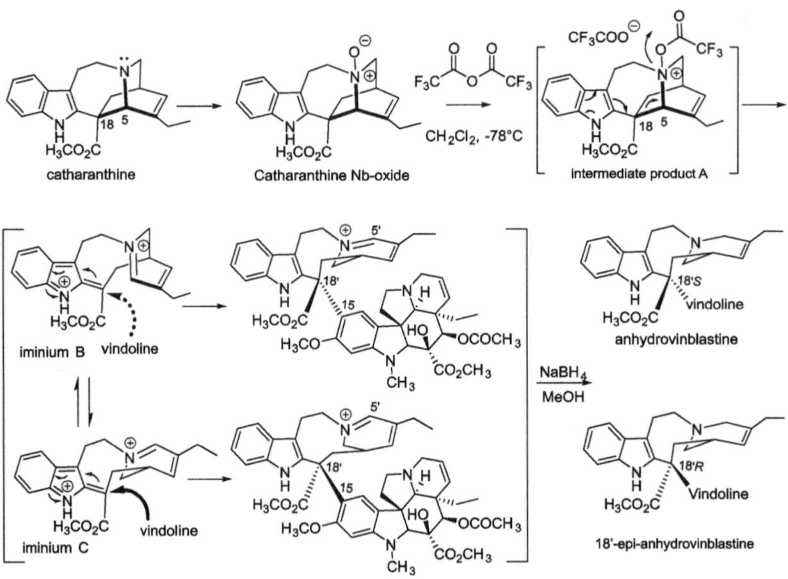

Scheme 3.10. Mechanism of anhydrovinblastine formation

The yields of the two epimers are temperature-dependent. Thus, the best yield of anhydrovinblastine (50%) is obtained when the Polonovski-Potier reaction is performed at -78°C. At a higher temperature, the epimer compound at the 18' carbon is predominantly obtained. This influence of temperature can be explained by the conformational differences of the intermediary iminiums B and C formed after the cleavage of the C_{18}-C_5 bond. At a low temperature, it is only the conformer B, the kinetic conformer, which forms. The nucleophilic attack of vindoline takes place on the least encumbered side, on the lower face, leading to the natural 18'*S* configuration At a higher temperature, the conformer C (the thermodynamic conformer) is obtained, leading to the 18'*R* epimer by vindoline attack on the upper face (Scheme 3.10).

Thus, the Polonovski-Potier reaction, applied to the coupling of vindoline and catharanthine N_b-oxide, for the first time, yielded a vinblastine-type alkaloid with the so widely sought configuration 18'*S*. The semisynthesis of anhydrovinblastine was later improved with a 77% yield by Kutney and Vukovic's team, who, in 1988, published the coupling of catharanthine with vindoline, initiated by ferric ions, entitled: "Production of 3',4'-anhydrovinblastine: a unique chemical synthesis"[150]. To explain the predominant formation of the 18'*S* epimer the authors suggest the involvement of a concerted mechanism, facilitating the attack of vindoline on the lower face of the intermediate product iminium obtained from catharanthine in the presence of iron chloride (Scheme 3.11).

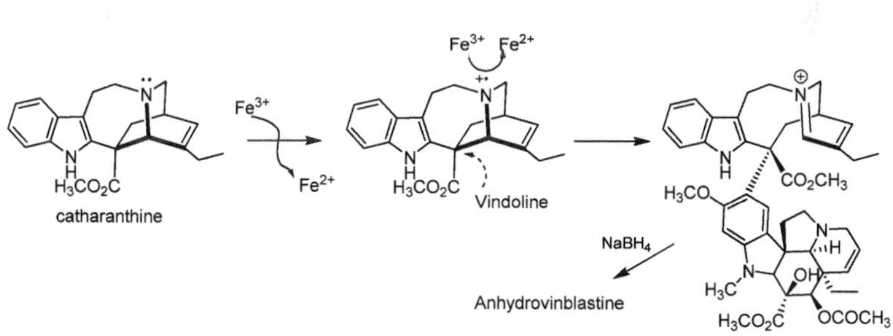

Scheme 3.11. *Semisynthesis of anhydrovinblastine by iron chloride ($FeCl_3$)*

Studies on the concerted mechanism of the reaction were then conducted, notably by R. Sundberg[151]. He suggested that at a low temperature, vindoline acted by a quasi-concerted process, as a base which deprotonizes the intermediate product A and as a nucleophile, accounting for the stereochemistry observed (Scheme 3.12).

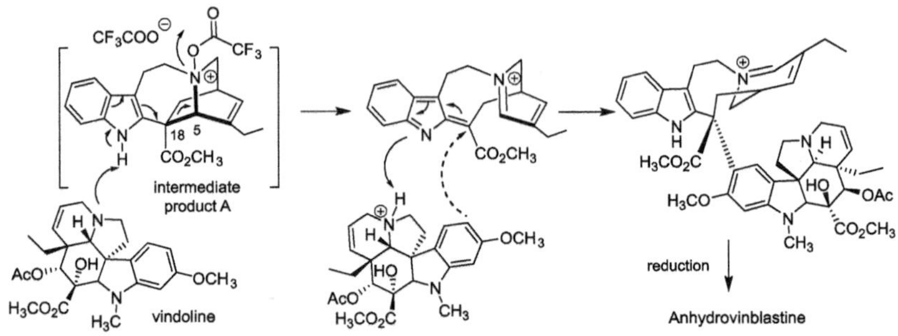

Scheme 3.12. *Involvement of vindoline in the quasi-concerted mechanism of anhydrovinblastine formation*[s]

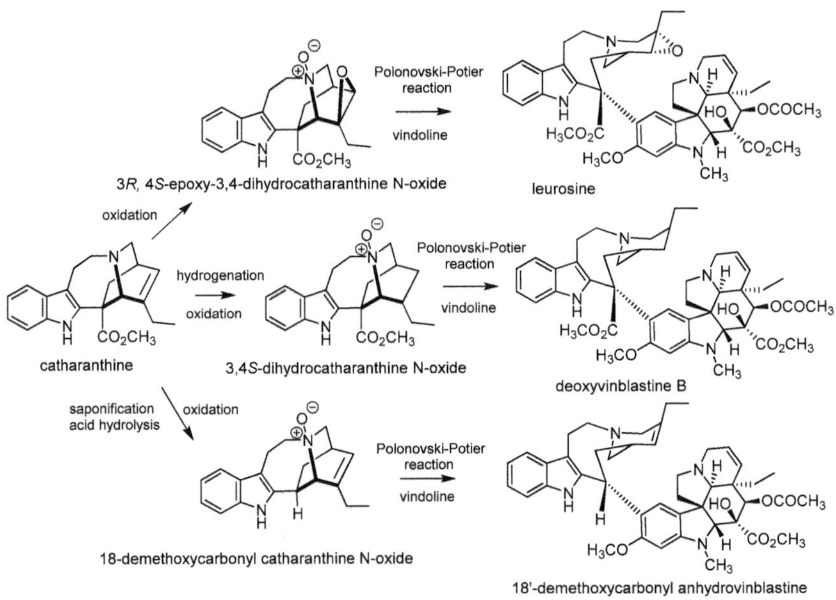

Scheme 3.13. *Semisynthesis of leurosine, deoxyvinblastine B and 18'-demethoxycarbonyl anhydrovinblastine*

s Scheme taken from the slideshow for P. Mangeney's lecture, "*Découverte de la Navelbine®*", at the *École nationale supérieure de chimie de Montpellier*, 10 February 2011.

The Polonovski-Potier reaction was then used, by Potier's team, to synthesize other bisindolic compounds, again with N. and Y. Langlois, and the doctoral students R.Z. Andriamialisoa[137b], P. Mangeney[152] and F. Guéritte[153]. Among other, natural bisindolic alkaloids such as leurosine[152,154] or deoxyvinblastine B[146b,153a], and non-natural ones such as 18'-demethoxycarbonyl anhydrovinblastine [137b,155] were obtained by coupling vindoline with catharanthine derivatives (Scheme 3.13).

At the same time, Kutney's team, in Canada, published the semisynthesis of the same alkaloids[156]; Atta-ur-Rahman's team[157] in Pakistan published the partial synthesis of vinblastine; and the team led by Y. Ban[158], in Japan, reported the coupling of derivatives of catharanthine with vindoline. Numerous other analogs of vinblastine were then synthesized using the Polonovski-Potier reaction.

3.4.4. *Determination of the configuration at C-18 (18'S versus 18'R): electronic circular dichroism*

The configuration at carbon 18' of bisindolic alkaloids plays a determinant role in their biological activity. For example, anhydrovinblastine in 18'*S* configuration is active, but its epimer 18'*R* is inactive (see section 3.4.5). In order to easily determine the absolute configuration of that carbon of the different bisindolic alkaloids obtained by semisynthesis, the use of electronic circular dichroism[t] has been of critical importance. Thus, the French team published the values of the Cotton effects of vinblastine (**1**), anhydrovinblastine (**8a**), and epi-18' anhydrovinblastine (**8b**) in Table 2 of the publication reporting the first semisynthesis of alkaloids with the 18'*S* configuration[146a] (Figure 3.17).

t Electronic circular dichroism is a differential polarized-light-absorption technique, which provides information about the configuration and conformation of chiral molecules.

TABLE 2

c.d. (EtOH)	(1)	(8a)	(8b)	(10)
λ/nm	254	258	258	260
Δε	+10·5	+13·3	−13·2	+12·0
λ/nm			280	
Δε			+3·2	
λ/nm	302	305	309	304
Δε	+4·8	+6·4	+8·0	+4·8

Figure 3.17. *Circular dichroism of vinblastine (1), anhydrovinblastine (8a) and its epimer at C-18' (8b) (table extracted from the publication J.C.S. Chem. Comm., 1975)*[146a]

The difference existing between compounds (**1**), (**8a**) and compound (**8b**), at the wavelength (λ) of 258–260 nm is the sign of the absorption (Cotton effect (Δε)), which is positive for bisindolic alkaloids with configuration 18'*S* ((**1**), and (**8a**)) and negative for the compound with configuration 18'*R* (**8b**). Thus, in 1978, in his doctoral thesis, R.Z. Andriamialisoa reported a detailed comparative study of the circular dichroism curves on numerous vinblastine analogs[137b]. This quick and easy method was also used by J.P. Kutney, D.E. Scott[159] and R. Parish[160] to determine the absolute configuration of the asymmetrical carbons on the cleavamine part of various vinblastine diastereoisomers.

3.4.5. *Antitumoral activity and evaluation with the tubulin test*

As previously mentioned, one of Potier and his team's objectives was to seek out new compounds with potential antitumoral properties. It was therefore essential to monitor the activity of the molecules obtained during the semisynthesis work conducted by the team.

To begin with, the collaboration with the oncology department at Rhône-Poulenc enabled the team to test the *in vitro* cytotoxicity, and then the *in vivo* activity in mice, of anhydrovinblastine, on grafted tumors and leukemias. Preliminary results found by Dr. René Maral show antitumoral activity for anhydrovinblastine against leukemia L1210, but a lesser effect than that of vinblastine[153a]. As these tests were lengthy and costly, it was crucial to find a substitute method by which to quickly and easily evaluate compounds' biological activity.

It happens that J. Harry Cutts, from the team at the University of Western Ontario, had, in 1961, published an article showing the effects of vinblastine on normally-dividing and tumoral cells, and concluded that vinblastine ought to function as a spindle toxin.[161] Then, the first publications dealing with the direct interaction of vinblastine with tubulin began to appear in the early 1970s.[67, 162]

This ubiquitous protein, which is present in eukaryotic cells, in the form of dimers (α and β) and in the polymerized form of microtubules, is the raw material for the mitotic spindle, along which chromosomes migrate during cell division.

Tubulin was first isolated in the late 1960s, by Edwin Taylor and Gary Borisy, using another natural product: colchicine[163]. Shortly afterwards, in the 1970s, a tubulin purification process was published by Michael Shelanski[164], based on the reversibility of the disassembly of microtubules into tubulin, induced by cold. Tubulin, which is made up of its two subunits α and β, assembles *in vitro* at 37°C, forming protofilaments. The lateral association of these protofilaments and their elongation creates microtubules, which disassemble at 0°C. This equilibrium is also disturbed by magnesium ions, by guanosine triphosphate (GTP) and by "microtubule-associated proteins" (MAPs) which lead to assembly, and by calcium ions, which disassemble the microtubules into tubulin (Figure 3.18).

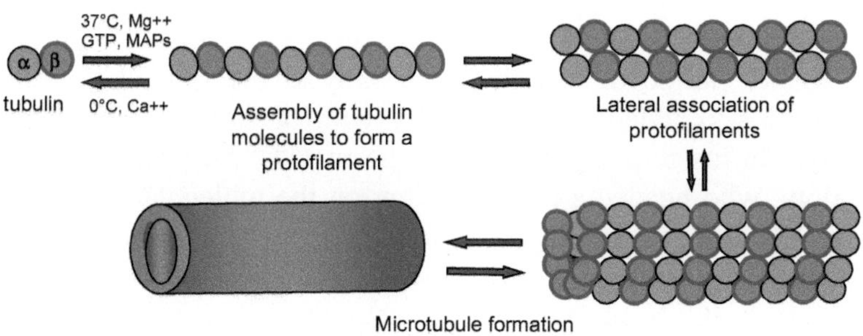

Figure 3.18. *Simplified representation of the equilibrium between tubulin and microtubules. For a color version of the figure, please see www.iste.co.uk/leroux/navelbine.zip*

In vivo, that dynamic equilibrium which exists between tubulin and microtubules is of crucial importance for the correct function of cell division, and any molecule which disrupts that equilibrium, by binding either to tubulin or to microtubules, will have a direct effect on a cell, preventing it from dividing. To observe this effect, certain teams – notably that led by M. Shelanski[165] – developed an *in vitro* test capable of monitoring the equilibrium between tubulin and microtubules, in certain conditions. Using that *in vitro* test, M. Shelanski[166] and R. Himes[167], in 1975 and 1976 respectively, published on the inhibiting effects of vinblastine and other analogs on the assembly of tubulin into microtubules. Then, B. Bhattacharyya and J. Wolff showed that vinblastine binds to two sites on tubulin[168]. The first, where it has high affinity, causes disassembly; the second, where it has weak affinity, induces the behavior of spiralization (or aggregation) of tubulin.

In light of these results, research pertaining to the use of that *in vitro* test to directly observe the action of bisindolic alkaloids on tubulin began at the ICSN in 1975, in Potier's team, with Daniel Guénard. This new area of study, quite different from that on which they had previously worked, was significant. The laboratory already had experts in botany, phytochemistry, analytical and structural chemistry and organic chemistry. All that was needed now was expertise in biochemistry to supplement the research under way, for tracking the biological activity of the isolated/synthesized compounds. At P. Potier's suggestion, D. Guénard, a chemist by training, undertook a period of post-doctoral study at the Institut Pasteur, to combine his knowledge in chemistry with that of biochemistry and biology. On his return to the ICSN, he met the biologist Dominique Pantaloni, who headed a team working on the molecular mechanisms of the dynamic assembly of tubulin into microtubules, at the enzymology laboratory at the CNRS. The close proximity of that laboratory to ICSN on the CNRS campus in Gif-sur-Yvette facilitated regular exchanges between the biologist and the chemist. Flora Zavala, a 3rd cycle doctoral student, under the supervision of P. Potier and D. Guénard, undertook a training course in D. Pantaloni's laboratory, to learn how to handle tubulin.

As tubulin can be obtained in relatively large quantities from mammal brains, trips to and from the nearest abattoir to Gif-sur-Yvette began. Once the tubulin had been purified using Shelanski's method[164], a test to visualize the effect of the compounds on the polymerization of tubulin was then adapted for bisindolic alkaloids. Using a UV spectrophotometer equipped with a temperature control cuvette chamber the turbidity of a tubulin solution can be measured at a wavelength of 350 nm. When raising the temperature of the tubulin solution from 4°C to 37°C, the assembly of tubulin into microtubules causes an increase in the optical density. Conversely, dropping the temperature causes the microtubules to disassemble into tubulin leading to a decrease in optical density. The addition of an inhibitor, such as vinblastine, to the tubulin solution is characterized by a drop in optical density, and by adding variable quantities of the inhibitor, it is possible to calculate the concentration which yields a 50% inhibition of the assembly of tubulin (IC_{50}). Figure 3.19, extracted from F. Zavala's thesis[169], shows the result obtained for vinblastine, inhibiting the assembly of tubulin into microtubules, with an IC_{50} equal to 1.7×10^{-6} Molar.

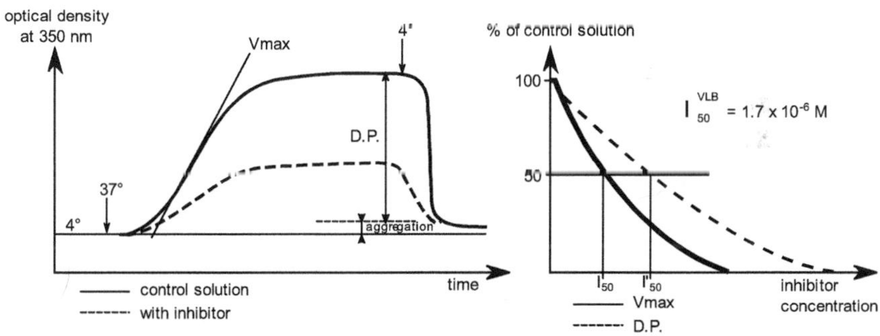

Figure 3.19. *Effect of an inhibitor on the assembly of tubulin (extract from Flora Zavala's thesis (p. 21)*[169]

For each compound, F. Zavala and D. Guénard also evaluated the induction of spiralization linked, as suggested by B. Bhattacharyya and J. Wolff[168], to the interaction of those compounds at the site with weak tubulin affinity. The dose of compound inducing 50% of the phenomenon of spiralization (S_{50}) can thus be measured.

Out of the compounds in the vinblastine series evaluated on tubulin, leurosine and leurosidine showed tubulin polymerization inhibition activities similar to that of vinblastine, whilst anhydrovinblastine is slightly less active. On the other hand, dimers with the C-18'*R* configuration, the inverse of that of natural bisindolic alkaloids, all prove to be completely inactive[169-170]. F. Zavala and D. Guénard also noticed that the polymerization inhibition activity was, in general, closely correlated with the induction of spiralization, in the vinblastine series.

From that point on, this simple test, known as the "tubulin test" – effective and quick – has systematically been used to evaluate the *in vitro* activity of natural compounds or those synthesized in the laboratory, with a view to selecting the best inhibitors for an in-depth pharmacological study.

3.4.6. *Biosynthesis of bisindolic alkaloids: anhydrovinblastine is a natural product*

Understanding the biosynthesis of natural products is an asset of crucial importance when chemists wish to realize their synthesis – in particular those having a particularly complex structure. This allows the development of biomimetic synthesis, imitating the different steps taken by the plant in transforming the initial precursor into the end product.

With regard to vinblastine, C.R Hutchinson[145] and A.I Scott[171], in 1974, in view of certain biosynthesis experiments, showed that catharanthine and vindoline might be precursors of vinblastine. Buoyed up by the success on coupling catharanthine with vindoline which P. Potier believed to be biomimetic, he offered F. Guéritte the chance to undertake a post-doctoral fellowship[u] at Professor

u That fellowship was undertaken at Yale University and then Texas A&M University between January 1977 and June 1978.

A.I Scott's team[v], to show that anhydrovinblastine was indeed a natural product.

Taking that hypothesis as a starting point, experiments on the incorporation of catharanthine and vindoline, marked with tritium (^3H) and carbon 14 (^{14}C) respectively, into the whole plant were conducted. Anhydrovinblastine marked with the two radioactive elements was obtained with satisfactory incorporation yields, as well as vinblastine and leurosine (Figure 3.20). These results, showing the natural origin of anhydrovinblastine, were published in 1978. [172]

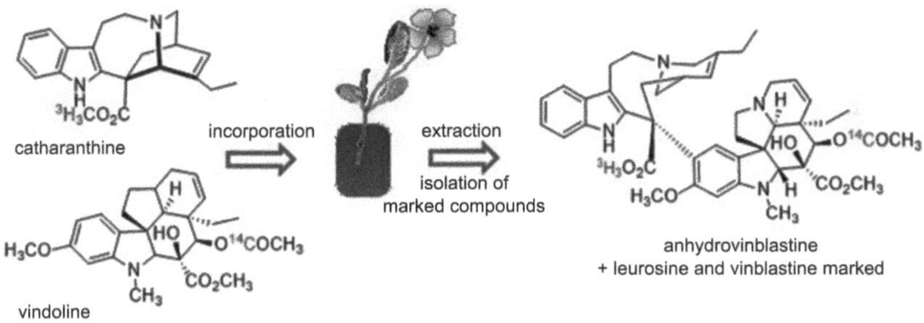

Figure 3.20. *Biosynthesis of anhydrovinblastine, leurosine and vinblastine*

The same year, J.P. Kutney reported similar results using extracts of cell cultures of *C. roseus* rather than the whole plant[173]. Many other biosynthetic studies were published in the wake of these results, including A.I. Scott *et al.*'s work on vinblastine formation from anhydrovinblastine,[174] and that of P. Potier *et al.* on the involvement of 4'-deoxyleurosidine in vinblastine formation[175]. Today, thanks to the progress in plant biotechnology and molecular biology made in the 1990s–2000s, certain steps of the biosynthesis of the hundreds of indolic alkaloids in *C. roseus* have been elucidated[176]. As regards bisindolic alkaloids, it has been shown that, in the plant, anhydrovinblastine was formed from catharanthine and vindoline, via a peroxidase, known as anhydrovinblastine synthase[177]. Comparing the biosynthetic scheme proposed for anhydrovinblastine

v Professor A. Ian Scott was a leading specialist recognized for his work on the biosynthesis of alkaloids, antibiotics and vitamin B12.

(Scheme 3.14)[79] against that described for semisynthesis (Schemes 3.10 and 3.12), we see that the same intermediate iminium is described. As P. Potier pointed out, in his book (page 97)[22]:

> The modified Polonovski reaction was indeed the biomimetic secret passage to achieve the correct configuration!

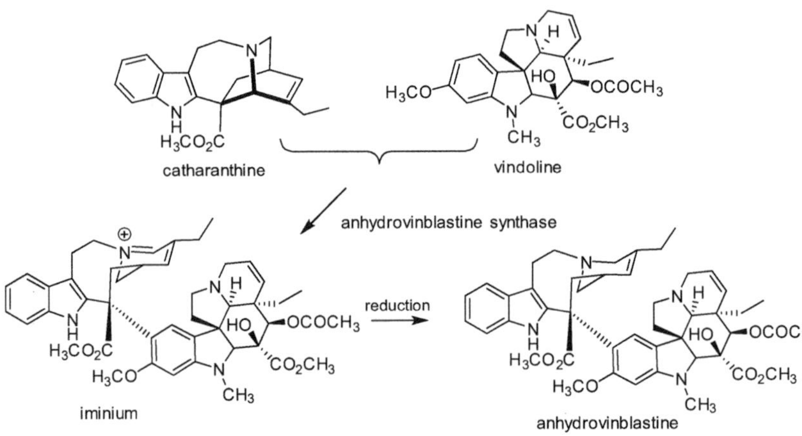

Scheme 3.14. *Dimerization of vindoline and catharanthine by anhydrovinblastine synthase*

Following the demonstration of the natural origin of anhydrovinblastine by the biosynthesis experiments[172], one question remained to be answered: in the numerous works devoted to the isolation of bisindolic alkaloids from the different parts of *C. roseus*, how could the absence of that compound be explained? In the 1970s, only the company Richter Gedeon[178] reported obtaining anhydrovinblastine from dry leaves of *C. roseus*. The answer was published by N. Langlois and P. Potier: anhydrovinblastine is unstable. Indeed, a solution of anhydrovinblastine, in different solvents, spontaneously yields natural bisindolic alkaloids – mainly leurosine and catharine – in lesser proportions to vinblastine and leurosidine[179]. The transformation of anhydrovinblastine into these compounds could be explained by oxidation/reduction steps, via intermediary iminiums, as indicated for leurosine (see Scheme 3.15)[179b].

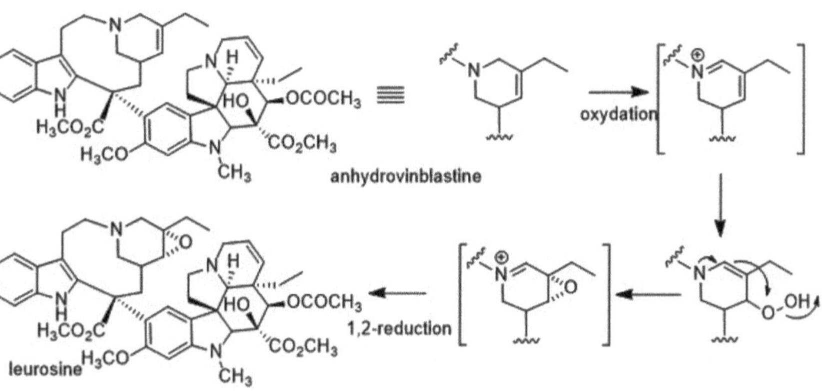

Scheme 3.15. *Formation of leurosine from anhydrovinblastine*

Finally, anhydrovinblastine was able to be isolated in fairly large quantities from the leaves of *C. roseus*, using conditions that prevent its oxidation *in situ by air*. Thus, Potier's team, in the late 1980s, focused on different methods for extracting alkaloids from the fresh or dried leaves of different plants of *C. roseus*, in order to evaluate the quantities of vindoline, catharanthine and anhydrovinblastine present in the alkaloidic extracts. A number of *C. roseus* plants were cultivated in the greenhouses at the Laboratoire du Phytotron, also situated on the CNRS' campus in Gif-sur-Yvette, very close to the ICSN. Extracts of the plant were obtained from the CNRS Medicinal Plant Laboratory – a satellite of the ICSN, in Nouméa, and others from the Research Center of the pharmaceutical company Laboratoires Pierre Fabre[69]. The alkaloids were quantified by high-performance liquid chromatography (HPLC), at the ICSN's chromatography department, then led by Marie-Thérèse Adeline. This unpublished study, conducted in February-March 1988 by F. Guéritte, D. Guénard and M.-T. Adeline showed, amongst other things, that an extraction from fresh *C. roseus* leaves in an acidic environment protected the anhydrovinblastine from parasitic oxidation. Thus, anhydrovinblastine could be isolated in an almost identical quantity to that of vindoline and catharanthine – the prevailing alkaloids in the plant (Figure 3.21)[w].

w Chromatogram taken from F. Guéritte's notebook "*C. roseus*", 29 February 1988. ICSN archives.

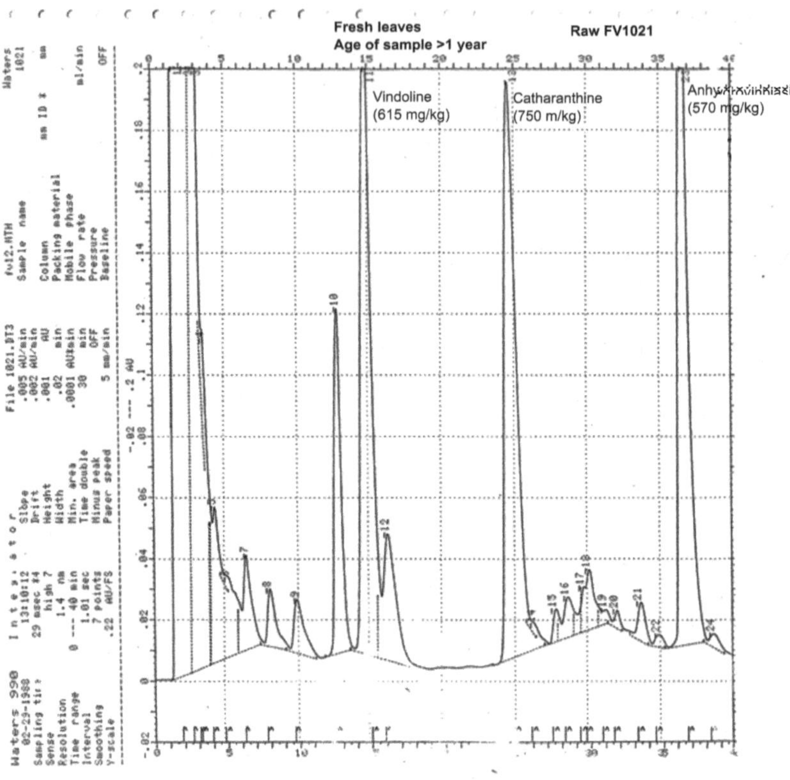

Figure 3.21. *Amount of vindoline, catharanthine and anhydrovinblastine in fresh leaves of C. roseus, found by HPLC*

When that study was conducted at the ICSN in early 1988, the researchers of the Canadian company Allelix, the same year, published the isolation of anhydrovinblastine by extraction, in an acidic medium, from *C. roseus* leaves, in similar conditions to those of the ICSN team[180].

3.5. From anhydrovinblastine to leurosine, leurosidine, vinblastine and the discovery of vinorelbine

Thus, thanks to the Polonovski-Potier reaction, bisindolic alkaloids – natural or synthetic – could easily be obtained from vindoline and catharanthine or their structural analogs. To make vinblastine, vincristine or the other antitumoral alkaloids leurosine and leurosidine, there was a different available strategy: the oxidation (other than air oxidation mentioned in the previous section) of the double bond $C_{3'}$-$C_{4'}$ in anhydrovinblastine, the first synthesized bisindolic alkaloid to possess the natural bioactive configuration (18'*S*) (Scheme 3.16).

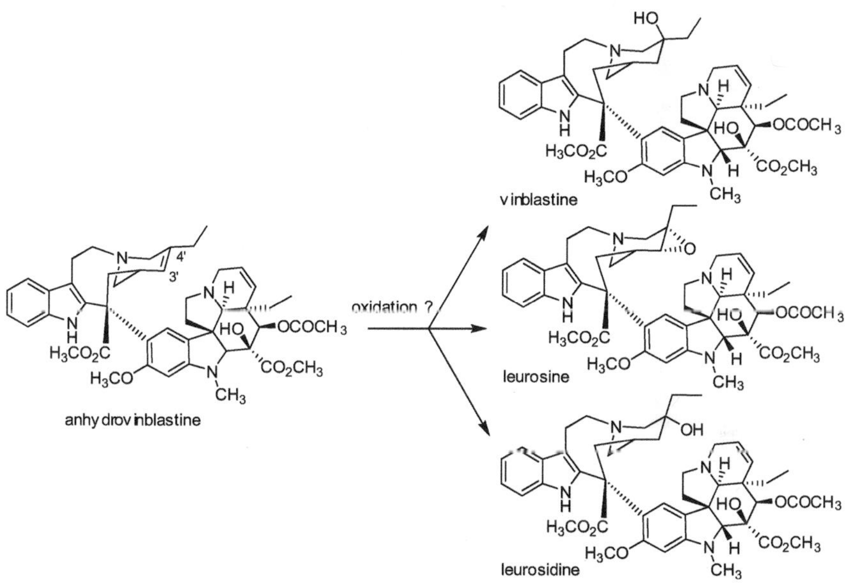

Scheme 3.16. *Oxidation of anhydrovinblastine*

Indeed, anhydrovinblastine appeared as a key product in the process of obtaining these bisindolic alkaloids, for the following reasons:

1) it can easily be obtained by coupling catharanthine N-oxide and vindoline – the most prevalent compounds isolated from *C. roseus*, using the Polonovski-Potier reaction;

2) its natural origin having been demonstrated by biosynthesis experiments, it could be the biogenetic precursor of the antitumoral bisindolic alkaloids, vinblastine and vincristine;

3) it spontaneously oxidizes in air to yield certain active alkaloids made by *C. roseus*.

3.5.1. *Transformation of anhydrovinblastine into leurosine, leurosidine and vinblastine*

Pierre Mangeney, N. and Y. Langlois and P. Potier, in 1976, published the semisynthesis of leurosine by direct epoxidation of anhydrovinblastine with an oxidant, paranitroperbenzoic acid, followed by reduction of the $N_{b'}$-oxide of leurosine formed (Scheme 3.17)[154]. Epoxidation takes place on the most easily accessible face of the double bond $C_{3'}$=$C_{4'}$: the lower face. The same year, J. Kutney also published similar work[181].

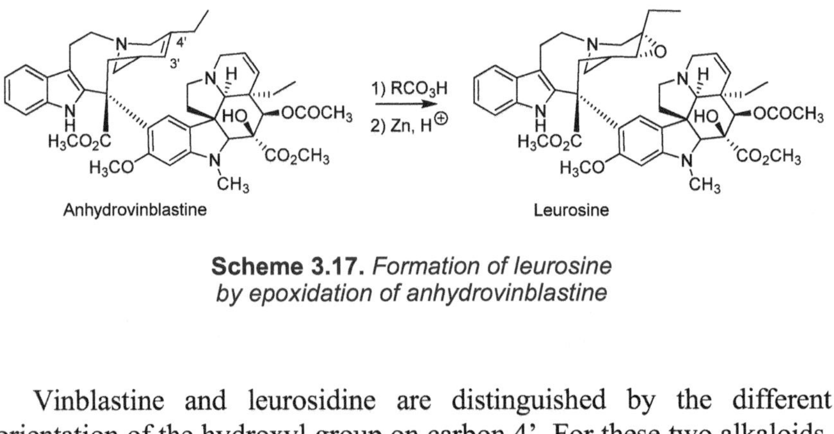

Scheme 3.17. *Formation of leurosine by epoxidation of anhydrovinblastine*

Vinblastine and leurosidine are distinguished by the different orientation of the hydroxyl group on carbon 4'. For these two alkaloids, a direct oxidation of anhydrovinblastine was not conceivable. Thus during his thesis research, P. Mangeney worked on the possibility of obtaining these two products from the enamine of deoxyvinblastine B, which could be oxidized at position 4' (Scheme 3.18)[152].

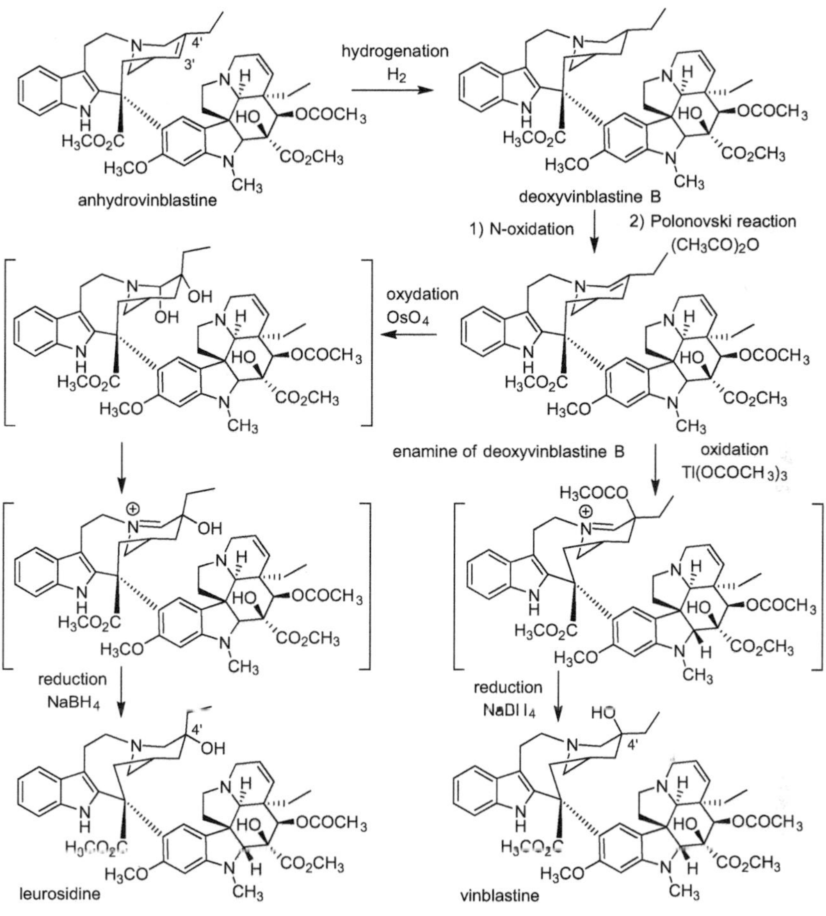

Scheme 3.18. *Formation of leurosidine and vinblastine from deoxyvinblastine B enamine*

Deoxyvinblastine B was easily obtained by catalytic hydrogenation of anhydrovinblastine. One of the strategies to obtain the enamine of deoxyvinblastine B was to conduct a Polonovski reaction on the $N_{b'}$-oxide of deoxyvinblastine B. As in the case of dregamine (Scheme 3.5), treating $N_{b'}$-oxide of deoxyvinblastine B with acetic anhydride, leads to an elimination reaction, thus producing enamine, which it was not possible to isolate because of its instability. Direct treatment of that enamine by osmium tetroxide (OsO_4) produces the unstable dihydroxyl derivative, which transforms into iminium. That iminium is reduced by sodium borohydride to give leurosidine[117,182]. Vinblastine was obtained from the same enamine by oxidation with thallium triacetate ($Tl(OCOCH_3)_3$), followed by the reduction of the iminium formed by sodium borohydride[182]. The difference between the oxidation conducted on the same enamine with osmium tetroxide and the thallium triacetate leading respectively to leurosidine and vinblastine, epimers at carbon 4', was explained as follows: the attack of osmium tetroxide takes place on the least encumbered face α of the double bond, whilst the attack of an electrophile (E) such as thallium acetate is controlled by the chirality of nitrogen whose stereochemistry is fixed, thus favoring an attack of the electrophile by the β face (Scheme 3.19).

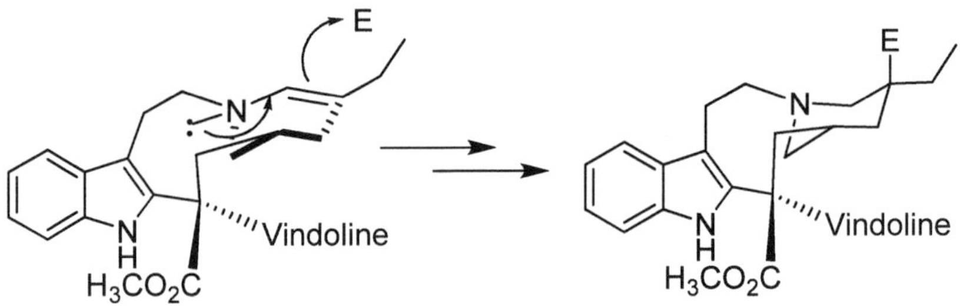

Scheme 3.19. *Attack of an electrophile on deoxyvinblastine B enamine*

The patent describing this synthesis of vinblastine and leurosidine was filed by Anvar, under the names of Nicole Langlois, Yves Langlois, Pierre Mangeney and Pierre Potier, on 8 December 1978[183].

3.5.2. *Discovery of 7'-nor-anhydrovinblastine or navelbine[x] and first pharmacological and clinical results*

During his thesis work on the semisynthesis of vinblastine[152], P. Mangeney, during summer and fall 1977[y], studied various other strategies to obtain the enamine of deoxyvinblastine B. One

x The different steps leading to the discovery of navelbine were communicated by P. Mangeney.

y Information from P. Mangeney, e-mail on 11 March 2014.

of the most direct ways was to realize a 1–4 reduction of the iminium obtained from anhydrovinblastine $N_{b'}$-oxide – iminium which could be formed by elimination of the $H_{5'}$ proton. In theory, the Polonovski reaction, i.e. the use of acetic anhydride, was the right method to use (Scheme 3.20).

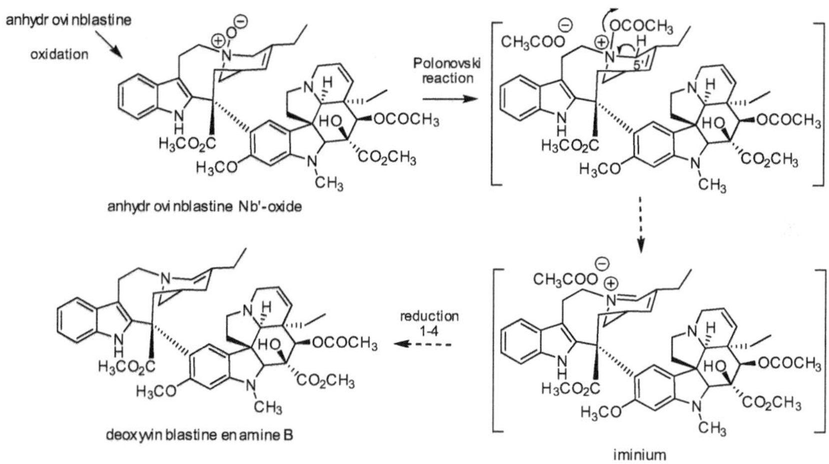

Scheme 3.20. *Polonovski reaction applied to anhydrovinblastine Nb'-oxide and 1–4 reduction*

However, and this was the first "stroke of luck", P. Mangeney used the flask of trifluoroacetic anhydride instead of acetic anhydride[z]. All attempts to isolate enamine, after 1–4 reduction of iminium, proved fruitless. There, P. Mangeney decided to directly treat the reactional medium by way of a whole series of oxidants in order to characterize the products obtained. New disasters occurred: multiple products were formed in the reaction mixture, but, in a second "stroke of luck", the thin-layer chromatography (TLC) analyses of the different experiments showed the ultra-minority existence of the same compound whose migration and color in the

z At that time, the laboratory's main activity was to carry out Polonovski-Potier reactions, and thus use trifluoroacetic anhydride, on numerous substrates.

CAS reagent (cerium ammonium sulfate)[aa], were similar to those of vinblastine (Figure 3.22).

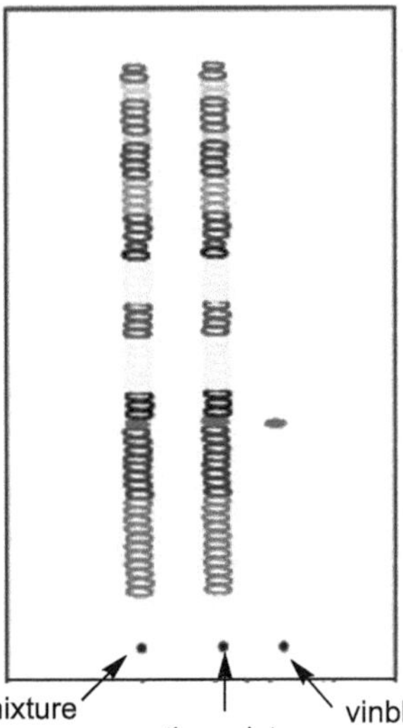

Figure 3.22. *TLC plate showing the comparison of the vinblastine retention factor with a reaction mixture [bb]. For a color version of the figure, please see www.iste.co.uk/leroux/navelbine.zip*

In the wake of these results, different nucleophiles (KCN, MeOH, hydrides, etc.) were added to the reaction mixture . This study showed that these reactions, for the most part, yield products coming from the cleavage of the $C_{7'}$-$C_{8'}$ bond. An example (reduction of the reaction medium by sodium borohydride ($NaBH_4$)) is shown in Scheme 3.21.

---

aa Ammonium cerium sulfate is a reagent which, when sprayed on a chromatography plate, allows us to visualize certain alkaloids by tinting them in different colors.

bb Schematic TLC plate from the presentation of P. Mangeney's lecture, "*Découverte de la Navelbine®*", *op. cit.*

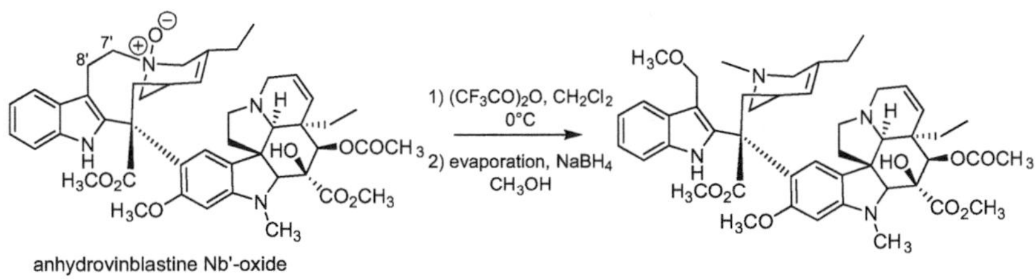

Scheme 3.21. *Example of the C7'-C8' bond cleavage*

All the reactions conducted by P. Mangeney led to results with a common feature: the ultra-minority presence of the compound exhibiting the same migration in TLC and the same color in CAS as vinblastine. This compound was able to be isolated and analyzed with mass spectrometry. The first experiments conducted by electron impact indicated a mass peak m/z equal to 808. That new product, for a while simply called "PM 808"[cc], was therefore not vinblastine, which has a molecular mass of 810. Nor was it leurosine, which does have a molecular mass of 808, but displays different migration in TLC.

At this stage, the tubulin test revealed the activity of that unknown product. Indeed, the products obtained through the work conducted by all members of the team were regularly subjected to the tubulin test, carried out by F. Zavala and D. Guénard. Thus, on 23 November 1977, F. Zavala's reported in her laboratory notebook a good level of activity inhibiting the assembly of tubulin by the compound PM 808[dd].

This observation encouraged P. Mangeney to search for new conditions facilitating the formation of this compound in larger quantities. Thus, he found that the only indispensable nucleophile was

---

cc PM for Pierre Mangeney and 808 for the mass peak obtained by electron impact.
dd Laboratory notebook of F. Zavala (November 1976 to December 1977, p. 142; December 1977 to January 1979, p. 147).

water[ee]. Thus, a 27% yield of the product was obtained by treating the reaction medium, evaporated to dryness and dissolved in tetrahydrofuran, directly by water. The structure of the compound was finally established thanks to NMR spectral analysis of the proton (Figure 3.23), with the help of Jean-Yves Lallemand[ff].

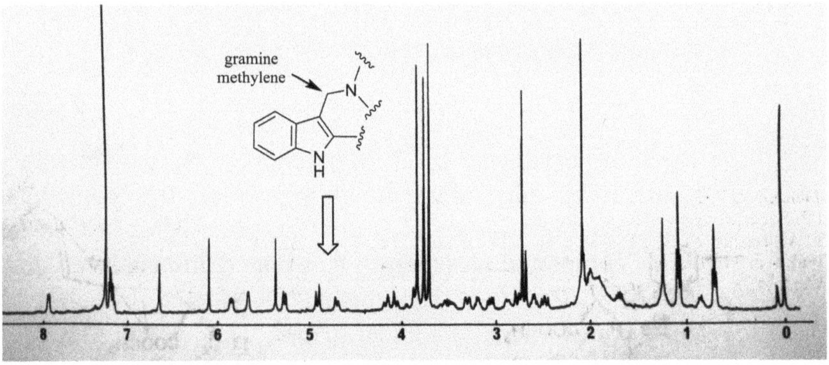

Figure 3.23. *NMR spectrum for the proton (250MHz) of the compound PM 808 (extracted from Tetrahedron, 1979*[184]

The presence of two signals corresponding to two doublets, integrating each one for one proton, around 4.5–5 ppm, was a clear indication of the presence of a methylene functional group (CH_2) as gramine. This methylene signal was also found in the carbon-13 NMR spectrum of the compound. In late December 1977[gg], this new compound (PM 808) was identified as 7'-nor-anhydrovinblastine[hh] (Scheme 3.22) – a structure confirmed by chemical correlations[152,184].

ee In the various experiments yielding PM808, the solvents used, such as methanol, were not anhydrous.

ff He set up a new NMR research group at the ICSN, in the late 1970s – see Chapter 2.

gg Information, P. Mangeney, e-mail, 11 March 2014.

hh 7'-nor-anhydrovinblastine (IUPAC numbering) was, at the time, named 5'-nor-anhydrovinblastine, because biogenetic numbering was used (Figure 3.6). As mentioned in section 3.4, IUPAC numbering has been chosen as the numbering system to be used throughout this book.

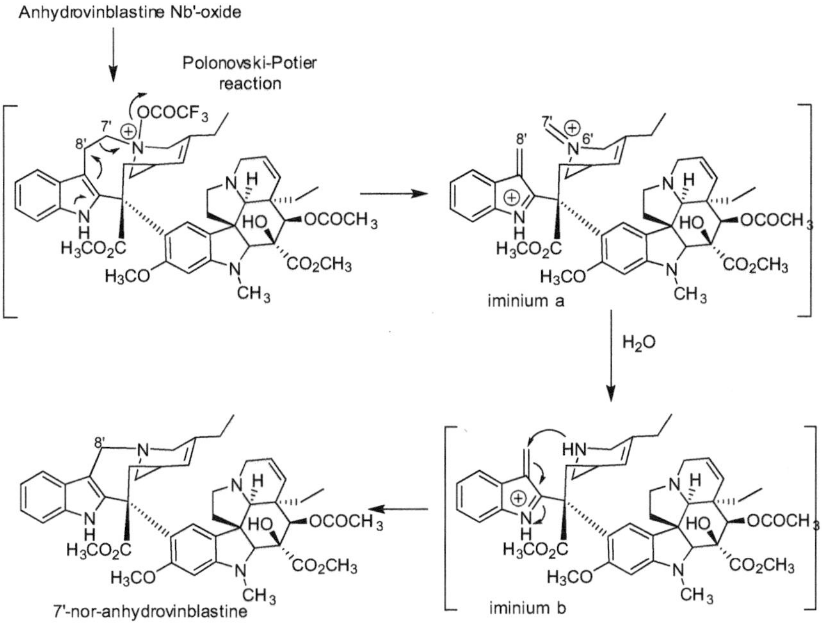

Scheme 3.22. *Formation of 7'-nor-anhydrovinblastine*

The formation of 7'-nor-anhydrovinblastine was easily explained: after cleavage of the $C_{7'}$-$C_{8'}$ bond, treatment of the iminium a with water led to the hydrolysis of the N6'-C7' bond, producing iminium b, and then the nucleophilic attack of the free amine on the indolic part forms 7'-nor-anhydrovinblastine (Scheme 3.22). As the molecular mass of 7'-nor-anhydrovinblastine is 778, the presence of the pic m/z at 808 in the electron-impact mass spectrum has been explained by the existence of intermolecular transmethylation (thermal) reactions[ii], which have already been described for vinblastine-type dimers[185] (Scheme 3.23).

ii Transmethylation is a reaction in which one or more methyl groups (CH3) is/are transferred from one molecule to another.

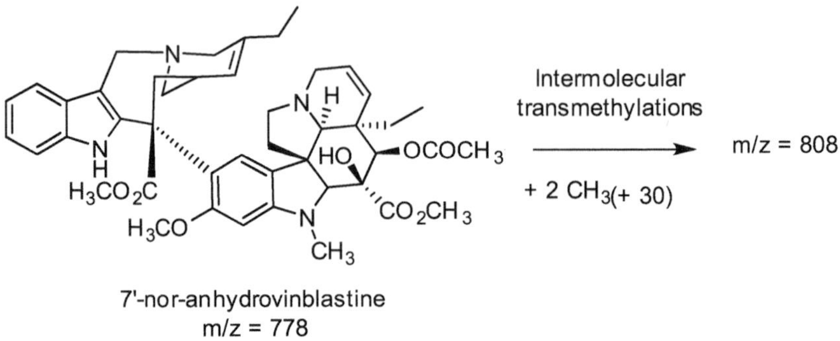

Scheme 3.23. *Reaction of intermolecular transmethylations*

During 1978, thanks to collaborations established by P. Potier with Suzanne Cros and Claude Paoletti, director of the *Laboratoire de pharmacologie et de toxicology fondamentale* (fundamental pharmacology and toxicology laboratory) of the CNRS in Toulouse, on the one hand, and with the teams of Professor Georges Mathé and Dr. René Maral from the *Institut de Cancérologie et d'Immunogénetique* at Paul Brousse Hospital in Villejuif, on the other, the tests on *in vivo* activity and toxicity in mice proved to be very promising. 7'-nor-anhydrovinblastine, administered to mice with leukemia (L1210 and P388), exhibited a degree of activity comparable to that of vinblastine and a toxicity lower than that of vincristine[152].

After that, everything happened very quickly: a first patent, reporting the preparation of 7'-nor-anhydrovinblastine along with the results of its activity on tubulin and those of the *in vivo* activity on murine tumors, was filed on 24 August 1978 by Anvar, with the names of Pierre Potier, Nicole Langlois, Yves Langlois and Pierre Mangeney as inventors (see Figure 3.24)[186].

On 22 December 1978, Professor Georges Mathé signed a commitment (see Figure 3.25) to carry out pharmacological and clinical studies of navelbine – a simplified name attributed, by Potier's team, to 7'-nor-anhydrovinblastine.

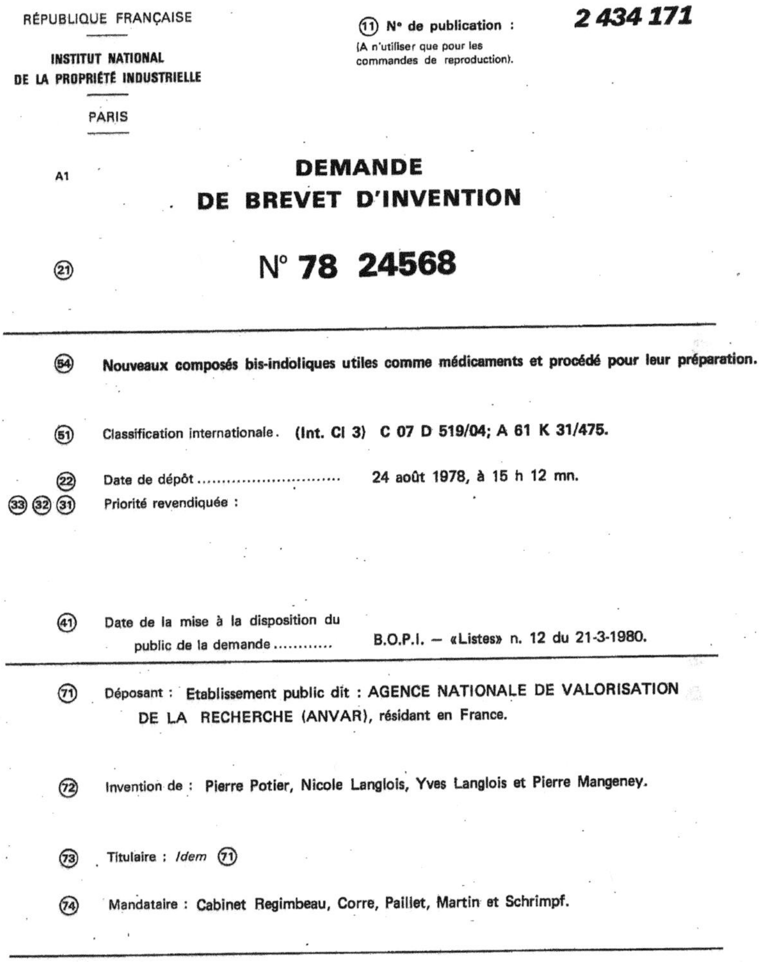

RÉPUBLIQUE FRANÇAISE

INSTITUT NATIONAL
DE LA PROPRIÉTÉ INDUSTRIELLE

PARIS

(11) N° de publication : **2 434 171**
(A n'utiliser que pour les commandes de reproduction).

A1

DEMANDE DE BREVET D'INVENTION

(21) **N° 78 24568**

(54) **Nouveaux composés bis-indoliques utiles comme médicaments et procédé pour leur préparation.**

(51) Classification internationale. **(Int. Cl 3) C 07 D 519/04; A 61 K 31/475.**

(22) Date de dépôt .... **24 août 1978, à 15 h 12 mn.**

(33) (32) (31) Priorité revendiquée :

(41) Date de la mise à la disposition du public de la demande .... **B.O.P.I. – «Listes» n. 12 du 21-3-1980.**

(71) Déposant : **Etablissement public dit : AGENCE NATIONALE DE VALORISATION DE LA RECHERCHE (ANVAR), résidant en France.**

(72) Invention de : **Pierre Potier, Nicole Langlois, Yves Langlois et Pierre Mangeney.**

(73) Titulaire : *Idem* (71)

(74) Mandataire : **Cabinet Regimbeau, Corre, Paillet, Martin et Schrimpf.**

Figure 3.24. *First page of the first patent pertaining to the preparation of 7'-nor-anhydrovinblastine*

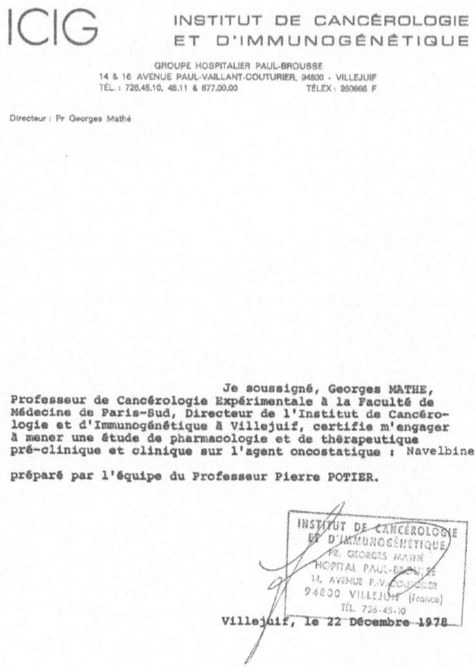

ICIG INSTITUT DE CANCÉROLOGIE ET D'IMMUNOGÉNÉTIQUE

GROUPE HOSPITALIER PAUL-BROUSSE
14 & 16 AVENUE PAUL-VAILLANT-COUTURIER, 94800 - VILLEJUIF
TÉL. : 726.45.10, 46.11 & 677.00.00 TÉLEX : 250666 F

Directeur : Pr Georges Mathé

Je soussigné, Georges MATHE, Professeur de Cancérologie Expérimentale à la Faculté de Médecine de Paris-Sud, Directeur de l'Institut de Cancérologie et d'Immunogénétique à Villejuif, certifie m'engager à mener une étude de pharmacologie et de thérapeutique pré-clinique et clinique sur l'agent oncostatique : Navelbine

préparé par l'équipe du Professeur Pierre POTIER.

Villejuif, le 22 Décembre 1978

Figure 3.25. *Letter of commitment from Professor Georges Mathé for the pharmacological and clinical study of Navelbine* [jj]

Next, the work on the semisynthesis of navelbine was published in 1979[184,187]. The same year, D. Guénard, F. Zavala and P. Potier presented the results of navelbine's activity on tubulin compared to those of other antitumoral alkaloids in the vinblastine group[188], and noted, in summary:

> A new analog, shown by its peculiar behavior in the presence of tubulin, has been shown *in vivo* – at least as active and less toxic than vinblastine.

P. Mangeney and F. Zavala defended their thesis in 1979, respectively on, amongst other things, the semisynthesis of this new compound[152] and its interaction with tubulin[169].

jj F. Guéritte's archives.

Navelbine presented a certain amount of interest as a potential antitumoral agent: its molecular structure was new, its activity on tubulin was specific and the first *in vivo* tests were highly promising.

To continue conducting the pharmacological trials and begin the clinical ones, many grams of navelbine were needed. In October 1978, F. Guéritte, returning from A.I Scott's laboratory, where she had studied the biosynthesis of bisindolic alkaloids, rejoined Potier's laboratory to work in Y. and N. Langlois' team on the preparation of navelbine, with P. Mangeney and R.Z. Andriamialisoa. Nguyen Van Bac, a researcher at the CNRS, also worked in the team. A few hundred milligrams of navelbine were thus prepared by the whole team, working from catharanthine and vindoline, following the semisynthetic path involving the Polonovski-Potier reaction twice (Scheme 3.24).

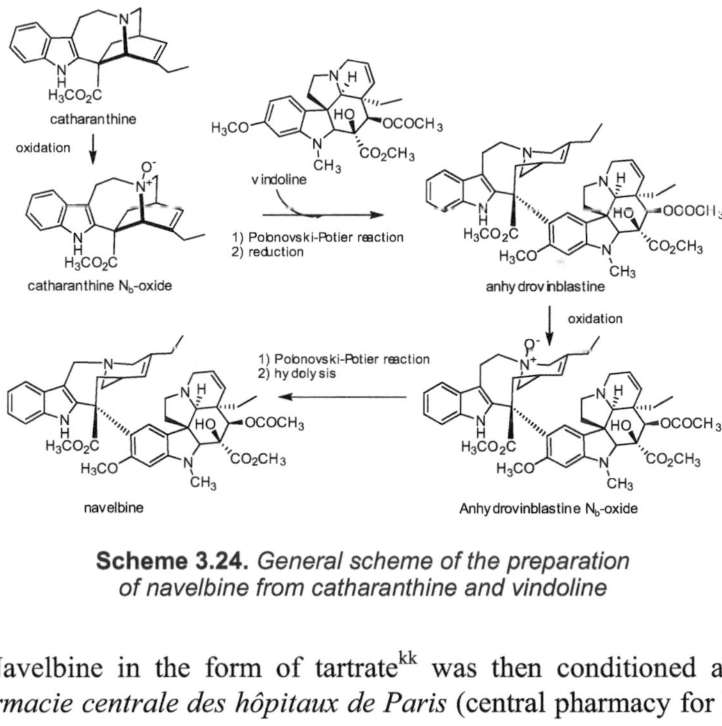

Scheme 3.24. *General scheme of the preparation of navelbine from catharanthine and vindoline*

Navelbine in the form of tartrate[kk] was then conditioned at the *Pharmacie centrale des hôpitaux de Paris* (central pharmacy for Paris

kk Navelbine is transformed into its salt of tartric acid (navelbine tartrate) to improve its solubility in water, thus facilitating its administration during pharmacological trials.

hospitals) before being delivered to Paul Brousse Hospital in Villejuif, to Professor Mathé's team. Regular exchanges between Potier's and Mathé's teams helped avoid interruptions in the supply of navelbine during pharmacological trials. Thus, in August 1979, Mathé's team reported that they had run out of stock of navelbine. Immediately, Potier's team prepared a few hundred mg of navelbine tartrate, which were sent to the central pharmacy for conditioning, before being passed on to Mathé's and Maral's team[ll]. *In vivo* experiments on cross-resistance between different Vinca alkaloids, including 7'-nor anhydrovinblastine, were also conducted by that team and published in 1981[189], and the first phase-I study was announced the same year[190].

However, there was one problem that remained to be solved: how to obtain navelbine in large quantities. Indeed, whilst the transformation of anhydrovinblastine into its $N_{b'}$-oxide was total, the yield in terms of navelbine obtained from it was only 27%, causing problems for the conducting of larger-scale pharmacological and clinical trials. Potier's team, therefore, turned its attention to finding a more effective way of preparing 7'-nor-anhydrovinblastine.

3.5.3 *The search for a new process to synthesize 7'-nor-anhydrovinblastine (vinorelbine)*

One of the likely methods for the formation of navelbine was to apply the Polonovski-Potier reaction to the coupling of vindoline with nor-catharanthine, modeled on the coupling of catharanthine with vindoline (Scheme 3.25).

Nor-catharanthine, obtained from catharanthine, was treated in the conditions of the Polonovski-Potier reaction with vindoline, but did not produce navelbine[191]. Other approaches continued to be studied by the team, and finally navelbine was obtained with high yields from anhydrovinblastine chloro-9' indolenine, treated by silver tetrafluoroborate in the presence of water (Scheme 3.26)[192]. This method of synthesis, studied by R.Z. Andriamialisoa, N. and Y. Langlois, involves the cleavage of the $C_{7'}$-$C_{8'}$ bond, with the departure of the chloride ion, yielding an iminium which is hydrolyzed to give navelbine.

ll Laboratory notebook, F. Guéritte (FG 551, August 1979). ICSN archives.

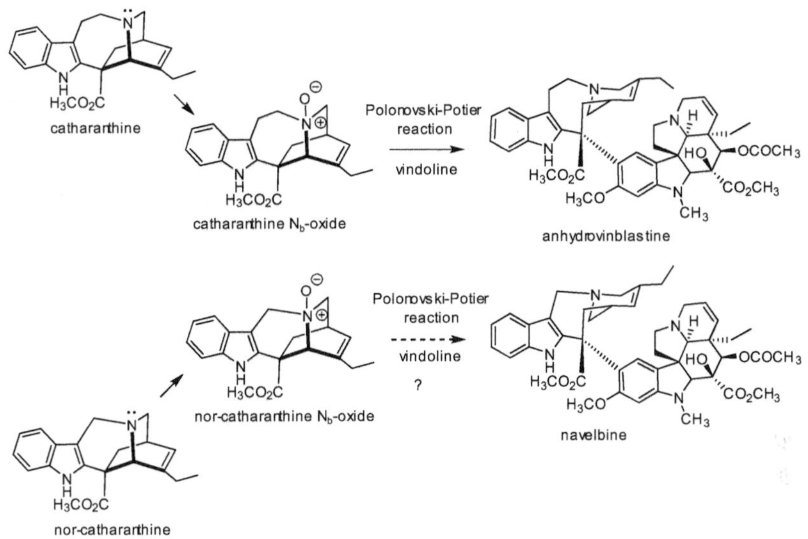

Scheme 3.25. *Proposed method for semisynthesis of navelbine from nor-catharanthine N_b-oxide*

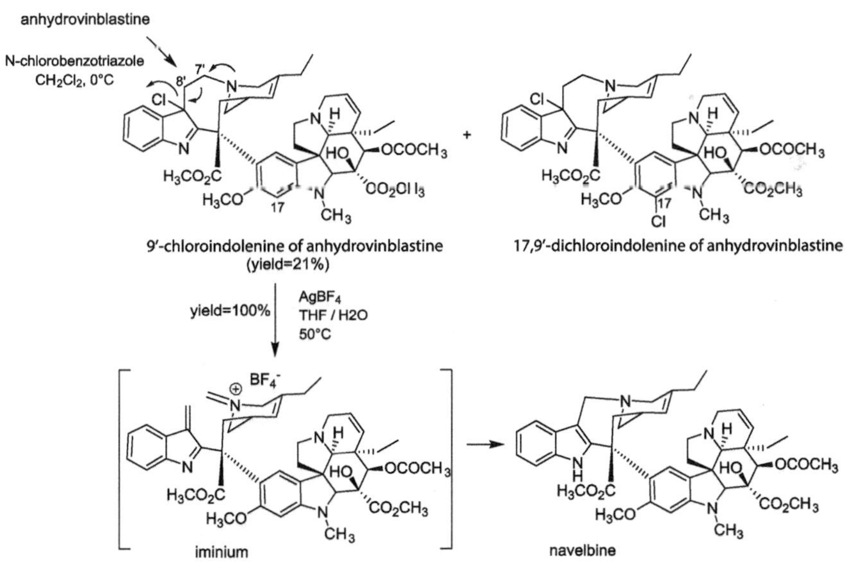

Scheme 3.26. *Semisynthesis of navelbine from 9'-chloroindolenine of anhydrovinblastine*

Whilst navelbine was obtained with a quantitative yield from 9'-chloroindolenine of anhydrovinblastine, the preparation of that product from anhydrovinblastine has proven to be less efficient, with a yield of 21%, the low yield obtained being due to a parasitic reaction leading to the formation of 17,9'-dichloroindolenine of anhydrovinblastine. By choosing a more voluminous electrophilic agent such as bromine (Br^+), and treating anhydrovinblastine with N-bromosuccinimide, it was possible to obtain navelbine with an excellent yield on the basis of anhydrovinblastine (Scheme 3.27)[192b,192c,193].

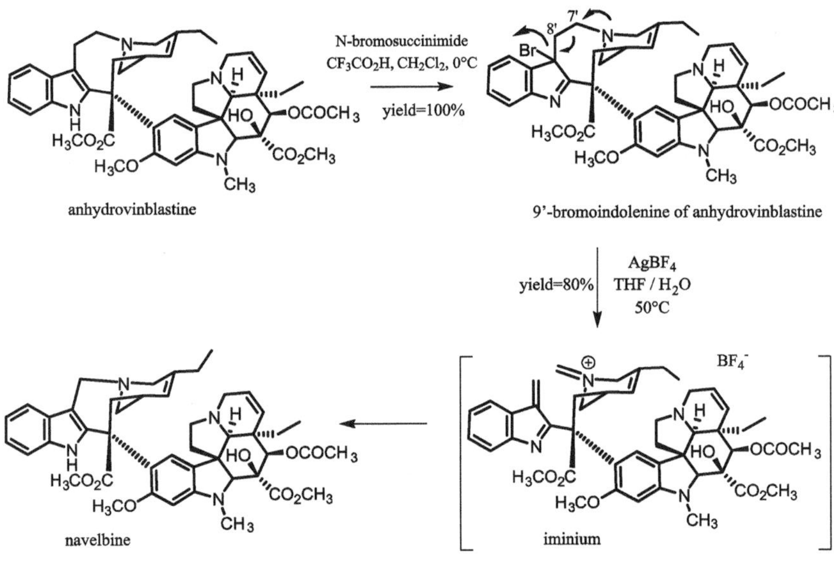

Scheme 3.27. *Semisynthesis of navelbine from 9'-bromoindolenine of anhydrovinblastine*

In August 1979, at the Twentieth Annual Meeting of the American Society of Pharmacognosy, at Purdue University (West Lafayette, Indiana), P. Potier presented most of these results under the title: *Synthesis of the antitumor dimeric indole alkaloids from Catharanthus species (vinblastine group)*[194].

Over the course of the years 1980–1983, over ten grams of navelbine were prepared by the team[mm]. The pharmacological, pre-clinical and clinical trials were able to continue. In 1982, a collaboration was begun between Potier's team and the group headed by Professor Jean-Paul Cano, director of the *Service commun national de toxicocinétique et pharmacocinétique* (National Toxicokinetics and Pharmacokinetics Branch) of Inserm (French National Institute of Health and Medical Research) in Marseille, which facilitated the pharmacokinetic study of navelbine[195]. For their part, in 1984, Mathé's and Maral's teams, continuing with their pharmacological and clinical studies, published the results of navelbine's antitumoral activity in mice[196], and a Phase-I clinical trial[197]. In 1985, Suzanne Cros, along with her colleagues, published a comparative study, *in vitro* and *in vivo*, of navelbine with vinblastine and vincristine[198], and G. Mathé published a Phase-I pharmacological study of navelbine[199].

Thus, thanks to the collaborations established by P. Potier, there were regular exchanges between the researchers at the ICSN and those belonging to the different laboratories involved in the clinical and pharmacological trials of navelbine. That scientific association, between chemists, biochemists and biologists at the CNRS and Inserm, on the one hand, and pharmacologists and clinicians at Paul Brousse Hospital, on the other, was indubitably essential to prove the role that navelbine could play as an antitumor agent.

In view of these results, after several meetings with pharmaceutical industrialists, thanks to Maurice Ponte from Anvar, Pierre Fabre and Pierre Potier met to discuss the possibility of a collaboration (see Chapter 2). After an agreement had been signed in July 1982 between the CNRS, represented by Anvar, and Laboratoires Pierre Fabre, exchanges began with the chemists from the pharmaceutical company. Notably, Jean-François Patoiseau came to ICSN to study the semisynthesis of navelbine. On the other hand, Annie Pouilhès went to the Laboratoires Pierre Fabre research center in Castres to participate in the production of navelbine. Pierre Fabre then took up the baton in the development of navelbine. During 1983, regular exchanges

mm Annie Pouilhès, a chemical engineer at the CNRS, joined P. Potier, N. Langlois and Y. Langlois' team, in July 1981.

continued between Potier's team, Patricia Ribaud from Mathé's team and Laboratoires Pierre Fabre, notably with Philippe Hatinguais, head of the phytochemistry department. Thus, in May of the same year, Hatinguais sent to F. Guéritte from Potier's team 1 gram of navelbine tartrate, to verify its purity before rewarding it to the team of Professor Mathé (see Figure 3.26)[nn].

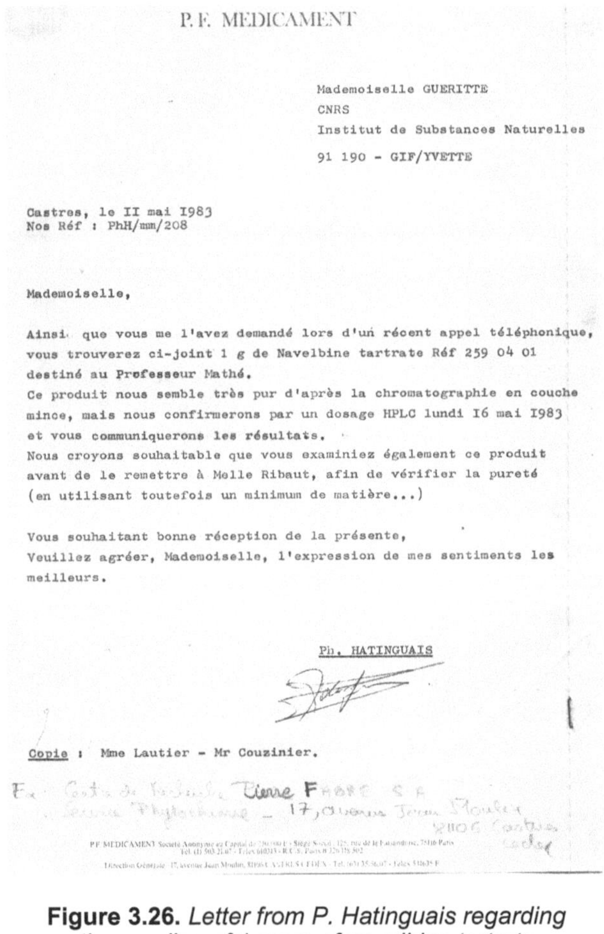

P. F. MEDICAMENT

Mademoiselle GUERITTE
CNRS
Institut de Substances Naturelles
91 190 - GIF/YVETTE

Castres, le II mai I983
Nos Réf : PhH/mm/208

Mademoiselle,

Ainsi que vous me l'avez demandé lors d'un récent appel téléphonique, vous trouverez ci-joint 1 g de Navelbine tartrate Réf 259 04 01 destiné au Professeur Mathé.
Ce produit nous semble très pur d'après la chromatographie en couche mince, mais nous confirmerons par un dosage HPLC lundi I6 mai I983 et vous communiquerons les résultats.
Nous croyons souhaitable que vous examiniez également ce produit avant de le remettre à Melle Ribaut, afin de vérifier la pureté (en utilisant toutefois un minimum de matière...)

Vous souhaitant bonne réception de la présente,
Veuillez agréer, Mademoiselle, l'expression de mes sentiments les meilleurs.

Ph. HATINGUAIS

Copie : Mme Lautier - Mr Couzinier.

Figure 3.26. *Letter from P. Hatinguais regarding the sending of 1 gram of navelbine tartrate*

nn F. Guéritte's laboratory notebook (FG 994 – FG 1004); ICSN archives. Letter from P. Hattinguais to F. Guéritte on 11 May 1983. F. Guéritte's archives.

In 1989, ten years after its discovery, navelbine became Navelbine® when it gained market authorization, for the treatment of non small-cell lung cancer, and in 1991, for that of metastatic breast cancer.

4

From the Pacific Yew (*Taxus brevifolia*) to the English Yew (*Taxus baccata*): Steps Towards the Discovery of Docetaxel (Taxotere®)

The earliest research which ultimately led to the discovery of Taxotere® (International Nonproprietary Name (INN): docetaxel) – an antitumoral drug developed by Rhône-Poulenc (now Sanofi) – began on the common yew (also called the English yew or European yew), *Taxus baccata*, in January 1980 in the team led by P. Potier. The starting point in this study comes from the demonstration, by Susan Horwitz and her collaborators, of the unique activity on microtubules of a natural compound: "taxol". Taxol had been isolated in the late 1960s from the Pacific yew, *Taxus brevifolia*, by the Americans Monroe Wall, Mansukh Wani and their collaborators. In December 1992, the Food and Drug Administration (FDA) approved the first use of Taxol® (INN: paclitaxel) from the Bristol-Myers Squibb Co, in the treatment of ovarian cancer.

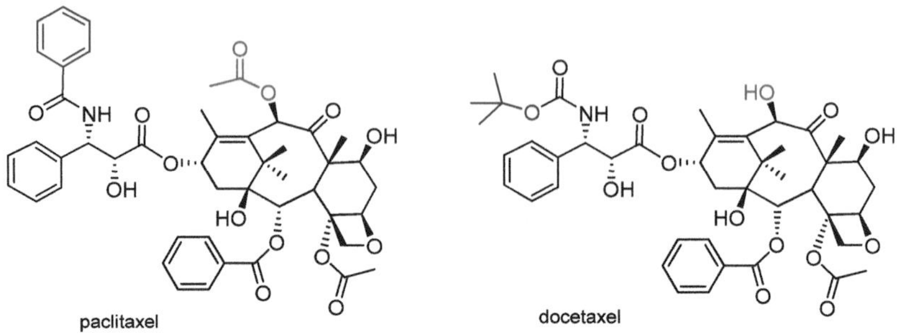

Figure 4.1. *Structures of paclitaxel and docetaxel. For a color version of the figure, please see www.iste.co.uk/leroux/navelbine.zip*

The structure of docetaxel differs from that of paclitaxel by the absence of the acetyl group ($COCH_3$), highlighted in red in the color version of Figure 4.1), and by the replacement, on the side chain, of the phenyl group by a tert-butyloxy ($OC(CH_3)_3$, shown in blue) – see Figure 4.1. Whilst paclitaxel is a natural compound, docetaxel does not exist in nature, but was obtained from a natural compound – 10-deacetylbaccatin III, isolated from the English yew, *Taxus baccata*. As in the case of vinorelbine (Navelbine®), the development of docetaxel as an antitumoral agent came from close collaborations between chemists and biologists in the public sector and a pharmaceutical company. The work which, in 1986, led to the discovery of docetaxel at the ICSN became reality thanks to worldwide-scale development by Rhône-Poulenc During the years 1995 and 1996, the use of Taxotere® as a single agent in the treatment of metastatic breast cancer was approved in over 40 countries. Taxotere® would then be approved for non small-cell lung cancer treatment, for prostate cancer and cancer of the digestive and gastric tracts.

4.1. The common yew, *Taxus baccata*

4.1.1. *Yews, botanics and toxicity*

The common yew, *Taxus baccata*, belongs to the Taxaceae family. Apart from the genus *Taxus*, five other genera are classed in that family: *Amentotaxus, Austrotaxus, Cephalotaxus, Pseudotaxus* and *Torreya.*

The taxonomy of the genus *Taxus* is still being debated even today. Whilst most botanists consider that there are nine species (*T. baccata* L., *T. cuspidata* Sieb & Zucc., *T. canadensis* Marshall, *T. brevifolia* Nutt., *T. floridana* Chapm., *T. globosa* Schltdl., *T. wallichiana* Zucc., *T. fuana* Nan Li and R.R. Mill, and *T. chinensis* (Pilger) Rehder)[200], Richard W. Spjut suggests the existence of 24 species belonging to the genus *Taxus*[201]. These species, whatever their number, are distributed mainly in North America, Europe and Asia.

The Taxaceae family is classified in the category of gymnosperms, so the genera in that family are coniferous and resinous. However, the yew does not have cones or produce resin! That is one of the peculiarities of the tree.

The yew is an evergreen dioecious tree[a], very strong and slow-growing. The female stems are characterized by the presence of red arils, and the male stems by yellowish catkins (Figure 4.2).

Figure 4.2. *The common yew, Taxus baccata*[b]

a Dioecious species have distinct male and female individual organisms.

b Original book source: Prof. Dr. Otto Wilhelm Thomé; *Flora von Deutschland, Österreich und der Schweiz* 1885, Gera, Germany.

Yew wood is much prized for its strength and flexibility – qualities which were notably exploited during the Hundred Years War by the English archers at the famous Battles of Crécy, Poitiers and Agincourt in France. The use of longbows, made from the wood of the yew, by the English archers was critical in their victory over the French crossbowmen.

The common yew has also long been known for its toxic properties (only the red flesh surrounding the seed in the aril is non-toxic). Numerous texts make reference to decoctions of yew leaves used as poison. Dioscorides, Pliny the Elder, Galen and Julius Cesar, for instance, reported "fortuitous accidents brought about by this poison"[202]. Poets and playwrights have also mentioned the yew, whose toxicity was well known. For example, in Shakespeare's *Macbeth*, the Third Witch says the following (Figure 4.3):

ALL

Double, double toil and trouble;
Fire burn and cauldron bubble.

Third Witch

Scale of dragon, tooth of wolf,
Witches' mummy, maw and gulf
Of the ravin'd salt-sea shark,
Root of hemlock digg'd i' the dark,
Liver of blaspheming Jew,
Gall of goat, and slips of yew
Silver'd in the moon's eclipse,
Nose of Turk and Tartar's lips,

Figure 4.3. *Macbeth, Act IV, Scene 1* [c]

c *Macbeth*, W. Shakespeare.

Similarly, in "A Pocket Full of Rye" by Agatha Christie, Dr. Bernsdorff reveals to Inspector Neele the name of the poison responsible for Mr. Fortescue's demise:

> "Taxine, my boy. Taxine." "Taxine? Never heard of it."
>
> "I know. Most unusual. Really delightfully unusual! I don't say I'd have spotted it myself if I hadn't had a case only three or four weeks ago. Couple of kids playing dolls' teaparties – pulled berries of a yew tree and used them for tea."
>
> "Is that what it is? Yew berries?"
>
> "Berries or leaves. Highly poisonous. Taxine, of course, is the alkaloid."[d]

In 1953, which is the date of publication of Agatha Christie's novel, then, the name *taxine*, the toxic alkaloid from the yew, was well known.

4.1.2. *First phytochemical studies of the common yew (T. baccata) and other species of* Taxus

The earliest phytochemical studies on *T. baccata* were conducted in the second half of the 17th Century. Thus, in 1856, H. Lucas, an apothecary in Arnstadt, Germany, published the first instance of obtaining an alkaloidic powder, which he called "Taxin", from the leaves of the common yew (Figure 4.4)[203].

In 1876 and 1881, W. Marmé[204], D. Amato and A. Capparelli[205] also noted the isolation of the alkaloid from the leaves of *T. baccata*, which molecular formula was given by A. Hilger and F. Brande[206], in 1890, as $C_{37}H_{52}NO_{10}$ (Figure 4.5).

d Collins Crime Club, 1st ed. 1953.

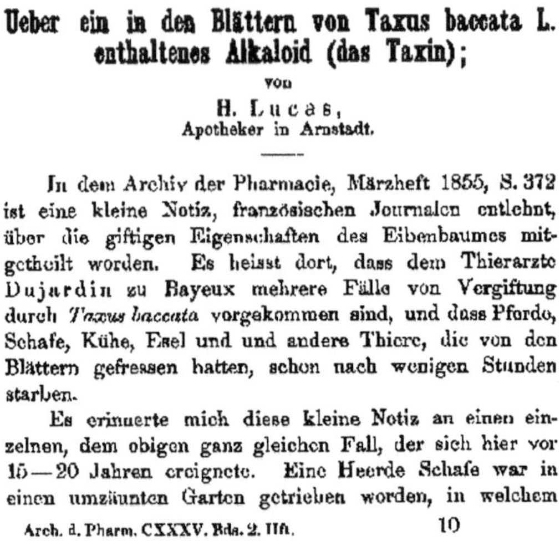

Ueber ein in den Blättern von Taxus baccata L. enthaltenes Alkaloid (das Taxin);

von

H. Lucas,
Apotheker in Arnstadt.

In dem Archiv der Pharmacie, Märzheft 1855, S. 372 ist eine kleine Notiz, französischen Journalen entlehnt, über die giftigen Eigenschaften des Eibenbaumes mitgetheilt worden. Es heisst dort, dass dem Thierarzte Dujardin zu Bayeux mehrere Fälle von Vergiftung durch *Taxus baccata* vorgekommen sind, und dass Pferde, Schafe, Kühe, Esel und und andere Thiere, die von den Blättern gefressen hatten, schon nach wenigen Stunden starben.

Es erinnerte mich diese kleine Notiz an einen einzelnen, dem obigen ganz gleichen Fall, der sich hier vor 15—20 Jahren ereignete. Eine Heerde Schafe war in einen umzäunten Garten getrieben worden, in welchem

Arch. d. Pharm. CXXXV. Bds. 2. Hft. 10

Figure 4.4. *Extract from H. Lucas' text on the isolation of Taxine. "On an alkaloid contained in the leaves of Taxus baccata L.". The text describes the poisonous properties of the yew tree. It details reports by a French veterinarian on the poisoning of various animals after eating the leaves of Taxus baccata, leading to death a few hours later*

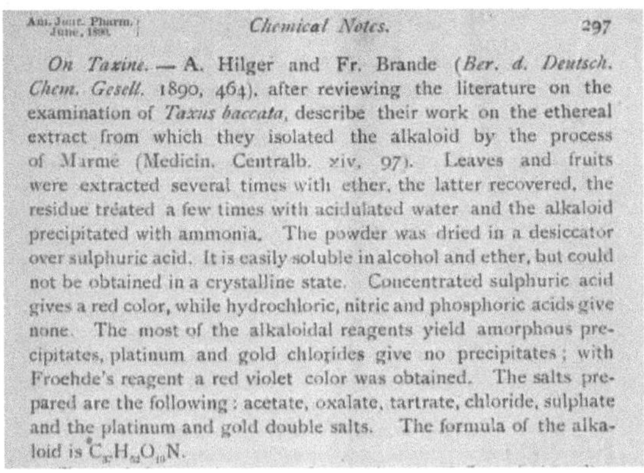

Am. Jour. Pharm. June, 1890. *Chemical Notes.* 297

On Taxine. — A. Hilger and Fr. Brande (*Ber. d. Deutsch. Chem. Gesell.* 1890, 464), after reviewing the literature on the examination of *Taxus baccata*, describe their work on the ethereal extract from which they isolated the alkaloid by the process of Marmé (Medicin. Centralb. xiv, 97). Leaves and fruits were extracted several times with ether, the latter recovered, the residue treated a few times with acidulated water and the alkaloid precipitated with ammonia. The powder was dried in a desiccator over sulphuric acid. It is easily soluble in alcohol and ether, but could not be obtained in a crystalline state. Concentrated sulphuric acid gives a red color, while hydrochloric, nitric and phosphoric acids give none. The most of the alkaloidal reagents yield amorphous precipitates, platinum and gold chlorides give no precipitates; with Froehde's reagent a red violet color was obtained. The salts prepared are the following: acetate, oxalate, tartrate, chloride, sulphate and the platinum and gold double salts. The formula of the alkaloid is $C_{37}H_{52}O_{10}N$.

Figure 4.5. *Note on the isolation of taxine by A. Hilger and F. Brande*

Winterstein's team in Zurich, in the 1920s, worked on the toxicity of the yew and on taxine[207]. To determine the structure of taxine, they studied its degradation products obtained in an acidic medium.

Thus, they identified β-dimethylamino-β-phenylpropionic acid (Figure 4.6) and believed taxine ought to be an ester of that acid.

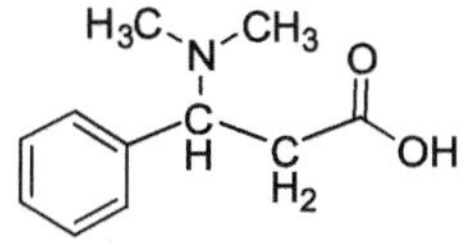

β-dimethylamino-β-phenylpropionic acid

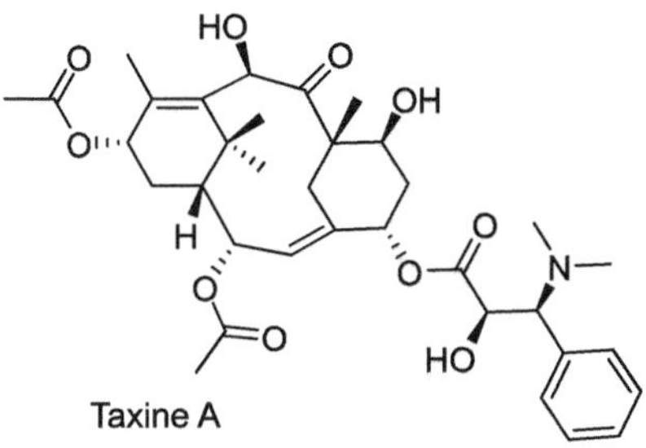

Taxine A

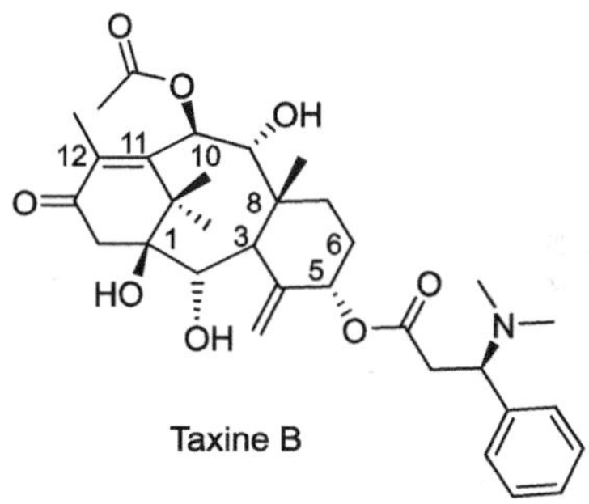

Taxine B

Figure 4.6. *Structure of β-dimethylamino-β-phenylpropionic acid and of taxines A and B*

Finally, it was the work of E. Graf at the University of Würzburg which, in 1956, revealed that taxine was, in fact, a complex mixture of alkaloids[208]composed of taxine A and taxine B, whose structures and absolute configurations would be determined much later, first by E. Graf himself and then by Alain Ahond and Christiane Poupat's team at Potier's laboratory[209] (Figure 4.6). It was then demonstrated that taxine B, acting as an antagonist to calcium channels[210], was mainly responsible for the cardiotoxic effects seen in cases of poisoning, in humans and animals[211].

In the 1950s and 1960s, several teams published their work on the isolation of different taxane molecules[e]. Notably, B. Lythgoe's team at

e The term "taxane" is used to denote all molecules possessing or deriving from a tricyclo[9.3.1.03,8]pentadecane ring system , as found in taxine B.

the University of Leeds worked on the components of *Taxus baccata*; the Japanese teams led by K. Nakanishi at the University of Sendai and Uyeo at the University of Kyoto studied the taxines isolated from *Taxus cuspidata*. All this work was published by Lythgoe in 1968, in the first review on taxanes[212]. In the 1970s, the structures of non-alkaloidic taxanes ("baccatin" series) isolated from *T. baccata*, such as baccatin III and baccatin V (epimer[f] on carbon 7 of baccatin III), were determined (Figure 4.7)[213].

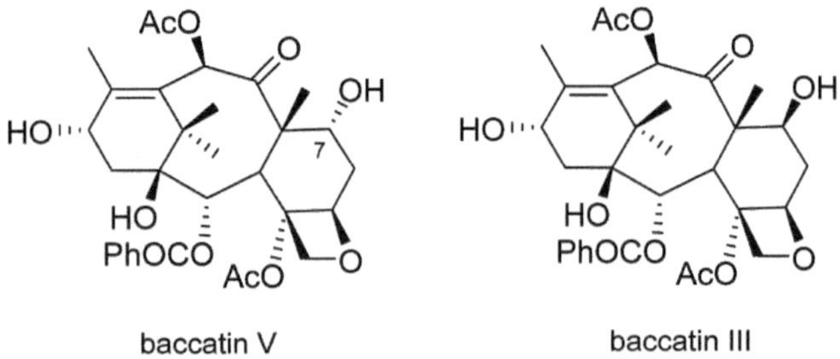

Figure 4.7. *Structures of baccatin V and baccatin III*

From the beginning of phytochemical studies until 1975, around 30 taxanes were isolated from different species of *Taxus*, and described in a review published by Miller[214]. In the 1970s and 1980s, research intensified at numerous laboratories following the appearances of two publications: one on the isolation, from the bark of the Pacific yew, *T. brevifolia*, of taxol – a new highly cytotoxic taxane; and the other reporting its unique mechanism of action (see section 4.2).

The authors of a review published in 2011 listed over 500 taxanes isolated from different parts of species of the genus *Taxus*, and reported ten taxane diterpenic skeletons found in the structures of the molecules isolated from yews[200].

f An epimer is a molecule which differs from another only through the absolute configuration of an asymmetrical carbon atom.

4.2. From the Pacific yew, *Taxus brevifolia*, to Taxol®, an anti-cancer molecule with a new mechanism of action

4.2.1. *Discovery of taxol, cytotoxic diterpene isolated from the Pacific yew*

Thus, in the late 1960s, a team of American researchers led by Monroe Wall, at the Research Triangle Institute (North Carolina), isolated taxol from an extract of bark from the trunk of the Pacific yew, *Taxus brevifolia Nutt.*, monitoring the cytotoxic activity of that extract. They published their work in May 1971[215]. That study originated in 1957, when Jonathan L. Hartwell from the National Cancer Institute (NCI) began an impressive program of screening of plant extracts devoted to finding anti-cancer molecules. That screening was performed *in vitro*, on cultures of human nasopharyngeal cancer cells (KB cells) and *in vivo*, on L-1210 and P-388 leukemias implanted in mice[216]. The plants were collected and their extracts prepared by collaborations with different institutions, including the United States Department of Agriculture (USDA). Thus, between 1957 and 1980, the activities of extracts from around 35,000 species of plants were evaluated both *in vitro* or *in vivo*[217]. The steps leading to the discovery of taxol have been described in great detail, notably by Matthew Suffness[g] and M. Wall[218], and of course by its actual "discoverers" M. Wall and Mansukh Wani[219], in Jordan Goodman and Vivien Walsh's book: *The Story of Taxol, Nature and Politics in the Pursuit of an Anti-Cancer Drug*[3], and, very recently, by M. Wani and S. Horwitz[220].

To briefly summarize the history of this discovery, in 1962, Arthur Barclay, a botanist working for the USDA, and his students, collected the first samples of stems, leaves and fruits of a Pacific yew, *Taxus brevifolia*, in Gifford Pinchot National Forest, in Washington State. As pointed out by Statz and Coon[221] and later by Goodman and Walsh[3], the extracts from the different parts of the Pacific yew were

---

g Matthew Suffness (1942–1995) was a crucially important actor in the development of taxol, at the National Cancer Institute. In 1976, he joined the NCI in the Natural Products Division, becoming head of that division in 1981. He edited the collective work *Taxol: Science and Applications,* CRC Press, 1995, to which he also contributed material.

prepared at the Wisconsin Alumni Research Foundation (WARF), and their cytotoxicity evaluated on KB cells at the Microbiological Associates Laboratory in Bethesda (Maryland). Out of all the parts studied, the bark from stems proved to be highly cytotoxic. In 1964, new collections of bark were organized, and the samples sent to Wall's laboratory with a view to finding the product(s) responsible for their cytotoxicity.

This work, done under contract with the NCI, led to the isolation, in 1966, of a new cytotoxic product, and first presented by M. Wall and M. Wani at a meeting of the American Chemical Society in 1967[222]. Although the structure of the compound isolated was not yet known at that time, M. Wall and his colleagues were certain that the new molecule had hydroxyl (OH) groups and that therefore it was an alcohol. Thus, it was named taxol: *tax* for *Taxus* and *ol* for alcohol.

From 12 kg of dry bark from *T. brevifolia*, 500 mg of taxol were initially isolated, monitoring the inhibitive activity on Walker 256 carcinosarcoma in mice, during the different steps of purification[218]. This very low yield (0.004%) was then improved, again by Wall's team, to 0.02%[215]. In mass spectrometry and elementary analysis, the molecule had a complex structure with 47 carbon atoms, 51 hydrogen atoms, 1 nitrogen atom and 14 oxygen atoms ($C_{47}H_{51}NO_{14}$). As NMR spectroscopy was unable to reliably determine the exact structure of the molecule, M. Wall and his collaborators tried to obtain crystalline derivatives of taxol to carry out X-ray analyses, but to no avail. They then studied methanolysis of taxol in a slightly basic medium (Scheme 4.1, path 1). This reaction yielded three compounds: a "tetraol"[h], N-benzoyl-β-phenylisoserine methyl ester and methyl acetate.

The first two products were converted into derivatives suitable for X-ray analysis, which helped identify their structure. Wall and his collaborators noted the structural similarity between tetraol and baccatin V – a taxane isolated from *T. baccata*, and whose crystallographic structure had been published in 1970

h "Tetraol": this compound was thus named because its structure included four "alcohol" (hydroxyl) functional groups. "Tetraol" will be identified as desacetyl–10 baccatin III.

(see Figure 4.7)[213a]. The tetraol was later named 10-deacetylbaccatin III – a desacetylated derivative at position 10 of baccatin III. Baccatin III had been isolated in 1966 from the wood of *T. baccata*[223]. Its erroneous structure had been revised once[213b], and was eventually established correctly in 1975[213c], as the epimer of baccatin V at carbon 7 (see Figure 4.7).

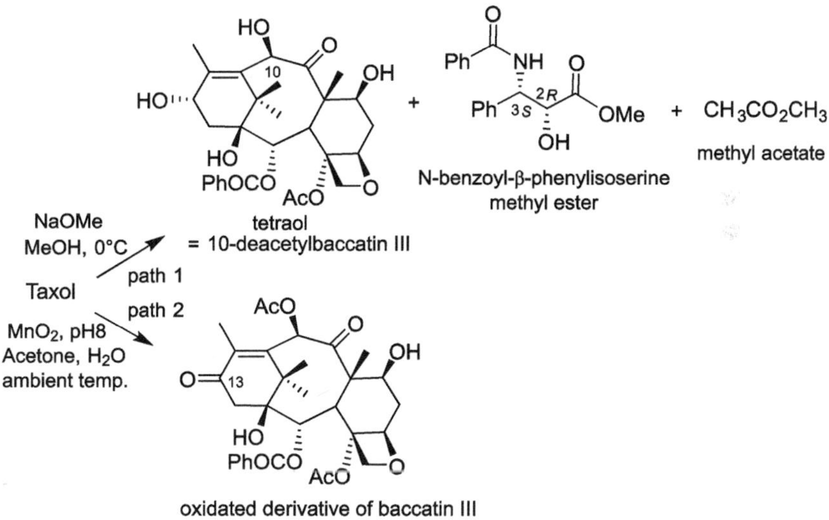

Scheme 4.1. *Methanolysis (path 1) and oxidation (path 2) of taxol*[215]

The absolute configuration of N-benzoyl-β-phenylisoserine methyl ester was determined as being the 2*R*,3*S* stereoisomer[i].

In order to determine the position of the acetate group and N-benzoy-β-phenylisoserine on tetraol (10-deacetylbaccatin III), M. Wall and his collaborators oxidized taxol in slightly basic conditions. A derivative of baccatin III, oxidized at the C-13 position, was obtained (Scheme 4.1, path 2). This reaction, in combination with the crystallographic structures of tetraol and N-benzoyl-β-phenylisoserine, allowed researchers to determine the structure of

---

i N-benzoyl-β-phenylisoserine methyl ester contains two asymmetrical neighboring carbons, so four stereoisomers are possible: 2*R*,3*R* ; 2*R*,3*S* ; 2*S*,3*S* and 2*S*,3*R*.

taxol, diterpene[j] with a complex structure having the tricyclic skeleton (A, B, C) of taxane with an oxetane ring (D) at carbons C-4 and C-5 (IUPAC numbering system), an isoserine side chain substituted at carbon 13, and an acetate functional group at carbon 10 (Figure 4.8).

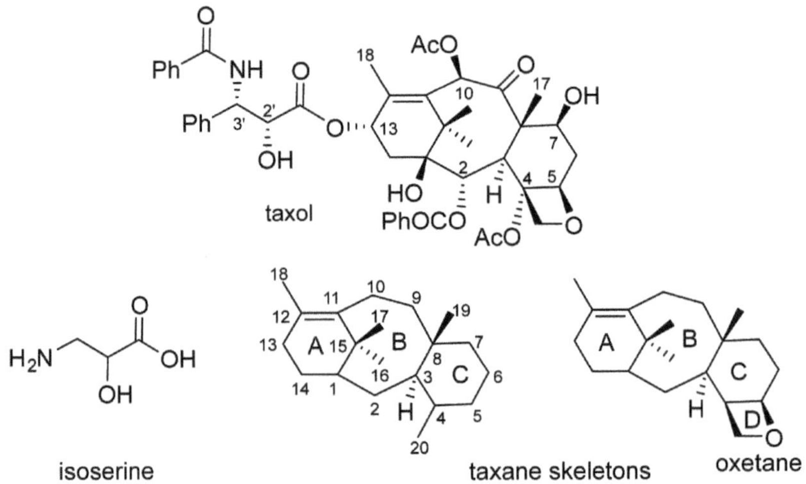

Figure 4.8. *Taxane skeletons, isoserine and Taxol with IUPAC numbering*

M. Wall and his collaborators published their work in 1971, entitled "*Plant Antitumor Agents. VI. The isolation and structure of Taxol, a Novel Antileukemic and Antitumor Agent from Taxus brevifolia*"[215].

4.2.2. *Taxol: a new mechanism of action and difficulties encountered during its development*

As soon as it was isolated in 1966, taxol was recognized as a highly cytotoxic agent against cultures of KB cancer cells. The next

j Diterpenes are natural molecules, formed by the association of four units of isoprene. Each isoprene unit contains five carbons. Thus, the skeleton of diterpenes has 20 carbon atoms.

year, its *in vivo* activity was confirmed on L1210 leukemia and Walker carcinosarcoma 256. In 1968, its activity on P1534 and P388 leukemias was mentioned, and then in 1975, the excellent antitumoral activity on B16 melanoma led the NCI to select taxol for in-depth studies, from 1977 onward.[218]

The earliest research pertaining to taxol's mechanism of action was published in 1978 by two researchers at the NCI, David Fuchs and Randall Johnson, with the title: *Cytologic evidence that taxol, an anti-neoplastic agent from Taxus brevifolia, acts as a mitotic poison*[224]. They showed that taxol, as a mitotic spindle poison, inhibits cell division. Shortly afterwards, the work of Susan Horwitz and her collaborators on the *in vitro* study of taxol's mechanism of action proved hugely important. Indeed, they discovered a unique mechanism of action, quite unlike that of the other antimitotic compounds known at the time: taxol promotes the assembly of tubulin to form microtubules, and stabilizes those microtubules irreversibly. These results, published in February 1979, entitled: *Promotion of microtubule assembly in vitro by taxol*[225], were crucially important in the NCI's decision to conduct preclinical studies on animals[226]. Finally, the first phase-I clinical trials began in 1984, and phase-II[k] trials two years later[226].

One of the major problems in conducting clinical trials in the 1980s and 1990s was how to obtain taxol in sufficient quantities. In 1989, the head of the Natural Products Branch at the National Cancer Institute, Gordon Cragg pointed out, in an article signed by Elaine Blume, "*Investigators seek to increase Taxol supply*", that 9 tons of bark, which would require the felling of 2,000–4,000 Pacific yews, would be needed to produce 1 kg of taxol (Figure 4.9)[227].

k In oncology, phase-I trials determine the optimal dose and the best conditions for administration of the product to patients. Phase-II trials evaluate the product's effectiveness against one or more types of cancers.

News

Investigators Seek To Increase Taxol Supply

Scientists are deploying their ingenuity to overcome a shortage of the promising anticancer compound taxol.

"Supply has been a major problem," said Gordon Cragg, Ph.D., acting head of the National Cancer Institute's Natural Products Branch. "We have been relying on bark of the Pacific yew tree, *Taxus brevifolia*, an evergreen that grows from Northern California up through British Columbia. But it takes 20,000 pounds of bark – that's two to four thousand trees – to produce one kilogram of taxol. And the trees must be sacrificed to produce the bark."

NCI bark collections to date (60,000 pounds in 1987–88 and another 60,000 pounds contracted for this year) have caused some concern among environmentalists. But the Pacific yew is neither sufficiently abundant nor sufficiently fast-growing to meet the needs of scientists waiting to conduct clinical trials with taxol.

Ways and Means

Selective breeding of yew trees could improve taxol yields, according to Matthew Suffness, Ph.D., program coordinator for NCI's natural products grants. "We have succeeded in getting Weyerhaeuser [a major forestry company] interested in growing yew trees as a crop," said Suffness. "In addition to breeding for higher yields of taxol, they would grow large stands of trees, which would be easier to harvest than the isolated wild trees we see today. Also, we have already found that taxol can be extracted from seedlings, so it would not be necessary to wait years for the trees to mature."

A 1988 article in the *Journal of the American Chemical Society* states that "Taxol is quite possibly the number one target today of synthetic organic chemists," and describes a "world-wide . . . prodigious effort toward its total synthesis." The same article goes on to note that "The various strategies revealed to date appear, however, to be of little practical value . . . ," a view shared by most observers.

Scientists are much more sanguine about the practicality of a partial synthesis, using a substance related to taxol as starting material. French researchers, for example, have identified a precursor of taxol in needles of the European yew, *Taxus baccata*. They are able to extract relatively large amounts of this compound, which they can then convert to taxol in a four-step procedure. In addition, these scientists have prepared a derivative of taxol that shows superior activity against murine tumors.

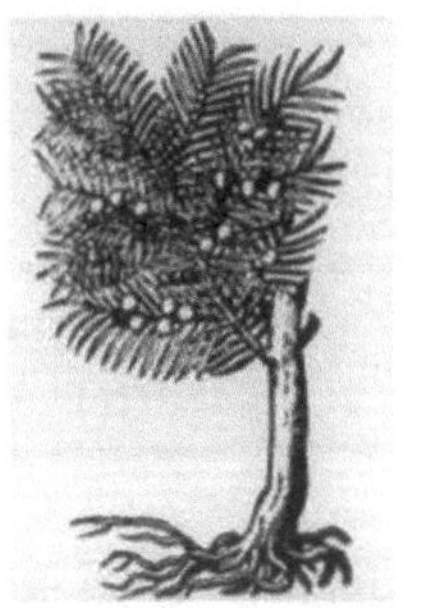

The yew tree, *Taxus baccata* (from J Gerard, *The Herball*, ed, 2, 1636).

Taxol From Tissue Culture

Alice Christen, Ph.D., a biologist at the U.S. Department of Agriculture in New Orleans, recently reported growing *Taxus brevifolia* in tissue culture and obtaining usable quantities of taxol from the growth medium. Her group has filed a process patent application for taxol production from cell culture and plans to obtain funds for further research by licensing the method.

"We are now trying to scale up our cultures," said Christen, who hopes that her novel approach will provide a viable solution to the taxol supply problem.

Officials in NCI's Cancer Therapy Evaluation Program are planning to solicit proposals for Collaborative Research and Development Agreements (CRADAs) from pharmaceutical companies for development of taxol. The company selected by NCI would be able to use data from NCI-supported trials to gain FDA approval of the drug, which it would develop and market. In exchange, the company would be expected to supply NCI with taxol for ongoing studies.

Unique Mode of Action

The efforts being devoted to increasing the supply of taxol attest to the interest investigators have in this compound. This interest dates from the late 1960s, when a crude extract of bark from the Pacific yew, which was being tested by NCI in a large-scale plant screening program, showed activity against a mouse leukemia.

1122 Journal of the National Cancer Institute

Figure 4.9. *First page of Elaine Blume's article: "Investigators Seek To Increase Taxol Supply"*[227]

Similarly, Bruce Chabner, head of the NCI's Division of Cancer Treatment, expressed the opinion, in an article in the same journal, signed by Randall Gentry, that 36,000 Pacific yews could produce enough taxol to treat 20,000 patients[228]. Hence, there was an enormous effort by the NCI and teams working in collaboration with that institute to increase taxol supply. However, it was not until a semisynthesis process was developed (see sections 4.4 and 4.5), following the discovery of 10-deacetylbaccatin III in the leaves of the

English yew *T. baccata* (see section 4.3), that the problem of taxol supply would be solved.

Finally, in December 1989, the pharmaceutical company Bristol-Myers Squibb (BMS) was chosen as the CRADA (Cooperative Research and Development Agreement) partner with the NCI for the development of taxol[229]. In 1992, BMS managed to register the name "Taxol®" as a trademark, and "paclitaxel" was the generic name of the molecule, though it had been called taxol when it was discovered by Wall and his collaborators[l]. In fact, the name Taxol had already been used in the 1920s by the French company Lobica[m], and in the 1930s by Continental in England[230]. This specialty – containing, amongst other things, bile extracts and aloe powder – was recommended in cases of constipation (Figure 4.10).

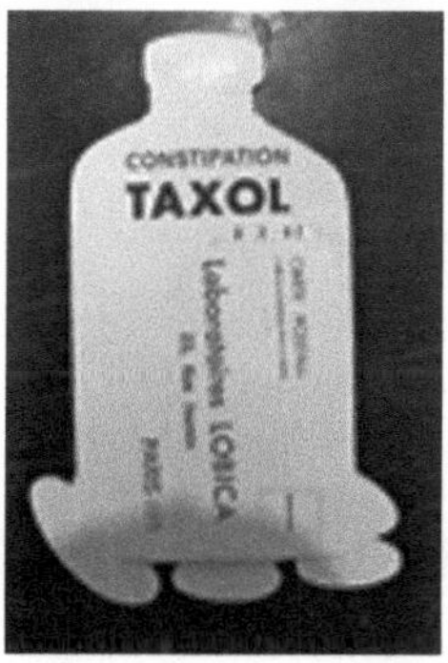

Figure 4.10. *Taxol as sold by Laboratoires Lobica[n] and Continental Laboratories Limited[o]*

l The name "taxol" used throughout this chapter denotes the chemical molecule (see Chapter 1, note a).

m *Journal Médical Français,* n°4, 01/04/1928. Santheose – Taxol. Laboratoires réunis- Lobica. Chronicle by Professor J. Castaigne.

n Advert sold on eBay (http://www.ebay.ca/itm/351040315595), consulted 14 April 2015.

o Image found online: http://www.sciencebase.com/science-blog/taxol-anticancer-drug.html.

Finally, in 1992, the FDA approved the use of Taxol® for the treatment of refractory ovarian cancer, and then in 1994 for that of breast cancer.

4.3. Phytochemical studies carried out at the ICSN: discovery of 10-deacetylbaccatin III in the natural state (1980s)

Work on the common yew[p], *Taxus baccata*, began at the ICSN in January 1980, in Potier's team, a year after the publication of S. Horwitz's article[225] on taxol's unique mechanism of action on microtubules. P. Potier and D. Guénard, who had developed the so-called "tubulin test" to evaluate the activity of vinca-alkaloids, had of course taken note of that article. D. Guénard recalls an encounter he had with Potier in early January 1980:

> It began at the start of 1980, at a meeting organized at Gif Castle – on the campus - with Paoletti where, on my way back from dinner, PP reminded me that he had sent me a recent publication (on taxol), and that we in Gif we well placed to work on it, given all the yews in the park[q].

D. Guénard then asked P. Potier for permission to begin research on the yew by studying all the extracts. P. Potier gave him an enthusiastic green light! D. Guénard then tells us:

> By happy coincidence, a few weeks later, I learned from the head gardener of the park (M. Dupont, whom I had approached to ask how to procure some yew wood) that

p The common yew (*Taxus baccata*) is also known as the English yew or European yew, as opposed to the Pacific yew (*Taxus brevifolia*).

q Information from D. Guénard, via e-mail on 7 January 2015. Gif for Gif-sur-Yvette, the town where is situated ICSN on the CNRS campus. .PP for Pierre Potier. The publication (taxol) was S. Horwitz's. Claude Paoletti (1928–1994), a friend of P. Potier, was head of the CNRS' pharmacology and fundamental toxicology laboratory in Toulouse, and later head of the CNRS Life Sciences Department.

> they were about to cut down a marvelous yew just at the crossroads between the road which runs down to the canteen and the road which leads to the castle, because that tree was blocking out light from the administrators' office windows![r]

4.3.1. *Extraction and purification of T. baccata, monitoring the activity on tubulin*

Thus, the first work on the common yew *Taxus baccata* began in January 1980, at the ICSN[s]. The yew nearest to the CNRS administrators' office windows was cut down, and D. Guénard prepared extracts from the leaves, and the bark, to evaluate their activity on tubulin. The main idea was to look for taxol or for similar compounds. In order to do this, he developed a modified tubulin test to reveal the presence or absence of taxol. Whilst the tubulin test had indeed been used beforehand in the laboratory with vinblastine-series alkaloids, it needed to be modified, as taxol's mechanism of action is different to that of vinblastine. S. Horwitz had, *in vitro*, shown the promoting effect taxol has on the kinetics of assembly of tubulin into microtubules, and its stabilization of those microtubules, by noting the increase in optical density (OD) (left, Figure 4.11)[225]. For practical reasons, D. Guénard chose to monitor the activity of yew extracts on the disassembly of microtubules into tubulin. Indeed, it was quicker and easier to examine the inhibitive effect on the disassembly of microtubules: when taxol was added to a solution of microtubules formed at 37°C, the compound's inhibitive effect could be seen in two minutes, at a cold temperature (right, Figure 4.11).

r Information from D. Guénard, *op. cit.*

s Information from D. Guénard, via e-mails on 7 January, 5 and 6 March, and 9 April 2015.

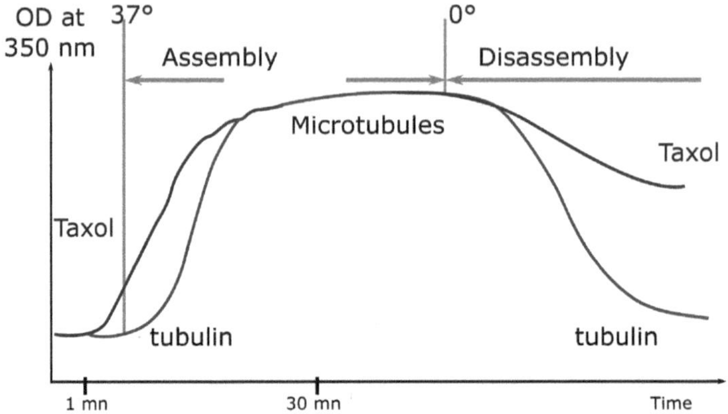

Figure 4.11. *Illustration of the in vitro test on the promoting effect of taxol (shown in blue) on the assembly of tubulin into microtubules (left) and its inhibitive effect on the disassembly of the microtubules into tubulin (right). For a color version of this figure, see www.iste.co.uk/leroux/navelbine.zip*

This *in vitro* test was, from then on, used systematically to evaluate the activity of the extracts and fractions during the different purification operations (bio-guided phytochemical study), and of the pure products thus isolated.

The first attempts at ethanol-based extraction were carried out on a few kilos of dry leaves and bark. The extracts prepared all proved to be active, inhibiting the disassembly of the microtubules into tubulin. From January to April 1980, D. Guénard worked on the extract from the leaves of *T. baccata*, whose cytotoxic activity had not been mentioned previously[t]. This extract had been obtained by following these steps: 1) drying of the leaves at 40°C, 2) grinding dry leaves, 3) extraction with alcohol, 4) evaporation at reduced pressure, 5) recovery of the extract in an aqueous medium, 6) filtering out of the insoluble material, and 7) extraction of the aqueous medium by methylene chloride (Figure 4.12).

t Remember that the researchers at the NCI and Wall's team had worked on extracts of the Pacific yew, *Taxus brevifolia*, monitoring its antitumoral activity *in vivo* and its cytotoxic activity *in vitro*.

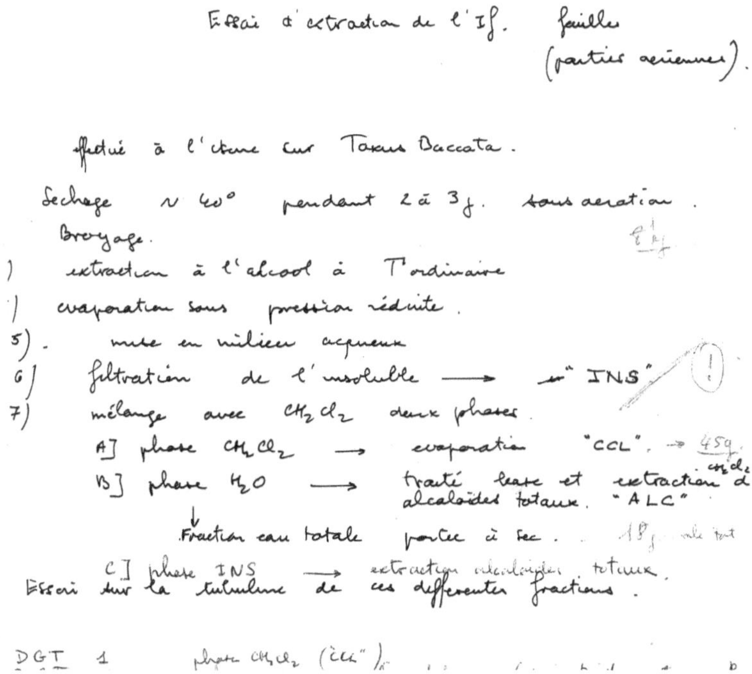
Essai d'extraction de l'If. feuilles
(parties aériennes).

effectué à l'étuve sur Taxus Baccata.

Séchage ~ 40° pendant 2 à 3 j. sous aération.
Broyage.
) extraction à l'alcool à T ordinaire
) évaporation sous pression réduite.
5). mise en milieu aqueux
6) filtration de l'insoluble → "INS"
7) mélange avec CH_2Cl_2 deux phases.
A] phase CH_2Cl_2 → évaporation "CCL". → 45g.
B] phase H_2O → traité base et extraction CH_2Cl_2 des alcaloïdes totaux. "ALC"
Fraction eau totale portée à sec.
C] phase INS → extraction alcaloïdes totaux.
Essai sur la tubuline de ces différentes fractions.

DGT 1 phase CH_2Cl_2 ("CCL")

Figure 4.12. *Extract from D. Guénard's laboratory notebook (8 January 1980)*[u]

4.3.2. *Isolation of 10-deacetylbaccatin III*

Dichloromethane extract, named DGT1 (for Daniel Guénard Taxus) was purified by different methods of chromatography, always monitoring the activity on tubulin, to yield a main compound – "tetraol" – of which 200 mg were obtained from 1 kg of dry leaves. By studying the mass spectrum and NMR spectrum, D. Guénard determined the structure of this compound, which turned out to be 10-deacetylbaccatin III – a compound never before obtained in the natural state, but already known as the product formed by the methanolysis of taxol[215] (see Scheme 4.1). As regards its activity on tubulin, 10-deacetylbaccatin III exhibited far less activity than taxol.

u D. Guénard's laboratory notes. 8 January 1980. ICSN archives.

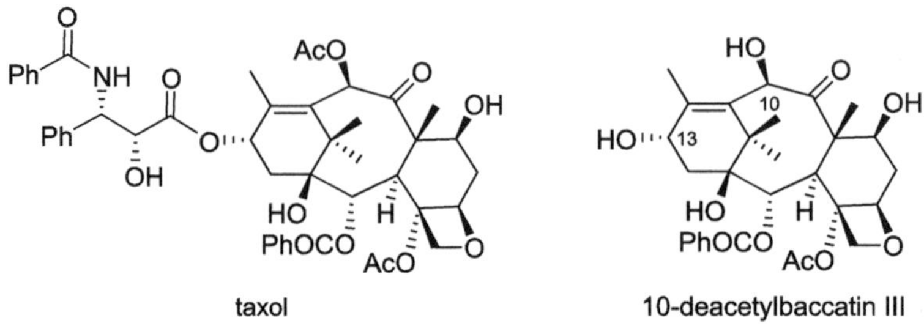

Figure 4.13. *Comparison of the structures of taxol and of 10-deacetylbaccatin III*

On seeing these results, P. Potier responded very enthusiastically. Indeed, the discovery of 10-deacetylbaccatin III, isolated from the leaves of the common yew, *T. baccata*, presented a twofold advantage: 1) the compound was easier to obtain than taxol, coming from a renewable source – the yew's leaves, so the tree did not need to be felled, 2) 10-deacetylbaccatin III could serve as a precursor for the semisynthesis of taxol, its molecular structure differing from natural taxol by the lack of an acetyl group at carbon 10 and the side chain at carbon 13 (Figure 4.13).

In order to speed up the research on this project, a student, Brigitte Bourdillat, and Gérard Chauvière, a researcher from the CNRS, joined Potier and Guénard's team during 1980, and worked on extraction from different parts of the yew. Françoise Picot, a technician at the ICSN, studying pharmacy, also joined the team to study the *in vitro* and *in vivo* activity of taxol isolated from the yew, in collaboration with Hélène Bériel – Professor of pharmacology and physiology at the *Faculté de Pharmacie* in Grenoble, and her collaborators. Later, P. Potier suggested to D. Guénard that they recruit a doctoral candidate, Véronique Sénilh, to work on the semisynthesis of taxol and to study the structure-activity relationships in the taxane series. In 1981, through a collaboration agreement between the pharmaceutical company Rhône-Poulenc (RP) and the CNRS[v], Michel Colin[w], an

v This contract, signed on 19 October 1981, pertained to the extraction and antitumoral activity of the natural products found in the yew and thuja (see Chapter 2).

engineer at RP, came to work with the team at the ICSN. P. Potier suggested he work on the extraction and purification processes at a larger scale, and then on semisynthesis for industrial purposes. In 1982, F. Guéritte, now INSERM's researcher on secondment to ICSN[x], at P. Potier's urging, joined D. Guénard's team to pursue the chemical study of taxanes with the objective to semisynthesis synthesize taxol and structural analogs.

To continue this work, a crucial point was how to obtain enough yews – an indispensable primary material in isolating and characterizing the taxanes contained in the different parts of the tree, and improving the yield of 10-deacetylbaccatin III to carry out the first tests on semisynthesis of taxol. A lucky coincidence was that, in the early 1980s, the city council of Gif-sur-Yvette acquired part of the CNRS' land to build a new road, in the center of the village[y]. As part of this work, a dozen yews (*T. baccata*) in the park were felled. D. Guénard negotiated directly with the person in charge of the felling, to recover all of those yews, which were deposited at the "factory"[z], situated below the ICSN. The whole team participated in "peeling" the yews, stripping the bark from the trunks, cutting leaves and stems, and sorting each part of the trees (Figure 4.14). The extraction of the plant material was then carried out in the "factory"[aa]. Over the course of 1983, thanks to contacts established with

w In accordance with the agreements between CNRS and Rhône-Poulenc in 1975 (see Chapter 2).

x At the suggestion of P. Potier, in order to facilitate exchange of personnel and develop cooperation between the CNRS and INSERM in the area of natural products at medicine, she had competed to join INSERM as a researcher in chemistry. F. Guéritte spent her entire career at ICSN, as an envoy from Inserm. Interview with PP – MLR, Paris, Maison de la chimie, 29 September 2003.

y *Archives municipales de Gif-sur-Yvette* (http://www.ville-gif.fr/cadre-de-vie/histoire-et-patrimoine/patrimoine/chateau-de-button/). Consulted on 24 April 2015.

z The factory, a building owned by the ICSN and located below it, was originally designed for the extraction of large quantities of plant material, its purification, and fermentation processes.

aa All this could never have happened in this way in the United States; see Le Roux & Walsh, "Contingency in Innovation and the role of National Systems: Taxol and Taxotère in the USA and France", *Research Policy*, 9, 3, 2004.

nurserymen in the region, many more kilos of yew leaves and bark were obtained, and extraction performed on them, under M. Colin's supervision, at Rhône-Poulenc's research center in Vitry-sur-Seine[bb].

Figure 4.14. *The team at work behind the "factory"... and the felled yews*

As previously mentioned, the earliest attempts at extraction and purification, thanks to monitoring of activity on tubulin, produced 200 mg of 10-deacetylbaccatin III, from 1 kg of dry leaves[231]. The isolation of desacetyl-10 baccatin was then transposed to a larger scale by M. Colin, and by way of example, 92 g of 10-deacetylbaccatin III could be obtained from 367 kg of undried hedge clippings[cc].

Later, the yield was further improved, and around 1 g of 10-deacetylbaccatin III was obtained from 1 kg of fresh leaves of *T. baccata*[dd].

bb Letter from J. Champy, head of the research center at Vitry, addressed to P. Potier, 1 February 1983. État des Travaux, (Status Report), M. Colin, 21/1 to 20/7/1983.
cc État des Travaux, M. Colin, November 1984. ICSN archives.
dd The conditions of extraction and purification leading to this improvement in the yield of desacetyl–10 baccatin III were never published.

4.3.3. *Isolation of other taxanes and biological activity on tubulin*

The bio-guided phytochemical study of the leaves and bark was conducted, in particular, by B. Bourdillat, in 1980[ee], by F. Harvard-Picot studying for her *Diplôme d'Etudes Approfondies* (DEA – Advanced Studies Diploma) obtained in 1981[ff], and by V. Sénilh, who, for her part, began work on her thesis in 1980[232].

After 10-deacetylbaccatin III, still in the early 1980s, 19-hydroxybaccatin III and 12*β*,16*β*-epoxy-11*β*-hydroxy-12, 12-dihydrotaxinin E , named taxagifine[231, 233], were isolated from the leaves of the common yew, *T. baccata*, by the team (Figure 4.15). Baccatin III, taxol, cephalomannine and their deacetylated derivatives, 10-deacetyltaxol and 10-deacetylcephalomannine (Figure 4.15) were obtained from the bark in small quantities[231], as were many other analogs of taxol[234]. In total, 16 taxol analogs, eight of them new, were isolated from the bark.

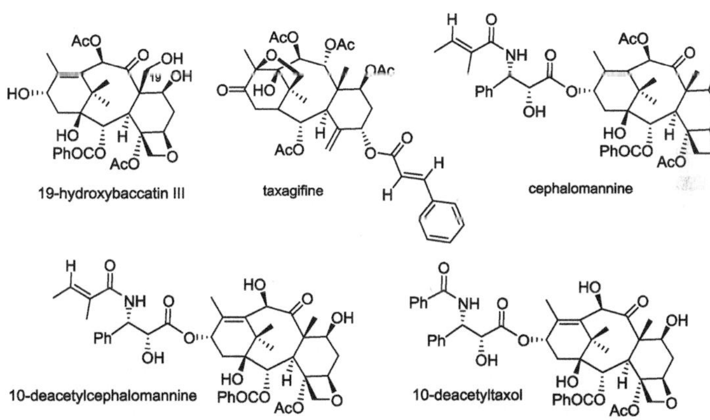

Figure 4.15. *Structures of 19-hydroxybaccatin III, taxagifine, cephalomannine, 10-deacetylcephalomannine and 10-deacetyltaxol*

ee Progress report by B. Bourdillat, February to July 1980, Isolement à partir des écorces d'if de substances naturelles antimitotiques. ICSN archives.
ff DEA report by F. Picot – Harvard, 1980–1981, Poisons de fuseau mitotique extraits de l'if *Taxus baccata* L., et leur interaction avec la tubuline. ICSN archives.

After verifying the purity of each of the products isolated, their activity evaluated on the inhibition of the disassembly of microtubules into tubulin offered an initial indication as to the groups, whether or not they were essential to the activity. By way of example, Figure 4.16 shows the structures and activities of taxol, 10-deacetyltaxol, baccatin III and 10-deacetylbaccatin III. The evaluated activity thus indicated that the presence of an acetoxy (AcO) group at carbon 10 had little influence on the activity[gg], On the other hand, the presence of the side chain at carbon 13 proved absolutely crucial for the activity: taxol and 10-deacetyltaxol do indeed have similar levels of activity, whilst baccatin III and 10-deacetylbaccatin III are much less active [231, 235].

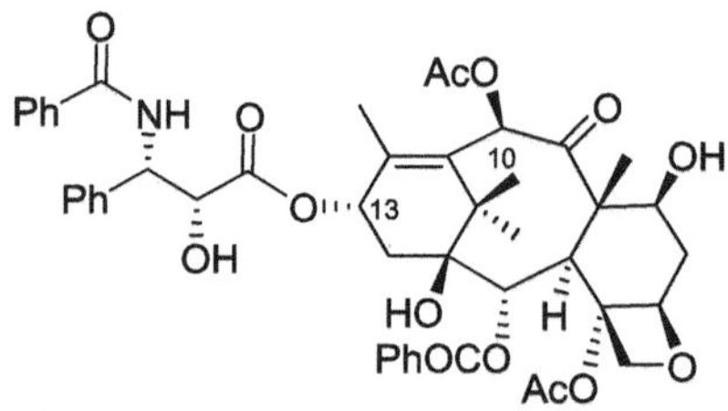

taxol
IC_{50}= 0.2 - 0.5 μM

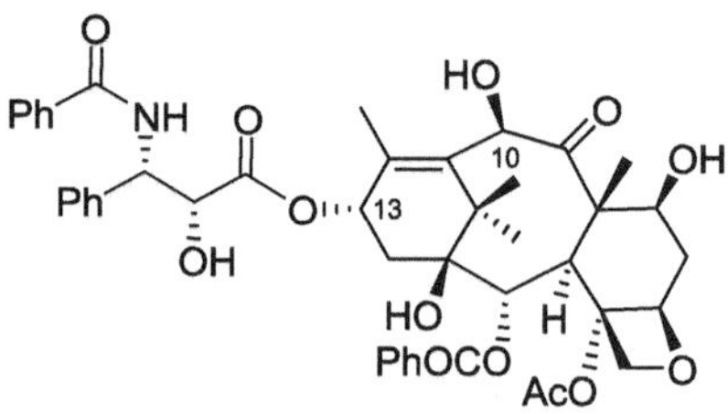

10-deacetyltaxol
IC_{50}= 0.7 μM

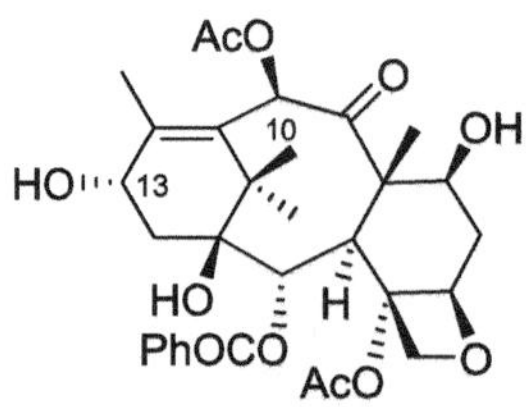

baccatin III
IC_{50}= 26 μM

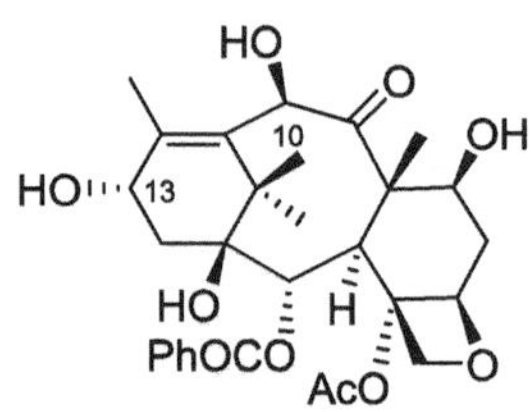

10-deacetylbaccatin III
IC_{50}= 23 - 30 μM

Figure 4.16. *Activity on tubulin by taxol, 10-deacetyltaxol baccatin and 10-deacetylbaccatin III , evaluated at IC_{50}*

gg The concentration of the product being evaluated causing a 50% inhibition of disassembly (IC_{50}) was systematically compared, the same day on the same batch of tubulin, to that of taxol, as these IC_{50} values may vary slightly depending on the batch of tubulin used.

In 1982, other *in vitro* tests were begun with Michel Wright's team at the CNRS *Laboratoire de Pharmacologie et de Toxicologie Fondamentales* (Fundamental Pharmacology and Toxicology Laboratory) in Toulouse, on microtubules of *Physarum polycephalum* – a unicellular organism in the myxomycetes class. This second series was expected to offer an idea about the potential anti-fungal power of the taxanes isolated. The results showed that, whilst the presence of the side chain at position 13 is essential for good activity on mammalian tubulin, its absence causes no loss of activity in the case of *P. polycephalum* tubulin[235].

At the start of the 1980s, besides the French team, there were teams in America working on the isolation of taxol and analogs from species of the *Taxus* genus: notably, that led by Cecil R. Smith at the US Department of Agriculture, and by David G.I Kingston of the Virginia Polytechnic Institute. By monitoring the cytotoxic activity during purification of extracts of *T. wallichiana,* the team at the U.S Department of Agriculture also isolated 19-hydroxybaccatin III[236], baccatin III, taxol, cephalomannine[237], and the desacetylated derivatives at C-10 of the latter two compounds[236], It should be noted that the name "cephalomannine" had been given to this product in 1979, as it was isolated from *Cephalotaxus mannii* – another genus belonging to the Taxaceae family[238]. Curiously, no taxane skeleton had previously been isolated from the genus *Cephalotaxus*, whose components belong to the chemical family characteristic of alkaloids in the cephalotaxine and harringtonine series. In 1981, the American team corrected the identity of the plant studied, renaming it *T. wallichiana*[236-237]. As the two species had morphological similarities, they had been confused, but the error was corrected thanks to structural characterization of the isolated metabolites isolated. The team at Kingston focusing on the phytochemical study of the species *T. brevifolia* isolated, amongst other things, 10-deacetylbaccatin III, a year after the French team had done[239], and in collaboration with S. Horwitz's team, studied the structure/activity relations of certain taxol analogs, with the *in vitro* activity being evaluated both on cytotoxicity and on the assembly of tubulin into microtubules[240]. They thus confirmed that the side chain in position 13 is indispensable for the activity, whilst the acetyl group in position 10 is not necessary.

4.3.4. *Study of the pharmacological properties of taxol at the ICSN and at the Faculté de Pharmacie in Grenoble*

From 1982 onwards, alongside the phytochemical studies and the evaluation of the activity of the isolated taxanes on microtubules, F. Picot studied the pharmacological properties of taxol, in collaboration with H. Bériel and her team at the *Faculté de Pharmacie* in Grenoble. A whole series of *in vivo* tests were notably developed on human tumors grafted into athymic mice (nude mice), which are characterized by the lack of an immune system[241]. The results obtained proved sufficiently encouraging to consider phase-I clinical trials in the service of Professors Michel Boiron and Michel Marty at St Louis hospital, in Paris[hh]. However, this project posed the same problem faced by the American teams: the difficulty of obtaining large quantities of taxol, from the common yew, *T. baccata*. This problem was noted in 1984 by D. Guénard, in his *Titres et Travaux*, in the chapter “Aspect technique du travail actuel” (technical aspect of work currently under way):

> Taxol is a product which is very much in demand right now: for biology, for pharmacological tests, for clinical trials; its semisynthesis did not succeed yet, nor its total synthesis although a number of major teams throughout the world are working on this. The only source, at present, then, is still the bark (or roots) of yews, whose yield is poor: around 100 mg/kg of dry bark. Therefore, this is the means which we have chosen to develop this product. There is nothing spectacular about

hh *Titres et Travaux* (Status Report), Daniel Guénard, Senior researcher, 1984. ICSN archives.

> this aspect of the research, but nevertheless, it is difficult: searching for yews (rarely ready for felling), and processing large quantities of material, necessitating the development of better-suited, better-performing equipment so as to lower the cost of the operation. Thus, over a ton of plant material has so far been processed (…)[ii]

The development of a semisynthesis process from 10-deacetylbaccatin III, which could more easily produce taxol, was therefore necessary.

4.4. Steps toward the first semisynthesis of 10-deacetyltaxol, of taxol and discovery of a highly active analog by the aminohydroxylation reaction

The isolation of 10-deacetylbaccatin III – a new natural taxane isolated from the leaves of the common yew, *T. baccata*, which grew relatively abundantly on the CNRS campus at Gif-sur-Yvette and in certain nearby nurseries – was essential for the continuation of the team's work in chemistry. Thus, several grams of 10-deacetylbaccatin III were obtained, so the team could begin studying the chemistry of that molecule. One of their objectives was to realize the semisynthesis of taxol, and comparing the two structures, it became clear that we simply needed to acetylate the hydroxyl functional group present at carbon 10 and esterify that at carbon 13, using the acid corresponding to the side chain on taxol – N-benzoyl-β-phenylisoserine in configuration 2*R*, 3*S* (Figure 4.17). However, before attempting semisynthesis, it was crucial to study the chemical reactivity of 10-deacetylbaccatin III.

ii *Ibid.*

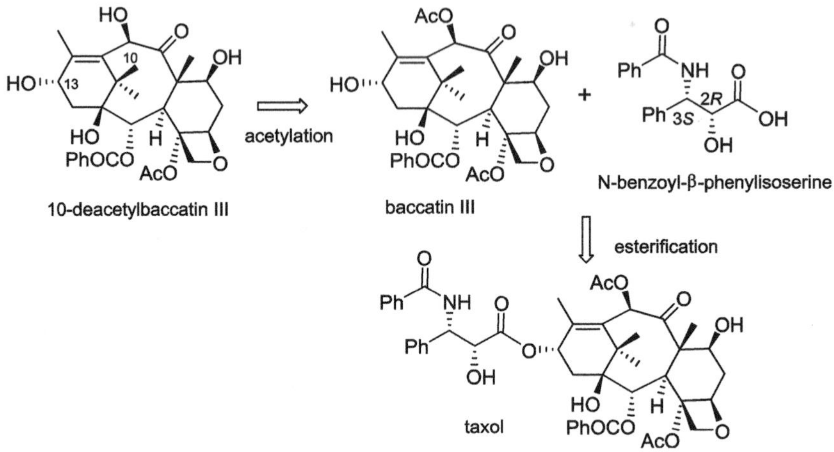

Figure 4.17. *Proposal of a path to the semisynthesis of taxol*

4.4.1. *Chemical studies of 10-deacetylbaccatin III*

When these studies began in 1981, little was known about the reactivity of 10-deacetylbaccatin III. An experiment had been conducted, by Wall's team, on that compound, obtained by the methanolysis of taxol (see Scheme 1.1): its transformation into iodoacetate derivative enabled researchers to determine its structure and its absolute configuration[215].

4.4.1.1. *First experiments pertaining to the chemical reactivity of hydroxyl groups: acetylation*

One of the first experiments carried out in Potier's team, by V. Sénilh, was devoted to the reactivity of the hydroxyl groups in 10-deacetylbaccatin III to an acylating agent: acetic anhydride (Ac_2O)[jj]. Four hydroxyl functional groups are present on this molecule's taxane

jj V. Sénilh's laboratory notes, September-October 1981. ICSN archives.

skeleton, in positions 1, 7, 10 and 13. As the hydroxyl group in position 1, on a tertiary carbon[kk] is not greatly reactive, if at all, only the hydroxyls at 7, 10 and 13 should more easily be acetylated. In mild conditions (ambient temperature for 24 hours), a 50:50 mixture of 7-monoacetate and 7-10-diacetate is obtained, with a significant yield. In much harsher conditions (60°C for 48 hours), 7, 10, 13 triacetate alone is isolated (Scheme 4.2)[242].

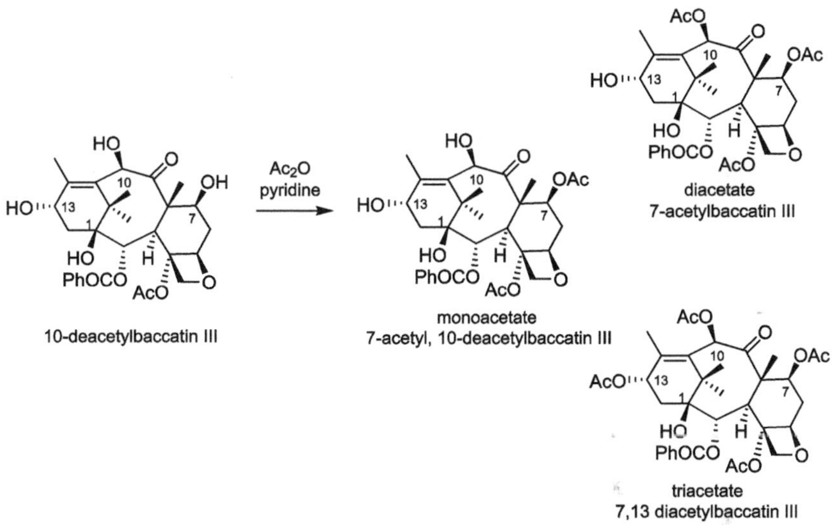

Scheme 4.2. *Acetylation of 10-deacetylbaccatin III*

The reason for the difference in reactivity of the hydroxyl groups becomes clear when we look at the molecular model of 10-deacetylbaccatin III, so we can visualize the molecule in three dimensions, and see its folded up conformation. Whilst the hydroxyls at positions 7 and 10 are easily accessible, that at position 13 is far less so, which may even lead to an intramolecular hydrogen bond with the acetate group in position 4 (Figure 4.18)[242].

kk A tertiary carbon is bonded to three other carbon atoms.

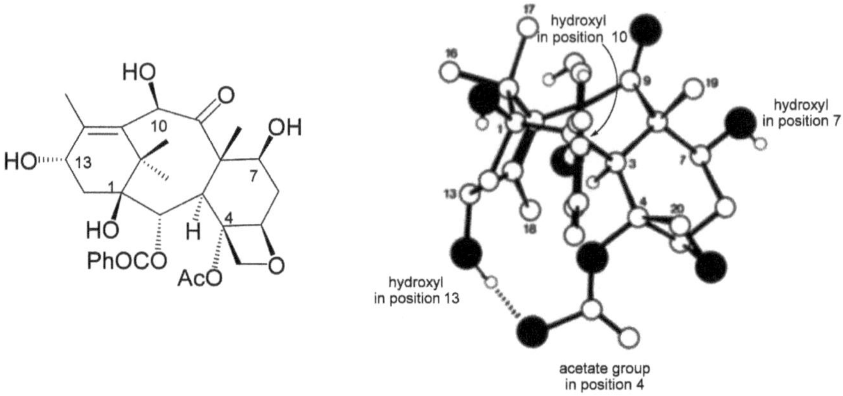

Figure 4.18. *2D structure and conformation of 10-deacetylbaccatin III*

Esterification of the hydroxyl in position 13 could be performed directly on 7-acetylbaccatin III (Scheme 4.2), which could serve as a precursor of 7-acetyltaxol. However, the lack of selectivity during the acetylation of 10-deacetylbaccatin III, and given that the presence of the acetyl group in position 10 had very little influence on the activity, semisynthesis studies were originally targeted at the obtaining of 10-deacetyltaxol. Thus, it was enough to protect the hydroxyl groups in positions 7 and 10 before performing esterification at 13 by the acid corresponding to taxol's side chain.

4.4.1.2. *Search for a protective group for the hydroxyls at C-7 and C-10 and their deprotection*

After many protection attemps, carried out by V. Sénilh, the trichloroethoxycarbonyl (troc) group was selected for how easily it can be deprotected in mild conditions[243]. Indeed, taxol had been shown to be unstable in basic conditions by M. Wall's team, as the side chain is easily hydrolyzed to give 10-deacetylbaccatin III[215]. In addition, again in a basic medium, the hydroxyl group in position 7 can be epimerized, by a retro-aldol / aldol mechanism (see Scheme 4.3)[236-237].

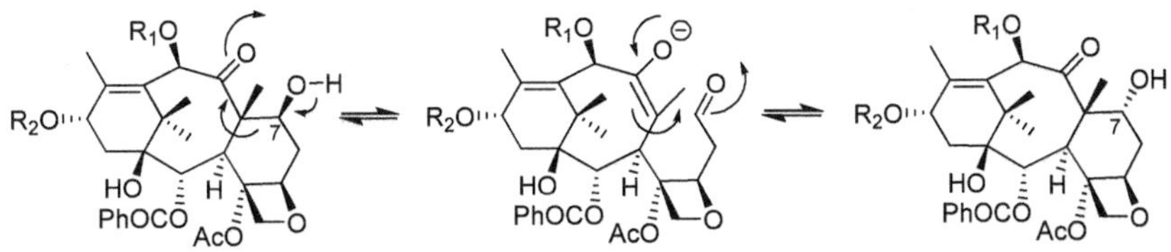

Scheme 4.3. *Mechanism of epimerization of the hydroxyl at C-7 in a basic medium*

By studying different conditions, the diprotected derivative at 7 and 10 (7,10-ditroc-10-deacetylbaccatin III) was obtained with yields greater than 90% from 10-deacetylbaccatin III in the presence of trichloro-2,2,2 ethyl chloroformiate, in pyridine at 80°C (Scheme 4.3)[11]. The deprotection of the troc groups was carried out with zinc in methanol or zinc in acetic acid[243]. As the use of zinc in methanol epimerizes the hydroxyl functional group at carbon 7, deprotection in acetic acid was chosen to give quantitatively 10-deacetylbaccatin III (Scheme 4.4)[232, 242, 244].

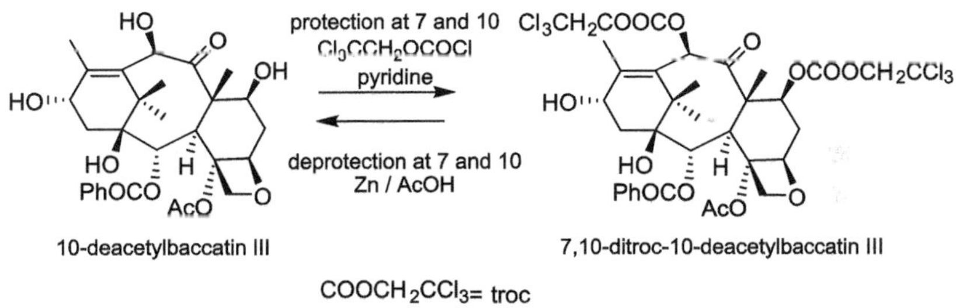

Scheme 4.4. *Protection of 10-deacetylbaccatin III and deprotection*

The excellent yields obtained in these attempts at protection and deprotection led the team to favor ditroc-7,10 10-deacetylbaccatin III as a key intermediary in their efforts to esterify the hydroxyl at position 13.

11 V. Sénilh's and F. Guéritte's laboratory notebooks, November 1982. ICSN archives.

4.4.2. *Studies on the esterification of 7,10-ditroc-10-deacetylbaccatin III. Semisynthesis of cinnamic ester of 10-deacetylbaccatin III*

During 1982 and 1983, the esterification of diprotected 10-deacetylbaccatin III (ditroc-7,10 DAB) by different acids was studied by V. Sénilh and then by F. Guéritte[mm]. As happened in the case of the acetylation studies, the hydroxyl in position 13 proved particularly inert to conventional esterification methods. Many experiments were conducted, notably with the acids 2*R*, 3*R* and 2*S*, 3*S* N-benzoy-β-phenylisoserine, diastereoisomers[nn] of the acid corresponding to taxol's side chain (2*R*, 3*S* N-benzoy-β-phenylisoserine) (Figure 4.19), and synthesized by Françoise Khuong-Huu's team, at the ICSN[oo], from trans-3-phenylglycidic acid obtained by a Darzens condensation[245].

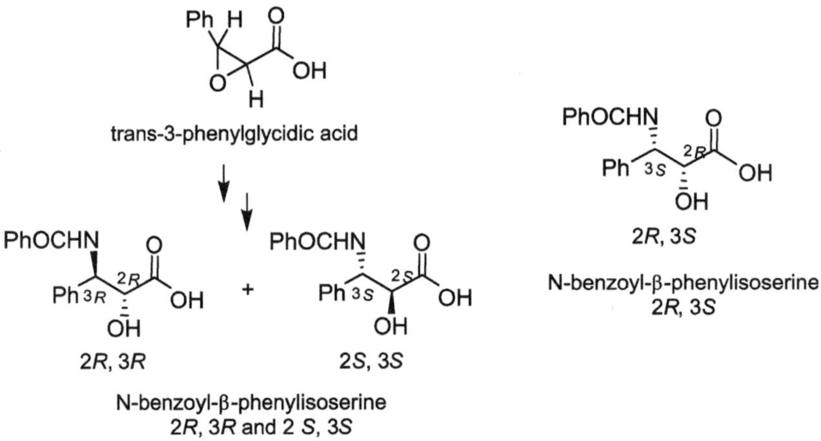

Figure 4.19. *Structure of N-benzoyl-β-phenylisoserine acids*

mm V. Sénilh's laboratory notebooks, May 1982, and F. Guéritte's notebooks, June-September 1983. ICSN archives.

nn Diastereoisomers are molecules identical in terms of the sequences of the atoms, but different in terms of the configuration of their chirality centers.

oo The synthesis of acids 2*R*, 3*R* and 2*S*, 3*S* N-benzoyl-β-phenylisoserine by the team at the ICSN led by F. Khuong-Huu was never published.

The very first attempts at esterification of 7,10-ditroc-10-deacetylbaccatin III with N-benzoy-β-phenylisoserines (2*R*, 3*R* and 2*S*, 3*S*), in the form of acid chloride and protected at the hydroxyl in position 2 by the trichloroethyloxycarbonyl (troc) group were unsuccessful. For example, in the presence of silver cyanide (AgCN) in toluene at 80°C (Scheme 4.5), the method of esterification developed by S. Takimoto's team in Japan for the preparation of encumbered esters[246], the desired esterification product could not be isolated[pp].

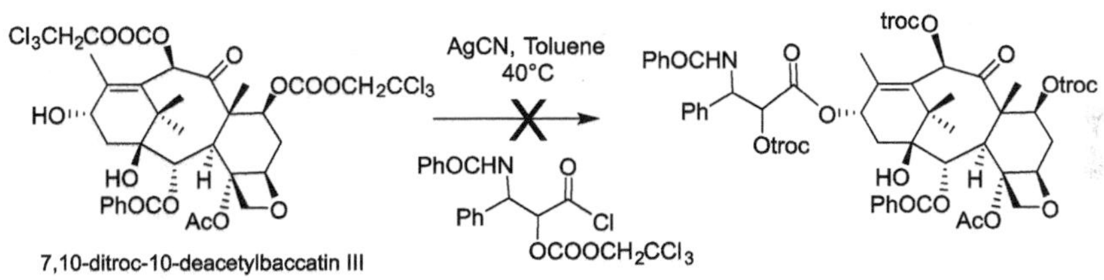

Scheme 4.5. *Failed attempt to esterify N-benzoyl-β-phenylisoserines (2R,3R and 2S,3S) protected by the troc group*

In retrospective, if that esterification reaction had met with success at that point (it would do later... see section 4.5), taxol could have been obtained, but taxotere would probably never have seen the light of day. Indeed, in order to study that esterification reaction, the team focused all their efforts on the esterification of 7,10-ditroc-10-deacetylbaccatin III with cinnamic acid chloride, which has a simpler structure than N-benzoy-β-phenylisoserine, and was commercially available. Thus, the cinnamic ester was obtained with no problems, with a 70% yield, by reacting 7,10-ditroc-10-deacetylbaccatin III with cinnamoyl chloride in the presence of silver cyanide (AgCN) in toluene at 80°C (Scheme 4.6)[232, 242, 244].

pp F. Guéritte's laboratory notebook, August 1983. ICSN archives.

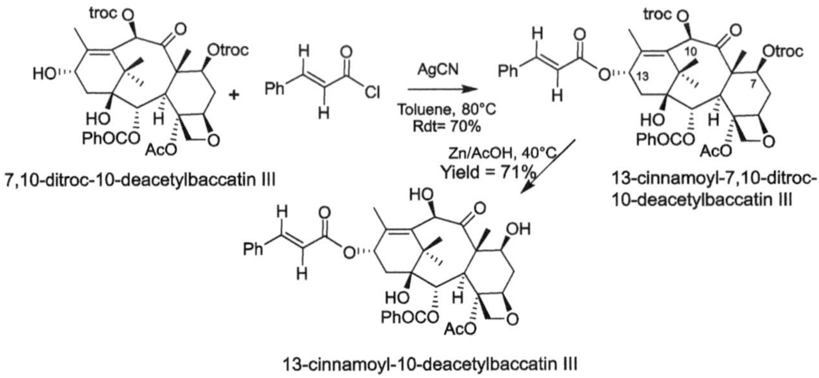

Scheme 4.6. *Semisynthesis of cinnamic ester of 10-deacetylbaccatin III*

The deprotection of the troc groups at 7 and 10 easily produced 13-cinnamoyl-10-deacetylbaccatin III (Scheme 4.6)[242, 244], – a compound which proved to be less active on the disassembly of microtubules into tubulin than taxol and 10-deacetyltaxol. The hydroxyl functional group in position 2' and the benzamide group in position 3' were therefore recognized to be necessary for strong interaction with tubulin. On 3 February 1984, V. Sénilh presented these results, along with her work on the isolation of new taxanes, in defense of her thesis, entitled: "Etude des constituants de l'if : *Taxus baccata* L. Relations structure-activité antitumorale *in vitro*"[232].

The development of the protection and esterification reactions to obtain 13-cinnamoyl-10-deacetylbaccatin III had been carried out on small quantities, ranging from around 10mg to around 100 mg of starting product. The transposition to a larger scale, facilitating the study of functionalization, was carried out within the ICSN itself, thanks to M. Colin's expertise. Thus, during 1984, several grams of cinnamic ester of 7,10-ditroc-10-deacetylbaccatin III were obtained from 10-deacetylbaccatin III, 92 g of which had been isolated from 367 kg of undried hedge trimmings[qq].

qq Results obtained in October/November 1984, État des Travaux, (Status Report), M. Colin, 22/07/1986 to 21/01/1987. ICSN archives.

The reaction of esterification of diprotected 10-deacetylbaccatin III with cinnamic acid was then improved. Using the same conditions as Steglish[247], the cinnamic ester of ditroc-7,10 desacetyl-10 baccatin III was obtained with a very good yield, using dicyclohexylcarbodiimide (DCC) as a coupling agent, and 4-dimethylaminopyridine (DMAP) as a catalyst (Scheme 4.7). These new conditions, avoiding the use of silver cyanide, raised the yield from 70 to 90%[rr].

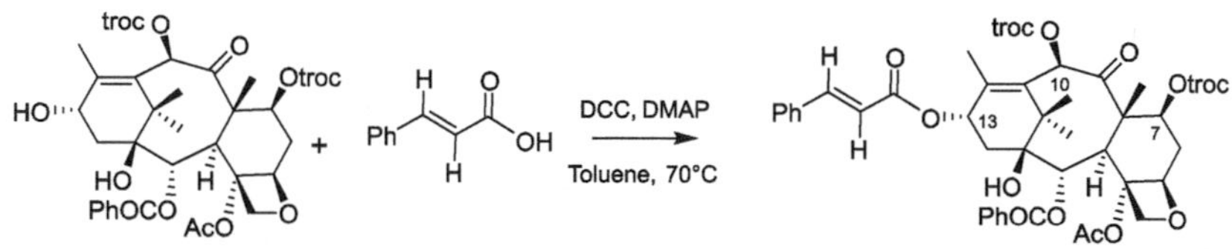

7,10-ditroc-10-deacetylbaccatin III

13-cinnamoyl-7,10-ditroc-10-deacetylbaccatin III

Scheme 4.7. *Optimization of the esterification reaction with cinnamic acid*

In these conditions, M. Colin successfully prepared several grams of the cinnamic ester in 1986 and 1987. For example, about 50 g of 7,10-ditroc-10-deacetylbaccatin III were esterified to give the cinnamic ester, with a yield higher than 90% (Figure 4.20)[ss].

4.4.3. *Functionalization of the cinnamic ester double bond: discovery of a compound (Oxy 1) more active than taxol*

Given that the first attempts of esterification with acids corresponding to the side chain of taxol proved difficult, the team focused their efforts on the functionalization of 10-deacetylbaccatin III cinnamic ester, protected at C-7 and C-10 – a potential precursor to 10-deacetyltaxol. Indeed, we merely needed to add appropriate groups to the double bond in position 2' and 3', and then deprotect the "troc" groups in positions 7 and 10 to create 10-deacetyltaxol. We then

rr État des Travaux (Status Report), M. Colin, 22/07/1986 to 21/01/1987. ICSN archives.

ss M. Colin's laboratory notebook, 5/03/1987. ICSN archives.

needed to obtain the correct configuration of the side chain at carbon 13: 2'*R*, 3'*S* (Scheme 4.8).

614

Cinnamate 13 diacyl DCT

5-03-87

Référence Réaction } MC 612

Appareil MC 612 en 2 l

Réactifs Ac. cinnamique 34,8 kg (240 mmol)
Toluène anhydre 1 l
DCC 48,6 g (240 mmol)
Diacyl MC 53,5 g (60 mmol)
DMAP 7,13 g (60 mmol)
Ac. Toxique

Opération

16 h chauffe par bain d'huile

à 75 → 69-70 dans la masse.

6-03-87 10 h ccm Toluène 7 Ether 3

3 x 100 ml

Concentre à sec. Reprend par

CH2Cl2 1 l

Lave avec HCl 2 % 3 x 150 ml

Concentre à sec → 92,2 g

Figure 4.20. *Extract from M. Colin's notebook: improved preparation of cinnamic ester using 53.5g of diacyl MC= 7,10-ditroc-10-deacetylbaccatin III*

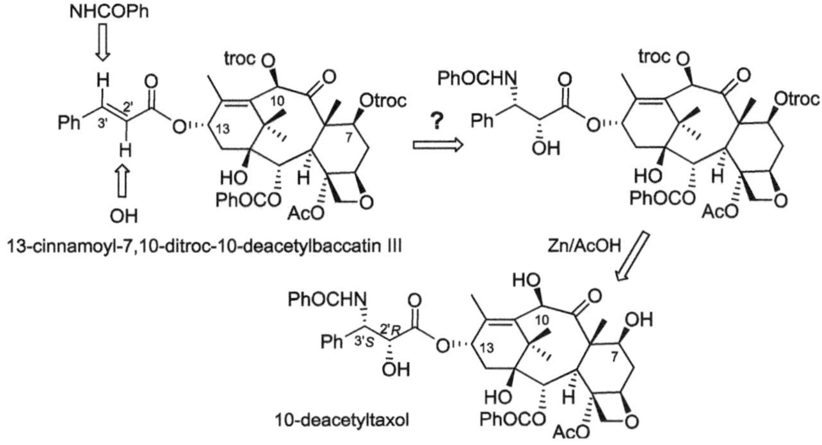

Scheme 4.8. *Proposed semisynthesis of 10-deacetyltaxol from the cinnamic ester of 7,10-ditroc-10-deacetylbaccatin III*

The double bond in the side chain of the cinnamic ester has a *trans* configuration[tt]. To obtain the correct configuration 2'*R*, 3'*S* of the side chain of taxol and of 10-deacetyltaxol, the only possibility was to perform a *syn* addition[uu] of the two substituents (hydroxyl (OH) and benzamide (NHCOPh)) onto the *trans* double bond, which ought to give the two isomers 2'*R*, 3'*S* and 2'*S*, 3'*R*, depending on whether the simultaneous addition of the two groups took place above or below the plane of the double bond (Scheme 4.9).

Before searching for the most practical method to carry out this reaction, V. Sénilh studied the dihydroxylation of the cinnamic ester, adding two hydroxyl groups to the double bond. The advantage to obtaining dihydroxylated derivatives at carbons 2' and 3' in the cinnamic ester was that it would allow us to know the influence of those two groups on the biological activity.

---

tt In this case, the configuration is *trans* because the two hydrogen atoms are situated on opposite sides of the double bond. It would be *cis* if those two atoms were present on the same side. The *cis* and *trans* stereoisomers are geometric isomers.

uu In the present case, the *syn* addition is the addition of both substituents on the same side of the double bond, and should yield the two isomers 2'*R*, 3'*S* and 2'*S*, 3'*R*. An addition *anti*, would lead to isomers 2'*R*, 3'*R* and 2'*S*, 3'*S*.

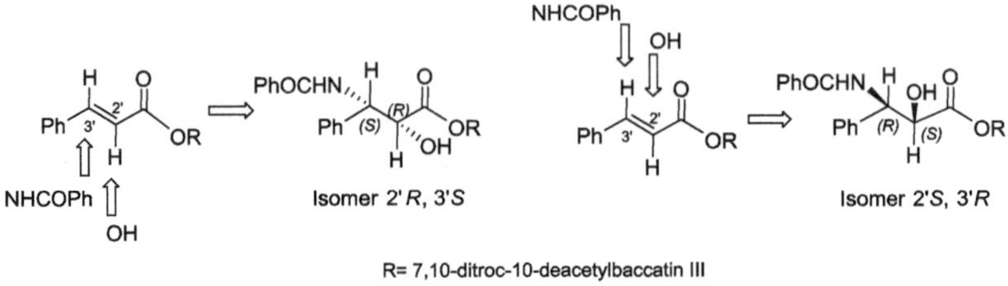

Scheme 4.9. *Syn addition on the double bond of the cinnamic ester*

4.4.3.1. *Dihydroxylation of cinnamic ester*

Thus, the action of osmium tetroxide in a pyridine medium on 13-cinnamoyl-7,10-ditroc-10-deacetylbaccatin III, followed by hydrolysis in the presence of sodium disulfite, yielded a mixture of diastereoisomers, dihydroxylated at carbons 2' and 3'. After deprotection by zinc in acetic acid and purification, the two dihydroxylated derivatives of 13-cinnamoyl-10-deacetylbaccatin III (2'*R*, 3'*S* and 2'*S*, 3'*R*) were obtained with good yields (Scheme 4.10)[232, 242]. Although they were significantly more active on tubulin than 10-deacetylbaccatin III cinnamic ester, these two dihydroxylated compounds exhibited lesser activity on tubulin than 10-deacetyltaxol. The presence of a benzamide group at carbon 3' was therefore essential...

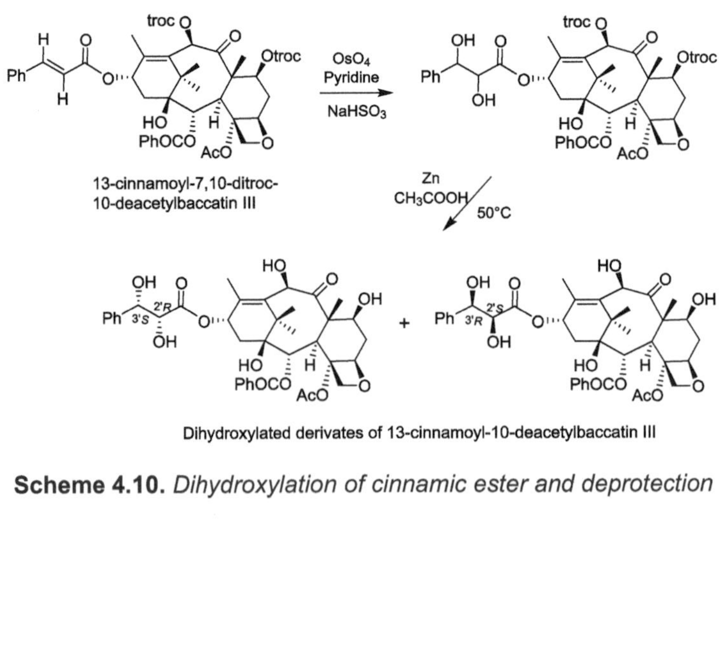

Scheme 4.10. *Dihydroxylation of cinnamic ester and deprotection*

4.4.3.2. *Aminohydroxylation of cinnamic ester and discovery of a compound more active than taxol on microtubules*

After a bibliographical search, one reaction seemed perfectly appropriate to perform a *syn* addition of a hydroxyl group and an aminated functional group to the double bond in cinnamic ester: the aminohydroxylation reaction discovered by K. Barry Sharpless and his collaborators, and known as "Sharpless oxyamination". This reaction offered direct and easy access to vicinal hydroxysulfonamides from olefins, using catalytic quantities of osmium tetroxide in the presence of chloramine-T and silver nitrate (Scheme 4.11)[248]. Similarly, vicinal hydroxycarbamates (ethyl carbamate or *tert*-butyl carbamate) were obtained in the same conditions using N-chloro-N-sodio-ethylcarbamate or N-chloro-N-sodio-*tert*-butylcarbamate (Scheme 4.11)[249].

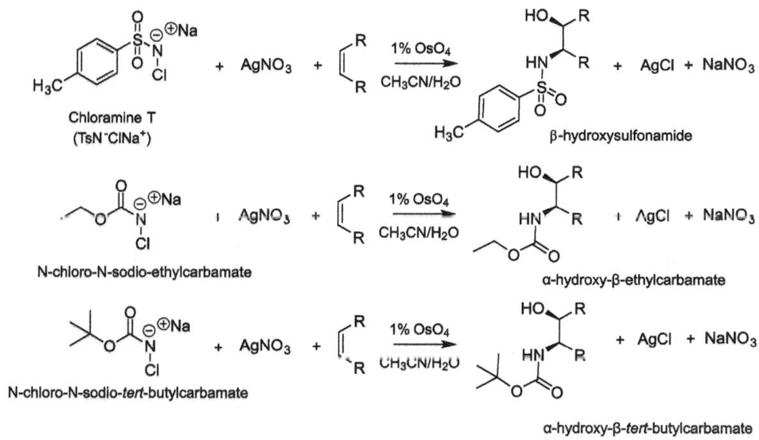

Scheme 4.11. *Sharpless aminohydroxylation*

Following the protocol laid down by K. Sharpless and his collaborators, the first attempts at aminohydroxylation of ditroc-7,10 desacetyl-10 baccatin III cinnamic ester were conducted, in March and April 1984, with chloramine-T and with N-chloro-N-sodio-ethylcarbamate, using catalytic quantities of osmium tetroxide[vv].

---

vv F. Guéritte's laboratory notebook, 22/03/1984, 28/03/1984, 3/04/1984. ICSN archives.

Each of the two experiments yielded four compounds (A, B, C and D), two couples of diastereoisomers, one possessing the hydroxyl group and the sulfonamide- or ethyl carbamate groups in position 2' and 3' (compounds A (2'*R*, 3'*S*) and B (2'*S*, 3'*R*)), and the other having these two groups in the opposite position (compounds C (2'*R*, 3'*S*) and D (2'*S*, 3'*R*)) (Figure 4.21).

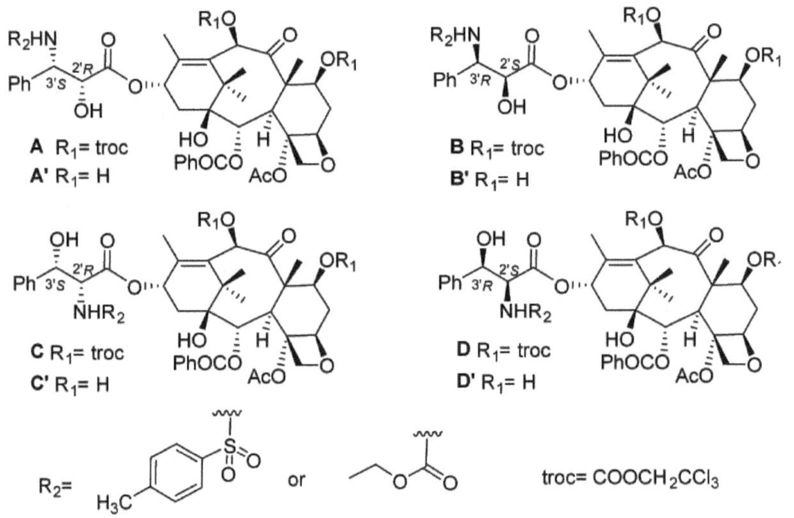

Figure 4.21. *Diastereoisomers formed during aminohydroxylation (A,B,C,D) and their deprotected derivatives (A',B',C',D')*

After deprotection by zinc in acetic acid, the corresponding deprotected derivatives A', B', C' and D' (Figure 4.21) were evaluated with the tubulin test. Although they exhibited activities greater than 10-deacetylbaccatin III cinnamic ester, none of them were as active as taxol and desacetyltaxol. These results were mentioned in a 1984 publication[242]. A different reaction of aminohydroxylation of cinnamic ester was then studied, in October 1984, using N-chloro-N-sodio-*tert*-butylcarbamate. In relation to the previous aminohydroxylation products, a compound with a *tert*-butyl carbamate functional group at position 3' exhibited the advantage of being a less problematic precursor to 10-deacetyltaxol. Indeed, the *tert*-butyloxycarbonyl group could more easily be eliminated, in mild conditions, to yield an aminated derivative whose benzoylation formed the benzamide function present in the structure of 10-deacetyltaxol (Scheme 4.12).

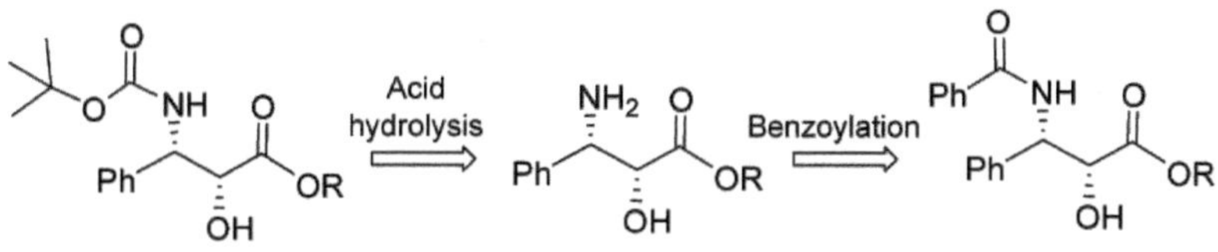

Tert-butyl carbamate   Aminated derivative   benzamide

Scheme 4.12. *From tert-butyl carbamate to benzamide*

Figure 4.22. *Extract from F. Guéritte's laboratory notebook: aminohydroxylation of cinnamic ester (cinnamate diacyl)*

Thus, the first aminohydroxylation reactions were conducted during October 1984, with N-chloro-N-sodio-*tert*-butylcarbamate, on 500 mg of the diprotected derivative of cinnamic ester (Cinnamate diacyl), and always with catalytic quantities of osmium tetroxide (Figure 4.22).

The four aminohydroxylation products (named 7,10-ditroc Oxy 1 to 7,10-ditroc Oxy 4, according to their polarity in thin-layer chromatography – TLC) were isolated by thick-layer chromatography, with yields ranging, in this first experiment, from 11.7% to 4.4% (Scheme 4.13).

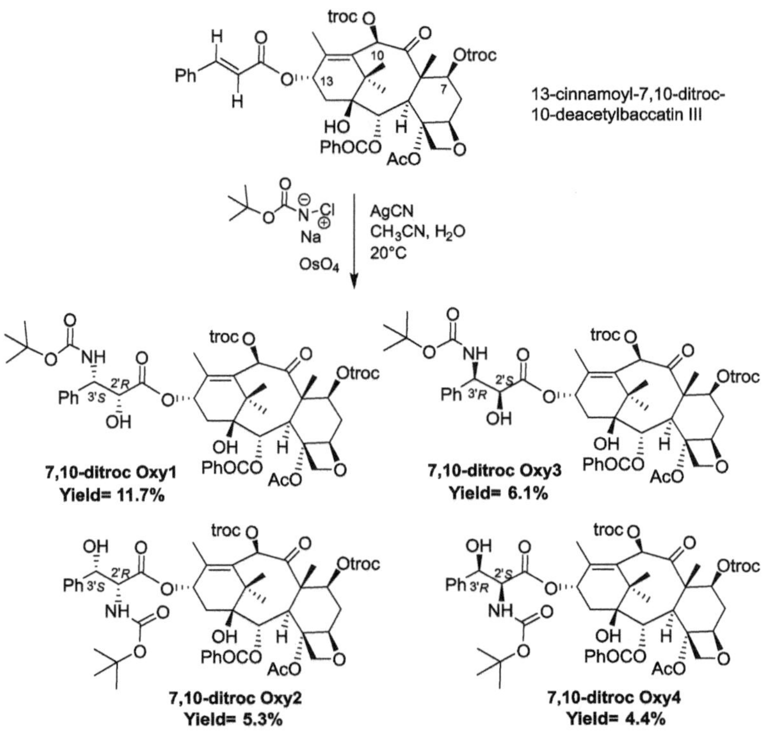

Scheme 4.13. *Aminohydroxylation of cinnamic ester with N-chloro-N-sodio-*tert*-butylcarbamate*

The yields obtained during the aminohydroxylation reaction were not very good... but the deprotection of the troc groups in positions 7 and 10 by zinc in acetic acid, realized in November 1984[ww], revealed a major surprise: one of the four compounds obtained (Oxy 1) exhibited activity inhibiting the disassembly of microtubules into tubulin that was much greater than that of the other three isomers, and greater even than that of taxol (Figure 4.23)[xx].

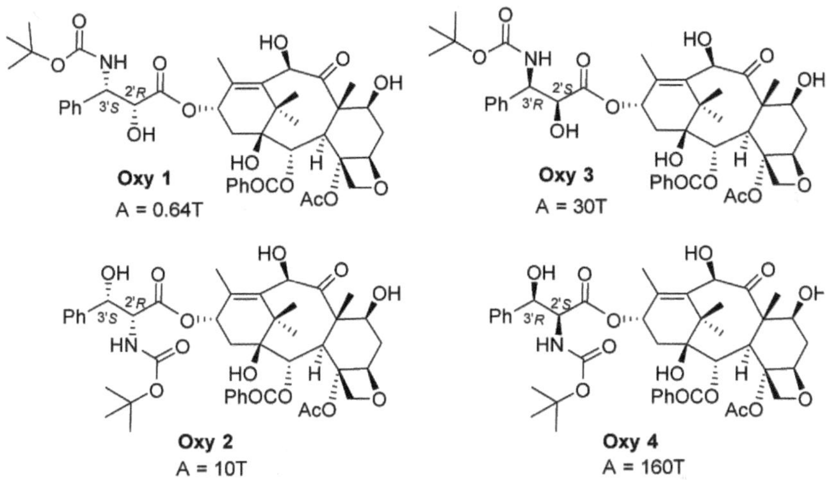

Figure 4.23. *Structure of aminohydroxylation products and their activity on tubulin in relation to taxol*

The structure of each compound (Oxy1, Oxy2, Oxy3 and Oxy4) was determined mainly by proton and carbon-13 NMR spectroscopy, and by decoupling experiments attributing the position of the hydroxyl and carbamate groups to carbons 2' and 3'. The 2'*R*, 3'*S*

ww F. Guéritte's laboratory notebook, 19/11/1984. ICSN archives.

xx The evaluations of the activity levels on tubulin were performed by D. Guénard. The activity (A) mentioned in Figure 4.23, expresses the results in relation to the activity of taxol (T): A= IC50 product / IC50 taxol, with these activities being evaluated on the same day and on the same batch of tubulin.

configuration, identical to that of taxol, was attributed to the product exhibiting the best activity on tubulin: compound Oxy 1. This configuration was then confirmed by chemical correlation of ditroc-7,10 Oxy 1 with 10-deacetyltaxol (see section 4.4.4).

Several students joined the team during the course of these studies, including Bruno David, a pharmacy student who worked one year from September 1984 on the esterification of baccatin III, notably by crotonic acid,[244] and then on the aminohydroxylation reaction leading to the compounds Oxy 1 to Oxy 4[250]. B. David presented his work to obtain his *Diplôme d'Etudes Approfondies* (DEA – Advanced Studies Diploma), on 23 September 1985[250]. Lydie Mangatal began her doctoral work in early 1986, notably studying the influence of chiral ligands on the aminohydroxylation reaction, and then on the chemical transformation of baccatin III into taxol by that reaction[251]. L. Mangatal also correlated the configuration in position 2' and 3' of the oxyaminated regioisomers Oxy 2 and Oxy 4 (Figure 4.23) to (D) and (L) 3-phenylserine[251-252]. L. Mangatal defended her thesis on 19 April 1989, entitled: "*Dérivés antitumoraux du Taxol. Hémisynthèse et relations structure-activité*" (Antitumoral derivatives of taxol. Semisynthesis and structure/activity relationships)[252]. Then, Marie-Thérèse Le Goff, a technician at the CNRS, joined the team in December 1986, also to work on the semisynthesis of new taxoids from 10-deacetylbaccatin III and on evaluating the activity on microtubules of the compounds synthesized by the team.

4.4.4. *First semisynthesis of 10-deacetyltaxol and taxol*

During November 1985, 7,10-ditrocOxy 1 was correlated with 10-deacetyltaxol, confirming the configuration 2'*R*, 3'*S* at the side chain[yy]. Scheme 4.13 shows the succession of the three steps leading

yy F. Guéritte's laboratory notes, FG1374, 12/11/1985. ICSN archives.

from 7,10-ditrocOxy 1 to 10-deacetyltaxol. As predicted, the *tert*-butyloxycarbonyl group was easily eliminated with iodotrimethylsilane to provide the β-aminoalcohol derivative with a 75% yield. This derivative, treated with benzoyl chloride, produced quantitatively the corresponding benzoylated derivative. Finally, the deprotection of the troc groups by zinc led to 10-deacetyltaxol, with a 90% yield (Scheme 4.14).

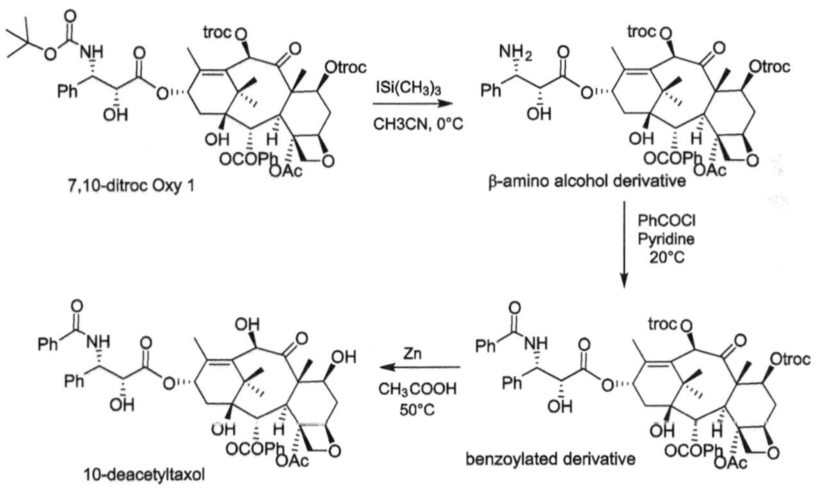

Scheme 4.14. *From ditroc-7,10 Oxy 1 to 10-deacetyltaxol*

Historically, the aminohydroxylation reaction was thus at the root of the first semisynthesis of 10-deacetyltaxol – a process which was extended to taxol and patented in July 1986 by Rhône-Poulenc[253].

The same series of steps carried out later by L. Mangatal, and applied to baccatin III, directly yielded taxol and 10-acetyl Oxy 1[zz],

zz Laboratory notebook, L. Mangatal, LM 72, 13/10/1988, LMIII 298, 10/11/1988, LMIII 298, 11/1988. ICSN archives.

which also has excellent activity on tubulin[251]. Scheme 4.15 illustrates these steps, going from 10-deacetylbaccatin III and baccatin III to 10-deacetyltaxol and taxol, respectively.

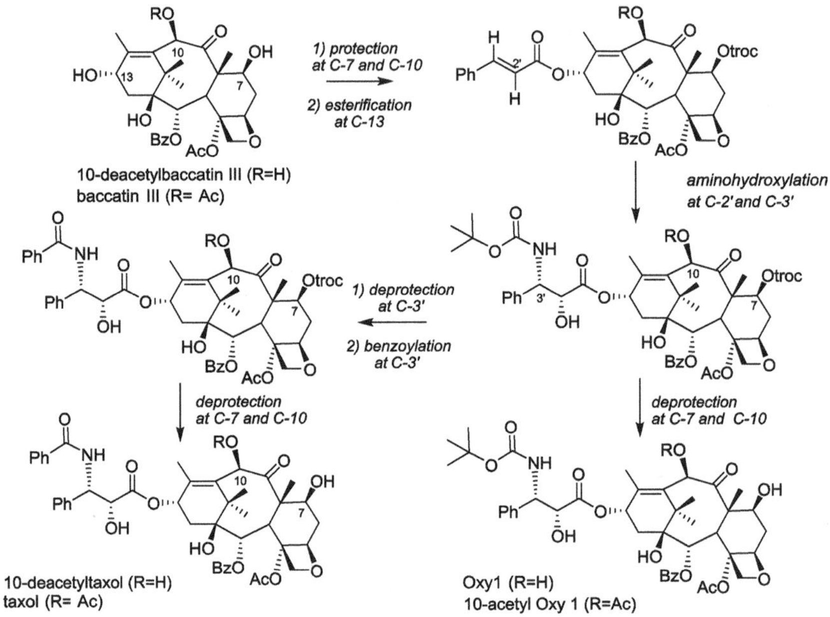

Scheme 4.15. *First semisynthesis of 10-deacetyltaxol, taxol, Oxy-1 and 10-acetyl Oxy 1*

Thus, the team had shown that 10-deacetylbaccatin III, present in appreciable quantities in the leaves of the common yew, *T. baccata*, could serve directly as a precursor not only for the natural compound, 10-deacetyltaxol, but also for a compound that was highly active on tubulin, Oxy 1, whose three-dimensional structure would be carried out later by X-ray analysis of the product crystallized in methanol[254]. However, this semisynthetic procedure could not be applicable for the large-scale production of taxol, as baccatin III is isolated only in very small quantities from *T. baccata*[213b, 234].

4.4.5. *Earliest pharmacological studies of Oxy 1 (56 976 R.P.)*

The progression of these studies was, of course, monitored, step by step, by P. Potier, who decided to pursue the pharmacological studies on compound Oxy 1, which was done in close collaboration with François Lavelle, head of the "Anticancer research program" run at Rhône-Poulenc's biology department. Indeed, one of the important points was to find out whether this new compound was as active as taxol in *in vivo* experiments. In January 1986, 80 mg of Oxy 1 were sent to F. Lavelle to conduct the first *in vivo* studies on mice with leukemias L1210 and P388. The code name 56 976 R.P. was attributed by the Rhône-Poulenc researchers to the compound Oxy 1. Figure 4.24 shows the results obtained for the *in vivo* activity of 56 976 R.P., in comparison to those of taxol and daunorubicin (an anti-cancer pharmaceutical used in France from the 1960s onwards)[aaa]. The results showed that 56 976 R.P. had an antitumoral activity greater than that of paclitaxel.

This new taxoid, obtained by the aminohydroxylation procedure, was patented with its *in vitro* activity on tubulin and *in vivo* activity in mice. The first patent, entitled "*Dérivés du taxol, leur préparation et les compositions pharmaceutiques qui les contiennent*" was filed on 17 July 1986 by Rhône-Poulenc[255], in accordance with the research agreement between the CNRS and the company[bbb]. The results regarding the semisynthesis of Oxy 1 (56976 R.P.) and its isomers were published later on[251], as was their activity on tubulin in a comparative study of the structure/activity relations of different analogs of taxol[256].

aaa Extract of the *in vivo* results on mice grafted with P388 tumor, and treated with 56 976 R.P., document provided by F. Lavelle to the ICSN team. T/C indicates tumor growth inhibition, with T representing the group of mice treated, and C (control) the group of mice left without treatment. ICSN archives.

bbb See Chapter 2, note ffff, and Chapter 4, note v.

FLA/FC/86/517

TABLEAU 2

Réf. Essai : 1058

Tumeur : P388

Greffe : 10^6 cell i.p.

Voie de traitement : i.p.

Séquence des traitements : +1,+2,+3,+4

Souris utilisées : B6D2F1

Durée d'observation : 63 jours

Mode d'administration : solubilisation éthanol, emulphor, sérum physiologique (1/1/18)

Code R.P.	Doses (mg/kg)	Variations pondérales j 8 - j 0 (g)	Toxicity	Activité T/C X 100 (%)
13 057 R.P. (daunorubicine	1	+ 0,8	-	153
48 725 R.P. (taxol)	10	- 0,5	-	133
	5	+ 1,3	-	125
	2,5	+ 0,2	-	136
	1,25	+ 1,7	-	118
	0,625	+ 0,4	-	118
	0,312	+ 2,0	-	116
56 976 R.P.	10	- 1,7	+/-	199(3v/5)
(FG 1392)	5	+ 0,4	-	218(1v/5)
↑	2,5	+ 1,0	-	200
	1,25	+ 0,7	-	160
Oxy 1	0,625	- 0,4	-	142
	0,312	+ 0,8	-	139

REMARQUES : légère chute de poids à 10 mg/kg 56 976 R.P.

Figure 4.24. *Extract of the in vivo results for Oxy 1 (56 976 R.P.), obtained in mice grafted with the tumor P388*

4.5. Second semisynthesis of taxol by a convergent process

As previously mentioned, in the 1980s and the early 1990s, the issue of taxol supply was problematic in the United States, in terms of conducting clinical trials. Such trials, run by the NCI, had begun in 1984 using taxol obtained from the bark of the yew, *T. brevifolia.*

Semisynthesis of taxol from baccatin III by way of the aminohydroxylation reaction, mentioned in the previous section and patented in 1986 by Potier's team and Rhône-Poulenc, could not be applied to large-scale taxol production as, much like taxol itself, baccatin is obtained only in small quantities.

On the American side, several teams of chemists were working, at the time, on the total synthesis of taxol – a very real chemical challenge, given the molecule's so-complex structure: the teams led by Robert A. Holton at Florida State University, by Charles Swindell at Bryn Mawr College, Paul Wender at Stanford University and Kyriacos C. Nicolaou at the Scripps Research Institute. Given the number of steps required for this total synthesis, however, this procedure would not be applicable for commercial production of taxol.

Therefore, mainly in France and the United States, studies began on how to obtain taxol by convergent semisynthesis, by directly coupling baccatin III, protected at position 7 or 7,10-diprotected 10-deacetylbaccatin III, with an acid corresponding to taxol's side chain[ccc].

4.5.1. *First convergent semisynthesis of taxol*

Thanks to a collaboration initiated by P. Potier with Andrew Greene, senior researcher at *Université Joseph Fourier* in Grenoble, the first convergent semisynthesis of taxol was developed. As director of the ICSN and of Pirmed[ddd], P. Potier suggested to A. Greene that he [Greene], through this program, support research on the synthesis of the acid corresponding to taxol's side chain. Thus, in 1986, A. Greene, Jean-Noël Denis and their colleagues published the first enantioselective synthesis of the side chain of taxol[257]. Scheme 4.16 illustrates the steps involved in that synthesis: 1) Sharpless

ccc In the case of molecules with complex structures, such as taxol, a convergent semisynthesis yields the desired product by assembling key intermediary products in a minimum number of steps.

ddd See Chapter 2, note zzz.

asymmetric epoxidation[258] carried out on cis-cinnamic alcohol; 2) oxidation and methylation of the epoxide thus obtained; 3) opening of the epoxide by azidation, followed by a benzoylation of the hydroxyl in position 2; 4) hydrogenation of the azide functional group, leading to transbenzoylation from position 2 to position 3.

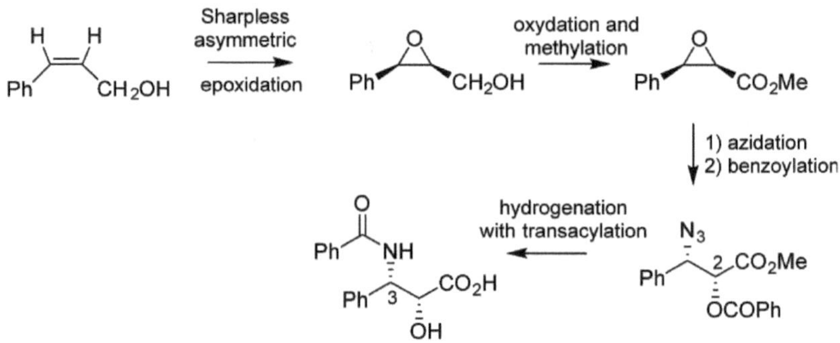

Scheme 4.16. *First enantioselective synthesis of the side chain of taxol*

A. Greene and his collaborators, in the same publication, also described the preparation of different esters with very good yields, using di-2-pyridyl carbonate (DPC) and dimethylaminopyridine (DMAP).[257]

Following this work by the team in Grenoble, a collaboration began with Potier's team, and in April 1988 led to the filing of the patent[259], on the first convergent semisynthesis of taxol from 10-deacetylbaccatin III (Scheme 4.17). The hydroxyl group in position 7of10-deacetylbaccatin III is protected to begin with, and then the hydroxyl in position 10 is acetylated. Esterification with the acid corresponding to taxol's side chain, protected at carbon 2, in the presence of DPC and DMAP, yields the corresponding ester. Taxol is then obtained after deprotection of the hydroxyls in positions 7 and 2', in an acidic medium, with an overall yield of 26% from

10-deacetylbaccatin III. This work was published, also in 1988, entitled "A highly efficient, practical approach to natural taxol"[260].

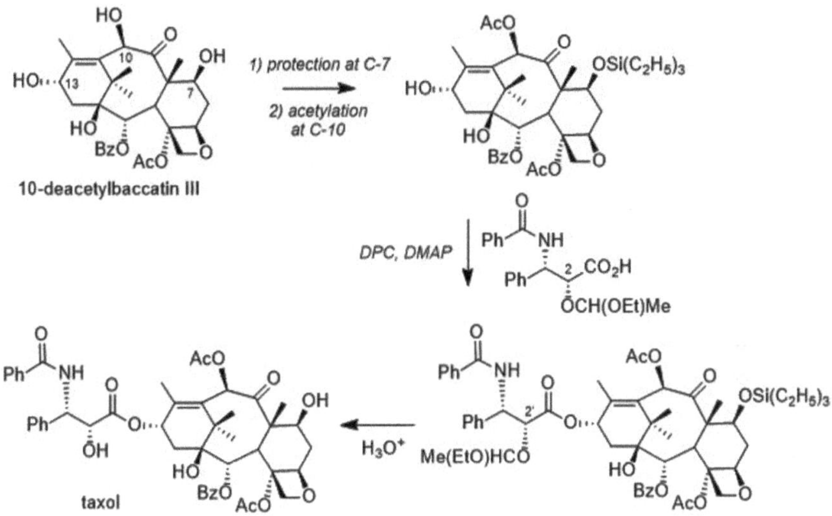

Scheme 4.17. *First convergent semisynthesis of taxol*

A. Greene and his colleagues later improved the synthesis of taxol's side chain[261], providing taxol with excellent yields[262].

4.5.2. *Other convergent semisynthesis and semisynthetic version of taxol approved by the FDA*

Following the publication of the convergent semisynthesis of taxol[260], Robert A. Holton from Florida State University began working on this procedure. In 1989, he filed two patents involved in coupling with protected baccatin III: one with an oxazinone[263], and the other a β-lactam[264]. Deprotection of the ester obtained, in an acidic medium, produced taxol (Scheme 4.18).

At the start of the 1990s, several other groups of chemists – notably Iwao Ojima's at Stony Brook University in New York[265], and Gunda I. Georg's from the University of Kansas[265a, 266], published the semisynthesis of taxol by the β-lactam method. A number of other enantioselective approaches to taxol's side chain were enacted by different teams, and between 1990 and 1993, K.C. Nicolaou and his collaborators published more than ten papers devoted to such synthesis in his journal, "Chemistry and Biology of Taxol"[267]. Finally, in 1993, the firm BMS adopted R. Holton's semisynthesis method for the first commercial production of taxol. In October 1994, the FDA approved the semisynthetic version of taxol produced by BMS, thus ending the problem of the supply of natural taxol[eee].

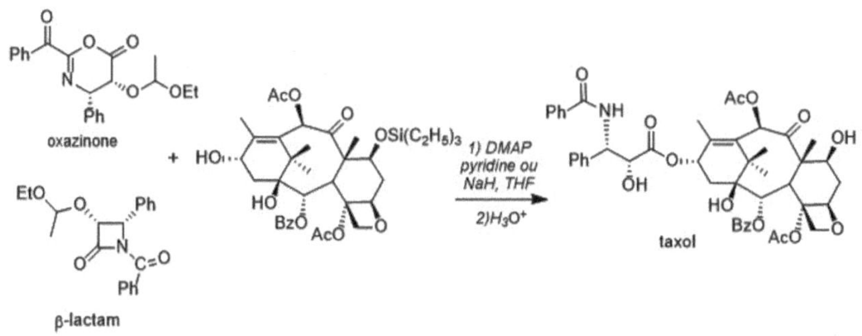

Scheme 4.18. *Convergent semisynthesis of taxol by R. Holton*

4.6. A step toward the development of 56 976 R.P., which was to become Taxotere®

Let us, though, step back to 1986 and look at the compound 56 976 R.P. After filing of the patent on the semisynthesis of this compound by aminohydroxylation and its biological activity[255], new attempts began being run at the ICSN in close collaboration with Rhône-Poulenc[fff], on a convergent semisynthesis of 56 976 R.P., which would allow the molecule to be obtained on a larger scale.

---

eee The New York Times, "New Version of Taxol is approved by F.D.A.", December 13, 1994 http://www.nytimes.com/1994/12/13/science/new-version-of-taxol-is-approved-by-fda.html. Readers can refer to Goodman and Walsh's book, *The Story of Taxol*, to find out about the problems encountered during the drive to isolate and synthesize the molecule and also to gain market authorization.

fff A new collaboration contract was signed in June 1987 between the CNRS and Rhône-Poulenc on, amongst other things, the development of a technique for

The ICSN team also continued to work on improving the processes of extraction and purification of 10-deacetylbaccatin III – the chemical precursor of 56 976 R.P. Numerous meetings organized by Jean-Louis Fabre[ggg], from the research division of Rhône-Poulenc, took place regularly between the team from the ICSN and that of the pharmaceutical company, to monitor the progress of the work.

4.6.1. *Large-scale extraction and purification of 10-deacetylbaccatin III*

In the first work on extraction carried out in 1980, on yews growing on the CNRS campus in Gif-sur-Yvette, 200 mg of 10-deacetylbaccatin III had been isolated from 1 kg of leaves[231]. In 1983, the large-scale extraction and purification of 10-deacetylbaccatin III from yews was undertaken by M. Colin, in direct collaboration with the Rhône-Poulenc team, and with V. Sénilh-Gastiger in particular[hhh].

Regarding the collection of leaves, thanks to collaborations with nurserymen and agronomic companies, multiple campaigns were carried out on *T. baccata* trees and hedges, notably in Ardèche, in Jura, in Brittany, in Var and on the CNRS campus in Gif-sur-Yvette. M. Colin noted, in his "Etat des Travaux" for 21 August 1984 to 20 January 1985:

> In September-October, on the Gif Campus, we collected nearly 400 kg of green leaves from *Taxus baccata*, from the trimming of hedges.

The extraction of 10-deacetylbaccatin III, begun at the ICSN factory, was pursued, notably, by the company Prosynthèse, in Beynes, and at Rhône-Poulenc's research center in Vitry.

---

convergent synthesis of 56 976 R.P. from desacetyl–10 baccatin III. ICSN archives, Guéritte's archives, Potier's archives.

ggg Jean-Louis Fabre, as head of the project and then as head of oncology research at Rhône-Poulenc, was involved with the development of 56 976 RP right up until its ultimate commercialization.

hhh V. Sénilh-Gastiger, having defended her doctorate at the ICSN in 1984, was recruited by RP to improve the procedures for extraction and purification of desacetyl-10 baccatin III, with which she was very familiar.

A method of dosing 10-deacetylbaccatin III present in extracts from yew leaves was developed by Marie-Thérèse Adeline, in charge of the high-performance liquid chromatography (HPLC) department at the ICSN, in order to quickly determine the quantities of the product present in the extracts obtained from leaves collected from different sources. Thus, many different extraction conditions were tried, to evaluate their impact on the amount of 10-deacetylbaccatin III found: ethanolic extraction or supercritical CO_2 extraction, season when harvested, choice of the yew (male or female trees, or hedges), place where the trees are growing, storage of the leaves (fresh or microwave dried). Following these studies, it was noted, for example, that the amount of 10-deacetylbaccatin III present varied considerably depending on the sources and the point in time at which the yew leaves had been collected: "young" leaves collected from hedges of yew could contain up to 1.25 g of 10-deacetylbaccatin III per kg[iii]. All of these aspects were, of course, taken into account to optimize the supply of this raw material, as the starting product to synthesize 56 976 R.P. Large-scale extraction and purification of 10-deacetylbaccatin III then took place at Rhône-Poulenc's research center in Vitry-sur-Seine. V. Sénilh-Gastiger noted, in conclusion of these studies, giving a final assessment of the first campaign to extract and purify 10-deacetylbaccatin III:

> In light of all these results and with a view to a new campaign of extraction and purification of 10-deacetylbaccatin III, batches of yew leaves from a variety of sources (the forests in Var) have been studied. The forest on the Sainte Baume Massif was selected as a result (content of around 500 mg/kg), and four tons were collected in mid-September 1987. The leaves which were collected and frozen will be processed from October 1987 onwards[jjj].

iii État des travaux (Status Report), M. Colin, 22/07/1986 to 21/01/1987 and minutes of RP meeting on 16 December 1987. ICSN archives.

jjj Note N°10 from V. Sénilh-Gastiger on 8/12/1987: report on the first campaign of extraction and purification of 10-deacetylbaccatin III (October 1986-July 1987). ICSN archives.

On 12 January 1988, the first batch of 376 g of 10-deacetylbaccatin III was therefore supplied to the ICSN by the Rhône-Poulenc team[kkk].

4.6.2. *Steps toward the convergent synthesis of 56 976 R.P.*

Some of the steps used in the first semisynthesis of 56 976 R.P., by way of the aminohydroxylation reaction, were far from advisable for a transposition to the industrial scale. For example, the aminohydroxylation reaction was to be avoided because of the toxicity of osmium tetroxide, even used in a catalytic quantity. Additionally, a convergent synthesis facilitating a direct esterification of an acid corresponding to the side chain of 56 976 R.P. (N-(*tert*-butyloxycarbonyl)-β-phenylisoserine (2*R*, 3*S*)), with 7,10-ditroc-10-deacetylbaccatin III was desirable, thus limiting the number of steps (see Scheme 4.19).

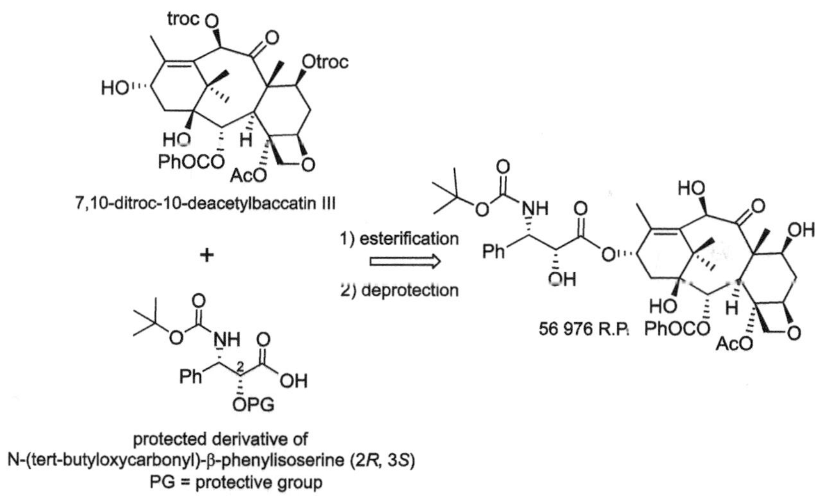

Scheme 4.19. *Proposal for convergent synthesis of 56 976 R.P.*

kkk État des Travaux, (Status Report), by M. Colin, 21/07/1987 to 20/01/1988. ICSN archives.

The team then worked on the synthesis of the acid corresponding to the side chain of 56 976 R.P., using 3-phenylglycidic acid *tert*-butyl ester synthesized by a Darzens reaction, as a starting product[268]. Scheme 4.20 illustrates the different steps leading from that compound to the racemic mixture (2'*R*, 3'*S* and 2'*S*, 3'*R*) of N-(tert-butyloxycarbonyl)-β-phenylisoserine: 1) formation of the azide derivative from 3-phenylglycidic acid *tert*-butyl ester; 2) hydrogenation of the azide derivative into β-aminoalcohol; 3) treatment of the β-aminoalcohol with di-*tert*-butyl dicarbonate (($(tBuOCO)_2O$); 4) protection at C-2 by ethyl vinyl ether (CH_2=CH(OEt)); and 5) saponification of the ester by lithin (LiOH). This synthesis, with an overall yield of 52%, giving the acid corresponding to the racemic side chain of 56 976 R.P, protected at carbon 2 by the ethoxy-ethyl group, was not published, but was patented in 1988[269].

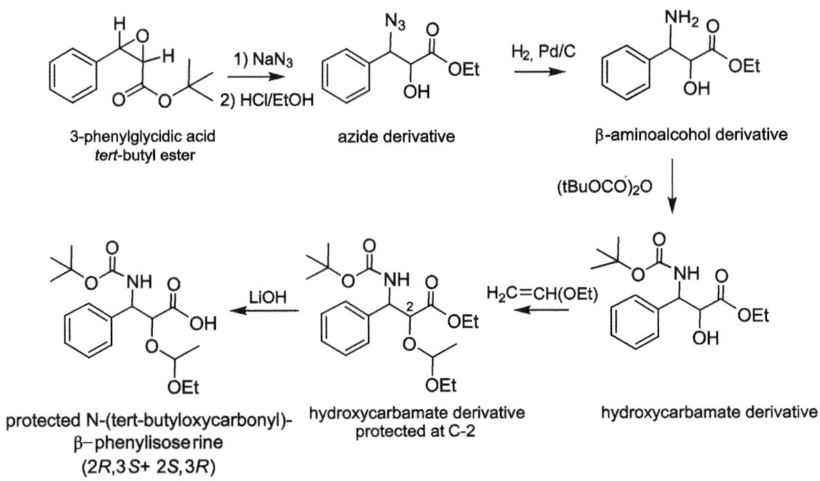

Scheme 4.20. *Racemic synthesis of the acid corresponding to the side chain of 56 976 R.P.*

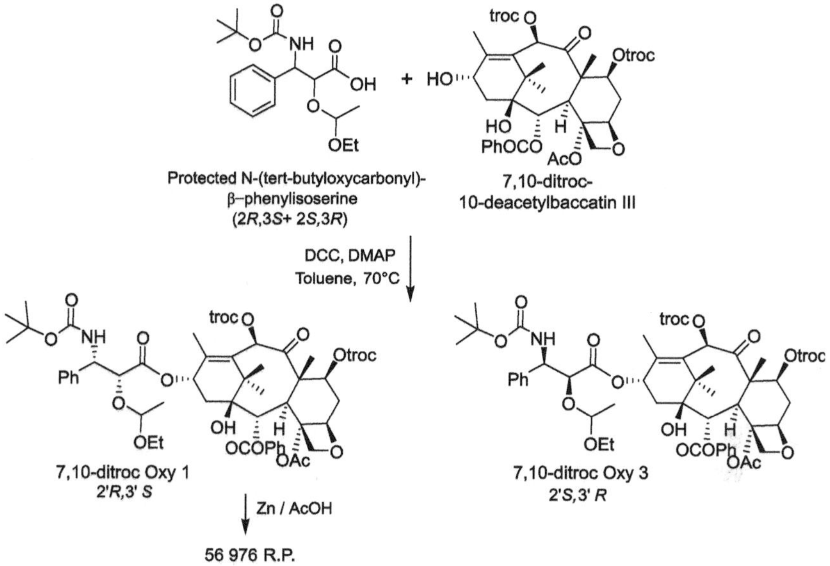

Scheme 4.21. *First convergent semisynthesis of 56 976 R.P.*

The treatment of that acid with 7,10-ditroc-10-deacetylbaccatin III, in the conditions of esterification outlined above, gave the team 7,10-ditroc Oxy 1 (2'*R*, 3'*S*), and its diastereoisomer, 7,10-ditroc Oxy 3 (2'*S*, 3'*R*) (Scheme 4.21). Finally, 56 976 R.P. was obtained after deprotection of the 7,10-ditroc Oxy 1, with an overall yield of 34% starting from 10-deacetylbaccatin III (Scheme 4.21). The patent on this first industrial synthesis of 56 976 R.P. was filed by Rhône-Poulenc on 6 April 1988, entitled: "*Procédé de préparation de dérivés de la baccatine III et de desacetyl-10 baccatine III*"[269].

Whilst, in the aminohydroxylation process, the use of osmium tetroxide presented a problem of toxicity, the preparation and use of the azide derivative in the synthesis of 56 976 R.P.'s side chain (Scheme 4.20) was also dangerous to do in the laboratory, given its toxic and explosive properties. For safety's sake, therefore, the synthesis of the β-aminoalcohol derivative was entrusted to the

Société Nationale des Poudres et des Explosifs, with the later reactions still being carried out at the ICSN. Then, Michel Mulhauser, a research engineer at Rhône-Poulenc in Lyon, and his colleagues studied ways to industrially synthesize 56 976 R.P.'s side chain. Between 1987 and 1989, 100 grams of 56 976 R.P. were obtained in this manner from 4 tons of *T. baccata* leaves[lll], with the cooperation of Rhône-Poulenc and the company Seripharm[mmm], specializing in the large-scale purification of plant-based products.

In November 1988, the name "taxotere" was submitted by J.-L. Fabre to the naming commission of *Pharmacopée Française* (French Pharmacopeia) as a proposed International Common Denomination (ICD) for 56 976 R.P. This proposition having been rejected by the World Health Organization (WHO), preferring the root "tax" to be used as a suffix rather than a prefix, docetaxel became the ICD (International Nonproprietary Name (INN)) of the molecule and Taxotere® became the brand name of the pharmaceutical specialty[nnn].

From the late 1980s onwards, significant improvements were made on this first semisynthesis, thanks to A. Greene and his team who improved, amongst other things, the enantioselective synthesis of taxotere's side chain[261, 270], and the team of chemists at Rhône-Poulenc. For instance, Alain Commerçon and his colleagues prepared taxotere, with excellent yields, by esterification of protected 10-deacetylbaccatin III with an oxazolidine (Scheme 4.22) – a process which they also applied to taxol semisynthesis[271].

lll The reactions for this semisynthesis were mainly carried out by M. Colin and then Augustin Hittinger, who was also dispatched by RP to join the ICSN team in early 1989. ICSN archives, P. Potier's correspondence.

mmm Seripharm (*Societé d'Etude et de Recherche en Ingénierie Pharmaceutique*), headquartered in Le Mans, was set up by Jean-Pierre Robin in 1987. Information from D. Guénard. Seripharm was bought by Rhône-Poulenc Rorer in 1996, and by Novasep in 2002.

nnn This information on the choice of names of the INN and brand was given by J.-L. Fabre to F. Guéritte via e-mail on 16 December 2015.

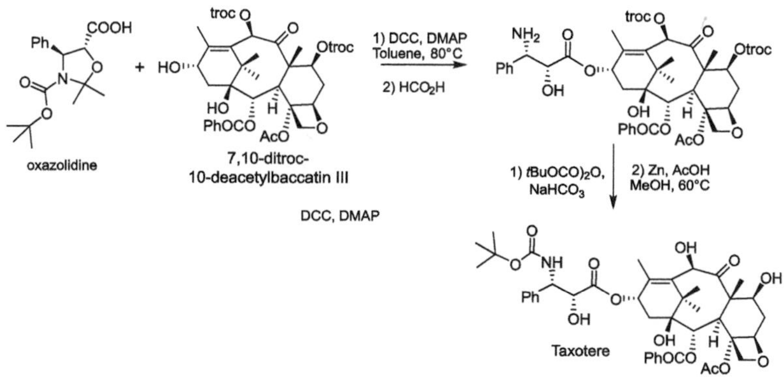

Scheme 4.22. *Semisynthesis of taxotere via an oxazolidine*

4.6.3. *From pharmacological and clinical properties to market authorization for Taxotere® (56 976 R.P.)*

At the Vitry research center, F. Lavelle and his colleagues continued to study the pharmacological properties of 56 976 R.P. In 1986, they had shown the compound's cytotoxicity *in vitro* on leukemia P388 cells, and antitumoral activity better even than that of taxol on certain tumors grafted into mice[272]. These studies were extended by F. Lavelle and his colleague, Marie-Christine Bissery, to numerous other tumors implanted in mice[273]. The results were conclusive, showing that 56 976 R.P. had a broad spectrum of antitumoral activity, and notably greater activity than taxol on B16 melanoma. These results, along with the fact that taxotere was easily obtainable by convergent synthesis from 10-deacetylbaccatin III, isolated from a renewable natural source (the leaves of *T. baccata*), were the crucial points in the product's selection to begin clinical trials.

On 16 February 1990, the first meeting bringing together the chemists from the ICSN involved in the discovery of Taxotere®, the pharmacologists from Rhône-Poulenc and the French, American and British researchers who were to be involved in the phase-I clinical evaluation of 56 976 R.P., was organized by the project manager of Taxotere®, J.-L. Fabre[ooo].

ooo Letter from J.-L. Fabre, 8 February 1990. ICSN archives, F. Guéritte.

The phase-I clinical studies of Taxotere® began shortly afterwards in Europe and the United States. The first results, published in 1991, indicated clinical activity notably against breast and ovarian cancers[274]. On 3 September 1992, Rhône-Poulenc Rorer (RPR)[ppp] staged, in Strasbourg, a satellite symposium of the 18th International Symposium on Natural Product Chemistry, entitled: Taxoids: From Chemistry to Medicine (Figure 4.25). Amongst the speakers, F. Lavelle presented the results of the preclinical testing and the first phase-I trials of Taxotere®, concluding:

> These encouraging initial results prompted Rhône-Poulenc Rorer to start phase II clinical trials in May 1992 at a dose of 100 mg/m^2 by 1 h I.V. infusion every 3 weeks.[qqq]

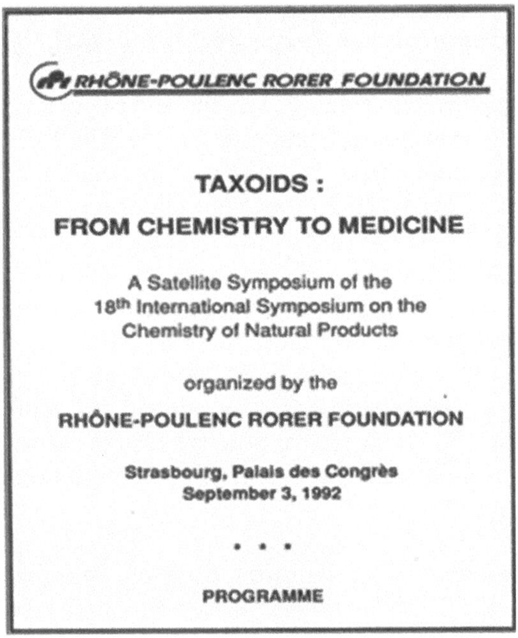
RHÔNE-POULENC RORER FOUNDATION

TAXOIDS :

FROM CHEMISTRY TO MEDICINE

A Satellite Symposium of the
18th International Symposium on the
Chemistry of Natural Products

organized by the

RHÔNE-POULENC RORER FOUNDATION

Strasbourg, Palais des Congrès
September 3, 1992

• • •

PROGRAMME

Figure 4.25. *Cover page for the satellite symposium organized by RPR on 3 September 1992*

---

ppp Rhône-Poulenc merged with the American pharmaceutical company Rorer in 1990.

qqq Catalog "Taxoids: from Chemistry to Medicine", compiling the summaries of the talks given at the symposium. F. Guéritte's archives.

In May 1994, the first registration dossier for Taxotere® was filed in Japan. The pharmacological and clinical studies continued, and fifteen years after the isolation of 10-deacetylbaccatin III from the leaves of the common yew, *T. baccata*, the first marketing authorizations for Taxotere®, commercialized by Rhône-Poulenc, were granted in over 40 countries between 1995 and 1996 (Figure 4.26).

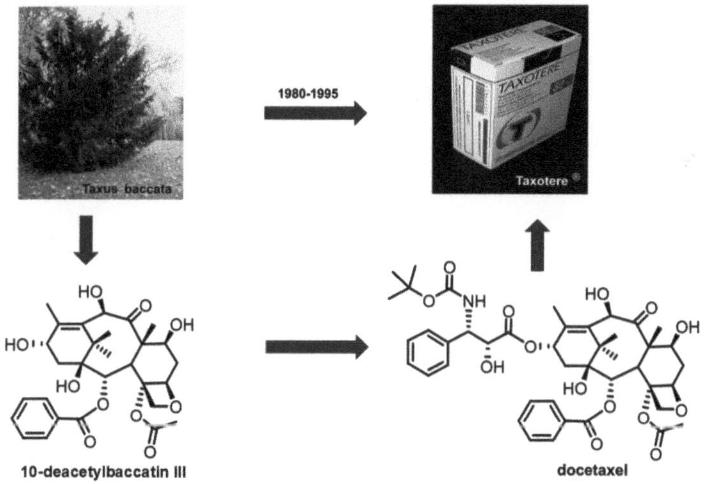

1980: phytochemical work on *T. baccata* begins at the ICSN
1980: deacetyl-10 baccatin III is isolated
1981: cooperation contract signed between the ICSN (CNRS) and Rhône-Poulenc Santé
1984: Oxy 1 synthesized by hydroxyamination. Found to be active against microtubules
1986: antitumoral activity of 56 976 R.P. (Oxy 1) confirmed
1986: patent filed on the product and its activities
1987: convergent synthesis of 56 976 R.P.
1988: patent filed on the product and its activities
1989: antitumoral activity demonstrated on B16 melanoma and other tumors
1990: clinical trials begin for Taxotere® (56 976 R.P.)
1995-96: first market authorizations granted for Taxotere®

Figure 4.26. *From the phytochemical study of T. baccata to the commercialization of Taxotere®*

As P. Potier remarks on the collaboration between the ICSN and Rhône-Poulenc teams, in his book "*Le magasin du Bon Dieu*": "The certitude of having promising molecules at our fingertips, and the relations of trust and friendship binding us together, won out over the difficulties we encountered along the way" (p. 113)[22].

Conclusion

From Science to Industry: the Full Story?

Until 2002, France did not have a central agency to coordinate the funding and the research conducted to combat cancer. The CNRS contributed to that mission, through financing projects or through the work of certain teams; in this context, the researchers working at the ICSN are merely one example. However, in this particular field, the results achieved by the ICSN researchers were exemplary. They discovered two important molecules which, under patent, gave rise to the manufacture of Navelbine® and Taxotere®. These pharmaceuticals have generated enormous turnovers for Laboratoires Pierre Fabre and Rhône-Poulenc (which is now Sanofi). Taxotere® alone produced €1.7 bn of turnover for that company in 2004, with the sales of Taxotere® having overtaken those of Taxol® in 2003. The CNRS was not left by the wayside, because in the years 2000–2005, these two pharmaceuticals represented 90% of royalties received (€450 m as at 1 January 2006)[a]. They have given rise to a financial manna which has provided the ICSN with a steady flow of income since the placement on the market of Navelbine® in 1989, until the patent of Taxotere® falls into the public domain. All the researchers directly involved in the discovery and development of the two drugs have received royalties, but still continue to search. After all, as P. Potier said, the CNRS was the ideal place to conduct research, given that researchers could come and go, were allowed the freedom to work, and the

a Interview with PP – MLR, 5 January 2006, at his home in Paris.

organization gave recognition for their work, helping them to protect their results[b].

These two pharmaceuticals were among the most widely sold antitumoral products worldwide, until they became public property in 2004 in the case of Navelbine®, though it has continued to generate sales profit, thanks to new associations with other medications, and also being produced in a new oral form, far more comfortable for the patient than the liquid form for injection. The patent on Taxotere®, for its part, lapsed in 2010, but it remains a hugely important product, either on its own or in combination. Despite their side effects, these two anticancer drugs remain important weapons in the therapeutic arsenal used to combat certain types of cancers, as it is so difficult to develop new molecules; the development of a medication requires around 15 years: five years of academic research, which may ultimately yield nothing, followed by ten years of research divided between academic and industrial centers before market authorization is obtained.

How are we to account for these successes, which go beyond the context of the ICSN? They were the fruit of collective work within a structure – the CNRS – which implemented a flexible form of organization (until the late 1990s) and which, in particular, facilitated a specific style of management. There was a collaboration between the CNRS – which, though sometimes the target of criticism, hosted research that was free, independent and not rigidly structured, allowing researchers the freedom to choose their own fields of study, their own partners – and entrepreneurs. There was a coming together of people with the shared ambition to succeed regardless of their professional attachments and obstacles. Finally, there was a meeting of minds, a partnership between an academic world and a business world in search of this type of knowledge[c]. Above all, though, could this not be said to be the result of a shared passion for scientific inquiry?

---

b *Op. cit.*

c These approaches will be discussed in a future book.

It would seem that this story can serve as an example, although some might protest, saying that the ICSN was not representative of the prevailing practices elsewhere in the CNRS. There is very little certainty on the matter, as it is so difficult to fathom what working strategies were devised by laboratories,[d] what the CNRS' connections with the industries were, and it is equally difficult to evaluate the true extent of the CNRS' role in the national process of innovation. The difficulties encountered in answering these questions result from a lack of transparency or an opacity which is not attributable only to CNRS. The frequent changes of tack by the State in terms of funding research, as well as the difficult dialog between the CNRS and the Finance Ministry – which refutes the specificity of research activity and often considers that it has been managed in the same way as any other activity – explain this obscurity surrounding the history of the financing of the CNRS, and more broadly, of research in general. However, a simple, illuminating fact becomes clear. For at least one generation, the CNRS' budget has no longer been able to finance the research under way, meaning that the majority of "hard science" laboratories (excluding the majority of human- and social-science laboratories) have developed their own strategies to procure the funding needed. Thus, the ICSN represents only one example among so many others[275,276].

All told, what sets the ICSN apart from other research institutions lies in the fact that its relations with the industrial sphere have always been well known, assumed and even lauded. For this reason, it has been easier to gain access to its archives – as kept in P. Potier's office – because a large part of its activity was based on this assumed relationship. Hence, it is worth examining the history of that relationship, looking at the point of view of the researchers and the industrialists. Therefore, this book on an aspect of the *history of*

d The evaluations dedicated to industrial research centers in the 1980s-1990s showed that it took less than ten years for researchers to make the organization their own, taking research in the direction of fields which interested them personally, defying the company's own guidelines. It is reasonable to imagine that the researchers at the CNRS have the same capability… See M. Le Roux, *Un siècle de recherche industrielle à Pechiney*, Paris, Rive droite, 1998, and archives of the R&D directorate at Pechiney.

sciences will be followed up by one on the history of that relation between the ICSN and industries.

The science discussed in this book arose in organizations designed in the 1950s, at a time when science and technology were synonymous with development and progress. There were very high hopes for science and medicine, expected to solve all manner of problems, and in this context, chemistry was a tool used for reconstruction during the "*trente glorieuses*" (France's recovery after WWII – 1945–1975), whilst its detractors began voicing their opinions in the late 1960s.

It must be recognized that, much like Zenobia of Palmyra – Queen of the Orient and a true Roman, who could not break off from the Roman Empire other than to fall under the yoke of another[277] – the chemistry of natural substances has a dual personality: it cannot be separated from the world of fundamental academic research without being assimilated into the highly capitalistic pharmaceutical industry, whose culture is different and where natural substances chemistry itself is subsumed within a vast ocean of other fields[e], even though it is one of the backbones of the existence of that industrial sector.

Having come to the end of this *compagnonnage*, the authors hope they have laid a stone in the building of the shared edifice that is the history of sciences, highlighting the degree to which the science practised today is dependent on its past. It would be a truism to say that its present is much more easily understood because it is illuminated by what has gone before. This journey through an important period of scientific history seemed to us all the more necessary, because today, when decisions are guided by financial criteria, we often hear the false sentiment expressed that today's science owes nothing to yesterday's...[25]

e Parallel inspired by Paul Veyne's text, p. 97.

Bibliography

1 LE ROUX M., "Hommage à Pierre Potier, dépasser les limites du présent", *Rayonnement du CNRS*, vol. 41, pp. 5–27, 2006.

2 LE ROUX M., "Genèse des textes de Pierre Potier, chimiste des substances naturelles", *Genesis*, vol. 20, pp. 91–125, 2003.

3 GOODMAN J., WALSH V., *The Story of Taxol. Nature and Politics in the Pursuit of an Anticancer-Drug*, Cambridge University Press, 2001.

4 BUD R., *Penicillin, Triumph and Tragedy*, Oxford University Press, 2007.

5 QUIRKE V., *Collaboration in the Pharmaceutical Industry. Changing Relationships in Britain and France, 1935–1965*, Routledge, New York and Abingdon, 2008.

6 CHANDLER A.D. Jr., *Shaping the Industrial Century: The Remarkable Story of the Evolution of the Modern Chemical and Pharmaceutical Industries*, Harvard University Press, Cambridge, 2005.

7 CARON F., *La dynamique de l'innovation*, Gallimard, Paris, 2010.

8 LE ROUX M., "From science to industry: the sites of aluminium in France from the nineteenth to the twentieth century", *Ambix, The Journal of the Society for the Study of Alchemy and Chemistry*, vol. 62, no. 2, pp. 114–137, 2015.

9 OECD, *Frascati Manual 2015: Guide and Expériemental Development, The Measure Acitivities*, 7th ed. (1st ed. 1963), OECD Publishing, Paris, 2015.

10 BENSAUDE-VINCENT B., SIMON J., *Chemistry, The Impure Science*, Imperial College Press, London, 2008.

11 THACKRAY A. (ed.), *Private Science. Biotechnology and the Rise of Molecular Sciences*, University of Pennsylvania Press, Philadelphia, 1998.

12 ZWEIG S., *Magellan*, Grasset, Paris, 2003, (1st ed. 1938).

13 KLEIN É., "L'avenir de la recherche scientifique", *Études*, vol. 6, no. 408, pp. 725–728, 2008.

14 BLOCH M., "Apologie pour l'histoire", in BECKER A., BLOCH E., *L'Histoire, la Guerre la Résistance*, Gallimard, Paris, 2006.

15 GAUDILLERE J.-P., *La médecine et les sciences, XIXe-XXe siècle*, La Découverte, Paris, 2006.

16 URFALINO P., "Introduction – Médicaments et société, enjeux contemporains", *Annales. Histoire, Sciences Sociales*, vol. 62, no. 2, pp. 269–273, 2007.

17 LE BIGOT É.-O., BLEVINS S.J., "Sur la genèse des résultats théoriques en physique", *Genesis*, vol. 20, pp. 129–144, 2003.

18 LAVAUD C., MASSIOT G., "Naming natural products: uses, abuses and a proposal for discussion", *Phytochemistry*, available at http://dx.doi.org/10.1016/j.phytochem.2016.09.001, 2016.

19 LE ROUX M., WELFELE O., "Les archives scientifiques contemporaines et l'écriture de la science, le cas du CNRS", *Genesis*, vol. 20, pp. 167–176, 2003.

20 VERSCHUEREN P., "Les écrits autobiographiques en sciences physiques après 1945: quelles sources pour l'historien ?", *Congrès de la Société Française d'Histoire des Sciences et des Techniques*, Lyon, France, 2014.

21 LEDERER E., *Itinéraire d'un biochimiste français de François Joseph à Gorbatchev*, Publibook, Paris, 2007.

22 POTIER P., CHAST F., GUERIN C., *Le magasin du Bon Dieu*, JC Lattès, Paris, 2001.

23 SALOMON-BAYET C., "L'histoire des sciences et des techniques", in BEDARIDAT F. (ed.), *L'histoire et le métier d'historien en France, 1945–1995*, Éditions de la Maison des sciences de l'homme, Paris, 1995.

24 BEDARIDAT F., "Post-face", in BEDARIDAT F. (ed.), *L'histoire et le métier d'historien en France 1945–1995*, Éditions de la Maison des sciences de l'homme, Paris, 1995.

25 POMIAN K., "Partir du présent", *Le Débat*, vol. 3, no. 175, pp. 79–92, 2003.

26 LANGLOIS N., LANGLOIS Y., *La découverte de la navelbine: histoire vécue*, self-published, 2015.

27 DALGALARRONDO S., "Savoir thérapeutique et logique commerciale, la cas de l'AZT", *Annales. Histoire, Sciences Sociales*, vol. 62, no. 2, pp. 299–326, 2007.

28 LE ROUX M., "Talking with the living: what methodology for today chemists' biographies in the present time history of chemistry?", *10th International Conference on the History of Chemistry: Chemical Biography in the 21st Century*, University of Aveiro, Portugal, 2015.

29 FARGE A., *Le goût de l'archive*, Le Seuil, Paris, 1989.

30 OZOUF M., "Récits des romanciers, récits des historiens", *Le Débat*, vol. 3, no. 165, pp. 13–25, 2011.

31 OLSON R., *Houston, We Have a Narrative*, The University of Chicago Press, 2015.

32 PICARD J.-F., *La république des savants – La recherche française et le CNRS*, Flammarion, Paris, 1990.

33 LE ROUX M., "The power of relationships, the emergence of contemporary science and technology policies in France during the first half of the 20th Century", *Économies et Sociétés, série: Histoire économique quantitative*, vol. XLII, no. 3, pp. 601−618, 2008.

34 GUTHLEBEN D., *Histoire du CNRS de 1939 à nos jours*, Armand Colin, Paris, 2009.

35 PROST A., Les origines des politiques de la recherche en France, *Cahiers pour l'histoire du CNRS*, vol. 1, 1988.

36 PICARD J.-F., "En France, grandeur et servitude du colbertisme scientifique", in BERTRAMS K., BIEMONT É., VAN TIGGELEN B., *et al.*, (eds), *Pour une histoire de la politique scientifique en Europe (XIXe–XXe siècle)*, Académie royale de Belgique, Brussels, Belgium, 2007.

37 PINAULT M., *Frédéric Joliot-Curie*, Odile Jacob, Paris, 2000.

38 Editorial, "La science dans la République – Colloques de Caen", *Les Cahiers de la République*, vol. 5, 1957.

39 CHATRIOT A., DUCLERCT V. (eds), *Le gouvernement de la recherche, histoire d'un engagement politique de Pierre Mendès France à Charles de Gaulle (1953–1969)*, La Découverte, Paris, 2006.

40 RIZZO J.-L., Pierre Mendès France et la recherche scientifique et technique, *La Revue pour l'histoire du CNRS*, vol. 6, pp. 60–67, 2002.

41 NYE M.J., *Science in the Provinces: Scientific Communities and Provincial Leadership in France, 1860–1930*, University of California Press, Berkeley, 1986.

42 GRELON A., "Pour une histoire des formations à la chimie en France", in BRAM G., CHAMOZZI F., FUCHS A., *et al.* (eds), *La Chimie dans la société, son rôle, son image*, CNRS – L'Harmattan, Paris, 1995.

43 LE ROUX M., *L'entreprise et la recherche, un siècle de recherche industrielle à Pechiney, 1808–1996*, Éditions Rive droite, Paris, 1998.

44 CRAWFORD E., OLFF-NATAHN J., (eds), *La science sous influence, l'Université de Strasbourg, enjeu de conflits franco-allemands 1872–1945*, La Nuée Bleue – Université Louis Pasteur, Strasbourg, 2005.

45 PICARD J.-F., *La fondation Rockefeller et la recherche médicale*, PUF, Paris, 1999.

46 LEHN J.-M., *Construire l'avenir – livre blanc sur la recherche présenté au Président de la République*, La Documentation française, Paris, 1980.

47 LESTEL L. (ed.), *Itinéraires de chimistes 1857–2007, 150 ans de chimie en France avec les présidents de la SFC*, SFC EDP Sciences, Paris, 2007.

48 TARTAKOWSKY D., TETARD F., *Syndicats et associations, Concurrence ou complémentarité?* PUR, Rennes, 2006.

49 CHARPENTIER-MORIZE M., "La contribution des 'laboratoires propres' du CNRS à la recherche chimique en France de 1939 à 1973", *Cahiers pour l'histoire du CNRS*, vol. 4, pp. 79–112, 1989.

50 PICARD J.-F., ELISABETH P., "La longue marche vers le CNRS (1901–1945)", *Cahiers pour l'histoire du CNRS*, vol. 1, pp. 7-40, 1988 and 2009.

51 LEDERER E., PICARD J.-F., PRADOURA E., "Edgar Lederer, La chimie des substances naturelles", *Cahiers pour l'histoire du CNRS, 1939–1989*, vol. 2, pp. 43–54, 1989.

52 LE ROUX M., "A chemist's community as a forerunner in management change and innovation in France during the second part of the twentieth Century? The case of the Institut de Chimie des Substances Naturelles, a CNRS Laboratory", *Business and Economic History On-Line*, vol. 7, 2009.

53 LANCIANO-MORANDAT C., Le mode de structuration du département des "sciences chimiques" du CNRS, Laboratoire d'Economie et de Sociologie du Travail – CNRS – Université Aix–Marseille and Département des sciences chimiques du CNRS, Aix-en-Provence, 1999.

54 NDIAYE P., *Du nylon et des bombes. Du Pont, l'État et le marché, 1900–1970*, Belin, Paris, 2001.

55 PESTRE D., *Sciences, argent et politiques. Un essai d'interprétation*, Éditions de l'INRIA, Paris, 2003.

56 PESTRE D., *À contre-science, Politique et savoirs des sociétés contemporaines*, Le Seuil, Paris, 2013.

57 PESTRE D., (ed.), *Le gouvernement des technosciences*, Paris, La Découverte, 2014.

58 POTIER P., "La création de l'Institut de Chimie des Substances Naturelles à Gif-surYvette par M.M. Janot", *Revue d'histoire de la pharmacie*, vol. 312, pp. 459–463, 1996.

59 TOURNES L., "Le réseau des boursiers Rockefeller et la recomposition des savoirs biomédicaux en France (1920–1970)", *French Historical Studies*, vol. 29, no. 1, pp. 77–107, 2006.

60 DOSSO D., "Louis Rapkine, biochimiste (Tchichenitch, près de Minsk, Russie, 14 juillet 1904 – Paris, 13 décembre 1948)", *Archives Juives, Revue d'histoire des Juifs de France*, vol. 32, no. 2, pp. 130–133, 1999.

61 PICARD J.-F., "Un demi-siècle de génétique de la levure au CNRS, de la biologie moléculaire à la génomique", *La revue pour l'histoire du CNRS*, vol. 7, pp. 42–49 2002.

62 NICAULT C., DURAND V., *Histoire documentaire du CNRS; Années 1950–1981*, vol. 2, CNRS Éditions, Paris, 2006.

63 CHAST F., MAURICE-BERNARD F., Pierre Potier (1934–2006), Formal sitting of the Académie nationale de pharmacie, Paris, 2007.

64 LE ROUX M., WALSH V., "Contingency in innovation and the role of national systems: taxol and taxotère in the USA and France", *Research Policy*, vol. 9, no. 3, pp. 1307–1327, 2004.

65 VILKAS C., Un laboratoire de recherche fondamentale en chimie, DEA, Institut d'études politiques de Paris, Paris, 1990.

66 MATHE G., *Dossier cancer*, Stock, Paris, 1977.

67 BERRY R.W., SHELANSKI M.L., "Interactions of tubulin with vinblastine and guanosine triphosphate", *Journal of Molecular Biology*, vol. 71, no. 1, pp. 71–80, 1972.

68 POTIER P., LANGLOIS N., LANGLOIS Y., *et al.*, Bi-sindolic compounds. Fr. Appl.74/43,221, 30 December 1974; Ger.Offen. 2,558,124 (Cl.C07D519/04), 1 July 1976.

69 PENAN H., *Histoire des laboratoires Pierre Fabre*, Éditions Privat, Toulouse, 2014.

70 MARKGRAF F., *Flore de Madagascar et des Comores: Apocynacées Firmin-Didot*, vol. 169, Paris, 1976.

71 LINNÉ C. (von), *Systema Naturae*, 10th ed., vol. 2, Stockholm, 1759.

72 REICHENBACH H.G.L., *Conspectus Regni Vegetabilis Per Gradus Naturales Evoluti,* vol. 1, Lipsiae, 1828.

73 ENDLICHER S., *Genera plantarum Secumdum Ordines Naturales Disposita*, Vindobonae, 1836–1850.

74 DON G., *General System of Gardening and Botany*, vol. 4, pp. 95–96, 1838.

75 STEARN W.T., "*Catharanthus roseus,* the correct name for the Madagascar periwinkle", *Lloydia*, vol. 29, pp. 196–200, 1966.

76 STEARN W.T., "Synopsis of the genus *Catharanthus*", in TAYLOR W.I., FARNSWORTH N.R. (eds), *The Catharanthus Alkaloids: Botany, Pharmacology, and Clinical Use*, Marcel Dekker, Inc, New York, pp. 9–44, 1975.

77 DE FLACOURT É., *Histoire de la grande isle Madagascar*, Nicolas Oudot, Troyes, 1661.

78 BOITEAU P., "Sur la première mention imprimée et le premier échantillon de *Catharanthus roseus* (L.) G. Don", *Adansonia*, vol. 12, no. 1, pp. 129–135, 1972.

79 VAN DER HEIJDEN R., JACOBS D.I., SNOEIJER W., *et al.*, "The *Catharanthus* alkaloids: pharmacognosy and biotechnology", *Current Medicinal Chemistry*, vol. 11, pp. 607–628, 2004.

80 PARIS R., MOYSE H., "Les pervenches indigènes et exotiques (fin)", *Journal d'agriculture et de botanique appliquée*, vol. 5, nos 1–3, pp. 35–43, 1958.

81 ASLAM J., KHAN S.H., SIDDIQUI Z.H., *et al.*, "*Catharanthus roseus* (L.) G. Don. an important drug: it's applications and production", *International Journal of Comprehensive Pharmacy*, vol. 1, no. 4, pp. 1–16, 2010.

82 WHITE C.T., "*Vinca rosea* – a reputed cure for diabetes", *Queensland Agricultural Journal*, vol. 23, no. 2, pp. 143–144, 1925.

83 WHITE C.T., "Le *Vinca rosea* ou Pervenche de Madagascar employé dans le traitement du diabète", *Revue de botanique appliquée et d'agriculture coloniale*, vol. 48, pp. 630–631, 1925.

84 JOHNSON I.S., ARMSTRONG J.G., GORMAN M., *et al.*, "*Vinca* alkaloids – a new class of oncolytic agents", *Cancer Research*, vol. 23, no. 8, pp. 1390–1427, 1963.

85 EPSTEIN D., "The action of *Vinca* on the blood sugar of rabbits", *South African Medical Record*, vol. 24, no. 2, pp. 35–38, 1926.

86 LEE D.H.K., DREW W.R.M., "*Vinca rosea*: its effect on the blood sugar levels of normal rabbits", *Medical Journal of Australia*, vol. 1, p. 699, 1929.

87 (a) NYE L.J.J., FITZGERALD M.E., "*Vinca* treatment of diabetes", *Medical Journal of Australia*, vol. II, p. 626, 1928;
(b) CORKILL A.B., DOUTCH A., "An investigation into the alleged therapeutic properties of *Vinca rosea* in the treatment of diabetes", *Medical Journal of Australia*, vol. I, no. 7, pp. 213–216, 1930.

88 NOBLE R.L., BEER C.T., CUTTS J.H., "Role of chance observations in chemotherapy: *Vinca rosea*", *Annals of the New York Academy of Sciences*, vol. 76, no. 3, pp. 882–94, 1958.

89 JOHNSON I.S., WRIGHT H.F., SVOBODA G.H., "Experimental basis for clinical evaluation of antitumor principles derived from *Vinca rosea* LINN.", *Journal of Laboratory and Clinical Medicine*, vol. 54, no. 5, p. 830, 1959.

90 SVOBODA G.H., "A note on several new alkaloids from *Vinca rosea* Linn. I. Leurosine, virosine, perivine", *Journal of the American Pharmaceutical Association*, vol. 47, no. 11, pp. 834, 1958.

91 SVOBODA G.H., "Alkaloids of *Vinca rosea* (*Catharanthus roseus*) Extraction and characterization of leurosidine and leurocristine", *Lloydia*, vol. 24, no. 4, pp. 173–178, 1961.

92 NOBLE R.L., "The discovery of the *Vinca* alkaloids, chemotherapeutic agents against cancer", *Biochemistry and Cell Biology*, vol. 68, no. 12, pp. 1344–1351, 1990.

93 (a) CUTTS J.H., BEER C.T., NOBLE R.L., "Biological properties of Vincaleukoblastine, an alkaloid in *Vinca rosea* Linn, with reference to its antitumor action", *Cancer Research*, vol. 20, pp. 1023–1031, 1960;
(b) JOHNSON I.S., WRIGHT H.F., SVOBODA G.H., *et al.*, "Antitumor principles derived from *Vinca rosea* Linn. I. Vincaleukoblastine and leurosine", *Cancer Research*, vol. 20, 1016–1022, 1960.

94 WARWICK O.H., DARTE J.M., BROWN T.C., *et al.*, "Some biological effects of Vincaleukoblastine, an alkaloid in *Vinca rosea* Linn. in patients with malignant disease", *Cancer Research*, vol. 20, pp. 1032–40, 1960.

95 COSTA G., HRESHCHYSHYN M.M., HOLLAND J.F., "Initial clinical studies with vincristine", *Cancer Chemotherapy Reports*, no. 24, pp. 39–44, 1962.

96 HODES M.E., ROHN R.J., BOND W.H., *et al.*, "Clinical trials with leurosine methiodide, an alkaloid from *Vinca rosea* Linn.", *Cancer Chemotherapy Reports*, no. 28, pp. 53–55, 1963.

97 DUFFIN J., "Poisoning the spindle: serendipity and discovery of the anti-tumour properties of the *Vinca* alkaloids", *Canadian Journal of Medical History*, vol. 17, pp. 287–308, 2000.

98 PARIS R., MOYSE-MIGNON H., "Sur une apocynacée sympatholytique, le *Vinca rosea* L.", *Comptes rendus hebdomadaires des séances de l'Académie des Sciences*, vol. 236, no. 20, pp. 1993–1995, 1953.

99 GRESHOFF M., "Berichte der Deutschen Chemischen Gesellschaft", vol. 23 p. 3543, 1890, in SVOBODA G.H., NEUSS, N., GORMAN, M. "Alkaloids of *Vinca rosea* Linn. (*Catharanthus roseus* G. Don)", *Journal of the American Pharmaceutical Association*, vol. 48, pp. 659-666.

100 BOORSMA W.G., Mededeulingen eit's Lands Plantentuin, 31, 42–45, 134, 1899, in PARIS, R., MOYSE, H., "Les pervenche indigènes et exotiques (suite)" *Journal d'agriculture tropicale et de botanique appliquée,* vol. 4, no 12, pp. 645-656, 1957.

101 COWLEY R.C., BENNET F.C., "*Vinca rosea*", *Australian Journal of Pharmacy*, vol. 9, p. 61, 1928.

102 (a) JANOT M.-M., LE MEN J., "Sur les alcaloides cristallises du *Lochnera (Vinca) rosea* (L.) Reichb. ou *Catharanthus roseus* G. Don", *Comptes rendus hebdomadaires des séances de l'Académie des Sciences*, vol. 243, no. 22, pp. 1789–1792, 1956;
(b) JANOT M.-M., LE MEN J., FAN C., "La vindolinine, alcaloïde du *Catharanthus roseus* G. Don – alcaloïde des pervenches – *Vinca* et *Catharanthus* (= *Lochnera*)", *Bulletin de la Société Chimique de France*, pp. 891–892, 1959.

103 PERNET R., MEYER G., BOSSER J.-M., *et al.*, "Les *Catharanthus* de Madagascar", *Comptes rendus des séances de l'Académie des Sciences*, vol. 243, pp. 1352–1353, 1956.

104 MORS W.B., ZALTZMAN P., BEEREBOOM J.J., *et al.*, "Alkaloid studies. 10. Alkaloids of 2 brazilian Apocynaceae, *Rauvolfia grandiflora* Mart. and *Lochnera* (*Vinca*) *rosea* (L) Reichb. var. alba (sweet) Hubbd", *Chemistry & Industry*, no. 11, pp. 173–174, 1956.

105 CHATTERJEE A., TALAPATRA S.K., "Constitution of vincain, a β-carboline alkaloid isolated from *Vinca rosea*", *Science and Culture (India)*, vol. 20, pp. 568–570, 1955.

106 KLOHS M.W., DRAPER M.D., KELLER F., *et al.*, "Alkaloids of *Rauwolfia* serpentina Benth. 2. The isolation of naturally occuring py-tetrahydroserpentine (Ajmalicine) and a contribution towards its structure", *Journal of the American Chemical Society*, vol. 76, no. 5, pp. 1332–1334, 1954.

107 SHIMIZU M., UCHIMARU F., "Isolation of alkaloids from *Vinca (Lochnera) rosea* L. Reichb", *Chemical & Pharmaceutical Bulletin*, vol. 6, no. 3, pp. 324–5, 1958.

108 KAMAT V.N., DESA J., VAZ A., *et al.*, "Isolation and characterization of chemical constituents from *Vinca rosea* Linn. (Apocynaceae)", *Indian Journal of Medical Research*, vol. 46, no. 4, pp. 588–97, 1958.

109 NOBLE R.L., BEER C.T., CUTTS J.H., "Further biological activities of vincaleukoblastine – an alkaloid isolated from *Vinca rosea* L.", *Biochemical Pharmacology*, vol. 1, no. 4, pp. 347–348, 1958.

110 NEUSS N., GORMAN M., "The structure of catharanthine, a novel variant of the iboga alkaloids", *Tetrahedron Letters*, vol. 2, no. 6, pp. 206–210, 1961.

111 GORMAN M., NEUSS N., BIEMANN K., "*Vinca* Alkaloids. X. The structure of vindoline", *Journal of the American Chemical Society*, vol. 84, no. 6, pp. 1058–1059, 1962.

112 (a) MONCRIEF J.W., LIPSCOMB W.N., "Structures of leurocristine (vincristine) and vincaleukoblastine. X-ray analysis of leurocristine methiodide", *Journal of the American Chemical Society*, vol. 87, pp. 4963–4964, 1965;
(b) BLAHA K., TROJANEK J., KOBLICOV Z, "Absolute configuration of Iboga and Voacanga alkaloids. Chiroptical approach", *Tetrahedron Letters*, vol. 13, no. 27, p. 2763, 1972.

113 (a) NEUSS N., GORMAN M., BOAZ H.E., *et al.*, "*Vinca* alkaloids. XI. Structure of leurocristine (LCR) and vincaleukoblastine (VLB)", *Journal of the American Chemical Society*, vol. 84, pp. 1509–1510, 1962;
(b) GORMAN M., NEUSS N., SVOBODA G.H., "*Vinca* alkaloids. 4. Structural features of leurosine and vincaleukoblastine, representatives of a new types of indole-indoline alkaloids", *Journal of the American Chemical Society*, vol. 81, no. 17, pp. 4745–4746, 1959.

114 MONCRIEF J.W., LIPSCOMB W.N., "Structure of leurocristine methiodide dihydrate by anomalous scattering methods; Relation to leurocristine (vincristine) and vincaleukoblastine (vinblastine)" *Acta Crystallographica*, vol. 21, pp. 322–331, 1966.

115 (a) ABRAHAM D.J., FARNSWORTH N.R., "Structure elucidation and chemistry of *Catharanthus* alkaloids. 3. Structure of leurosine, an active anticancer alkaloid", *Journal of Pharmaceutical Sciences*, vol. 58, no. 6, pp. 694–698, 1969;
(b) WENKERT E., HAGAMAN E.W., LAL B., *et al.*, "13C-NMR. Spectroscopy of naturally occurring substances. XXXII. Vincaleucoblastine and related alkaloid", *Helvetica Chimica Acta*, vol. 58, no. 6, pp. 1560–1567, 1975.

116 KUTNEY J.P., WORTH B.R., "Studies on synthesis of bisindole alkaloids. VII. Stereochemistry and alternative total synthesis of leurosine", *Heterocycles*, vol. 4, no. 11, pp. 1777–1782, 1976.

117 LANGLOIS N., POTIER P., "Hemisynthesis of leurosidine, antitumorigenic alkaloid isolated from *Catharanthus roseus* G.DON (Apocynaceae)", *Tetrahedron Letters*, vol. 17, no 14, pp. 1099–1102, 1976.

118 HERTZ R., LIPSETT M.B., MOY R.H., "Effect of vincaleukoblastine on metastatic choriocarcinoma and related trophoblastic tumors in women", *Cancer Research*, vol. 20, pp. 1050–1053, 1960.

119 ARMSTRONG J.G., DYKE R.W., FOUTS P.J., "Initial clinical experience with leurocristine, a new alkaloid from *Vinca rosea", Proceedings of the American Association for Cancer Research*, vol. 3, p. 301, 1962.

120 CARBONE P.P., BONO V., FREI E., *et al.*, "Clinical studies with vincristine", *Blood*, vol. 21, no. 5, pp. 640–647, 1963.

121 SVOBODA G.H., "The role of alkaloids of *Catharanthus roseus* (L.) G. Don (*Vinca rosea*) and their derivatives in cancer chemotheray", *Workshop Proceedings Plants: The Potentials for Extracting Proteins and Other Useful Chemicals*, Congress of the United States Office of Technology Assessment, Washington, DC, pp. 154–159, 1983.

122 POLONOVSKI M., POLONOVSKI M., "Sur les aminoxydes des alcaloïdes. III. Action des anhydrides et chlorures d'acides organiques. Préparation des bases nor", *Bulletin de La Société Chimique de France*, vol. 41, pp. 1190–1208, 1927.

123 HAGEMAN H.A., "The von Braun cyanogen bromide reaction", *Organic Reactions*, vol. 7, pp. 198–262, 1953.

124 WENKERT E., "The role of oxidation in the biogenesis of alkaloids", *Experientia*, vol. 10, no. 8, pp. 346–350, 1954.

125 HUISGEN R., BAYERLEIN F., HEYDKAMP W., "Die acylierung der N, N-dimethyl-arylamin-oxyde. Der mechanismus der Polonovski reaktion", *Chemische Berichte-Recueil*, vol. 92, no. 12, pp. 3223–3241, 1959.

126 (a) CAVÉ A., Analyse structurale des alcaloïdes du *Kibatalia gitingensis* (ELM) Woods. (Apocynacées). Etude de certaines réactions d'oxydation appliquées à ces alcaloïdes, PhD thesis, faculté des sciences de l'université de Paris, 1968;
(b) CAVÉ A., KAN-FAN C., POTIER P., *et al.*, "Modification de la réaction de Polonovski. Action de l'anhydride trifluoroacétique sur un aminoxyde", *Tetrahedron*, vol. 23, no. 12, pp. 4681–4689, 1967.

127 (a) MICHELOT R., "Etude du mécanisme de la réaction de Polonovski. Influence de la structure de l'oxyde d'amine sur le déroulement de la réaction", *Bulletin de la Société Chimique de France*, vol. 12, pp. 4377–4385, 1969;
(b) MICHELOT R., Etude des oxydes de méthylamines et du dimethylsulfoxyde en tant que sources de formaldéhyde et étude du mécanisme de la réaction de Polonovski, PhD thesis, faculté des Sciences d'Orsay, University of Paris, 1969.

128 CAVÉ A., MICHELOT R., "Influence of acylating agents on course of Polonovski reaction", *Comptes rendus des séances de l'Académie des Sciences*, vol. 265, no. 13, pp. 669–672, 1967.

129 AHOND A., De la réaction de Polonovski à la réaction de Mannich: étude de réactions de fragmentation et d'hydroxylation en série stéroïde, PhD thesis, faculté des sciences de Paris, 1969.

130 (a) AHOND A., CAVÉ A., KAN-FAN C., *et al.*, "Facile N-O bond cleavage of amine oxides", *Journal of the American Chemical Society*, vol. 90, no. 20, pp. 5622–5623, 1968;
(b) AHOND A., CAVÉ A., KAN-FAN C., *et al.*, "Modification of Polonovski reaction. Preparation of a new Mannich reagent", *Bulletin de la Société Chimique de France*, no. 7, pp. 2707–2711, 1970.

131 POTIER P., "Is the modified Polonovski reaction biometic?", *Annual proceedings of the Phytochemical Society of Europe*, vol. 17, pp. 159–169, 1980.

132 AHOND A., CAVÉ A., KAN-FAN C., *et al.*, "Fragmentation of N, N-dimethyltryptamine oxide and related compounds. A possible implication in indole alkaloid biosynthesis", *Journal of the Chemical Society D-Chemical Communications*, vol. 9, pp. 517–517, 1970.

133 MANGENEY P., "Study of Polonovski reaction on a model molecule, dregamine", *Tetrahedron*, vol. 34, no. 9, pp. 1359–1361, 1978.

134 (a) LANGLOIS N., POTIER P., "Alkaloids of *Catharanthus ovalis* (Apocynaceae) and particularly cathovaline", *Comptes rendus hebdomadaires des séances de l'Académie des Sciences. Série C*, vol. 273, no. 16, pp. 994–996, 1971;
(b) LANGLOIS N., POTIER P., "Plants from Malagasy Republic. Alkaloids from *Catharanthus ovalis*", *Phytochemistry*, vol. 11, no. 8, pp. 2617–2618, 1972;

(c) LANGLOIS N., POTIER P., "New alkaloid of *Catharanthus ovalis* Markg. (Apocynaceae)", *Comptes rendus hebdomadaires des séances de l'Académie des Sciences*, Série C, vol. 275, no. 3, pp. 219–222, 1972.

135 (a) RASOANAIVO P., POTIER P., LANGLOIS N., "Plants from Malagasy Republic. Alkaloids from *Catharanthus longifolius*", *Phytochemistry*, vol. 11, no. 8, pp. 2616–2617, 1972;
(b) RASOANAIVO P, LANGLOIS N., POTIER P., "Plants from Malagasy Republic 1. New alkaloid from *Catharanthus longifolius* Pich. (Apocynaceae)", *Tetrahedron Letters*, vol. 16, pp. 1425–1428, 1973.

136 (a) DIATTA L., LANGLOIS Y., LANGLOIS N., *et al.*, "Alkaloids of *Catharanthus ovalis* MGF. Reactivity of Vindolinine type alkaloids and correlation with deacetylcathovaline", *Bulletin de la Société Chimique de France*, vols 3–4, pp. 671–674, 1975;
(b) ANDRIAMIALISOA R.Z., LANGLOIS N., POTIER P., "Nouvel isomère de la vinblastine: la vincovaline isolée de *Catharanthus ovalis* Mgf. (Apocynaceae)", *Tetrahedron Letters*, vol. 33, pp. 2849–2852, 1976;
(c) CHIARONI A., RICHE C., DIATTA L., *et al.*, "Malagasy plants. New alkaloid from *Catharanthus ovalis* Mgf. (Apocynaceae). Cathovalinine or 14α, 15α-epoxy-19*S*-hydroxytabersonine", *Tetrahedron*, vol. 32, no. 15, pp. 1899–1902, 1976;
(d) LANGLOIS N., POTIER P., "*Catharanthus ovalis* MGF. alkaloids. Piperidinic ring contraction of Aspidospermane alkaloids", *Bulletin de la Société Chimique de France*, vols 3–4, pp. 144–146, 1978;
(e) LANGLOIS N., DIATTA L., ANDRIAMIALISOA R.Z., "Malagasy Plants. Mono-indolic alkaloids of *Catharanthus ovalis*", *Phytochemistry*, vol. 18, no. 3, pp. 467–471, 1979;
(f) LANGLOIS N., ANDRIAMIALISOA R.Z., NEUSS N., "Plantes malgaches. 22. Bis-indolic alkaloids of *Catharanthus ovalis*", *Helvetica Chimica Acta*, vol. 63, no. 4, pp. 793–805, 1980.

137 (a) RASOANAIVO P., Etude chimique d'alcaloïdes de *Catharanthus longifolius* Pich. (Apocynacée malgache). Hémisynthèse d'alcaloïdes bis-indoliques, PhD thesis, Université de Paris-Sud, centre d'Orsay, 1974;
(b) ANDRIAMIALISOA R.Z., Etude chimique d'alcaloïdes de *Catharanthus ovalis* Mgf. et hémisynthèse, PhD thesis, université de Paris-Sud, centre d'Orsay, 1978.

138 (a) RASOANAIVO P, AHOND A., COSSON J.P., *et al.*, "Structure of catharine", *Comptes rendus hebdomadaires des séances de l'Académie des Sciences*, Série C, vol. 279, no. 2, pp. 75–77, 1974;

(b) GUILHEM J., DUCRUIX A., RICHE C., *et al.*, "Bis-indole alkaloid catharine", *Acta Crystallographica Section B*, vol. 32, pp. 936–938, 1976.

139 ANDRIAMIALISOA R.Z., LANGLOIS N., POTIER P., *et al.*, "Structure of catharinine, bis-indole alkaloid isolated from several species of *Catharanthus*", *Tetrahedron*, vol. 34, no. 6, pp. 677–683, 1978.

140 (a) KUTNEY J.P., TROTTER J., TABATA T., *et al.*, "Chemistry of catharanthine. Evidence for a novel and remarkable acid rearrangement", *Chemistry & Industry*, vol. 16, pp. 648–649, 1963;
(b) CAMERMAN N., TROTTER J., "Stucture of cleavamine. X-ray analysis of cleavamine methiodide", *Acta Crystallographica*, vol. 17, no. 4, pp. 384–391, 1964.

141 HARLEY-MASON J., ATTA-UR-RAHMAN, "Total synthesis of (+/−)-16-Hydroxydihydrocleavamines and partial synthesis of demethoxycarbonyldeoxyvinblastine", *Chemical Communications*, vol. 20, pp. 1048–1049, 1967.

142 NEUSS N., GORMAN M., CONE N.J., *et al.*, "*Vinca* alkaloids. XXX (1). Chemistry of the deoxyvinblastines (deoxy-VLB), leurosine (VLR) and pleurosine, dimeric alkaloids from *Vinca rosea* LINN. (*Catharanthus roseus* G DON)", *Tetrahedron Letters*, vol. 9, no. 7, pp. 783–787, 1968.

143 KUTNEY J.P., BECK J., BYLSMA F., *et al.*, "Studies on synthesis of dimeric *Vinca* alkaloids", *Journal of the American Chemical Society*, vol. 90, no. 16, pp. 4504–4505, 1968.

144 ATTA-UR-RAHMAN, "Partial synthesis of Δ15,20-anhydrovinblastine", *Pakistan Journal of Science and Industrial Research*, vol. 14, no. 6, pp. 487, 1971.

145 DADDONA P.E., HUTCHINSON C.R., "Biosynthesis of dimeric indole alkaloids. Vincaleukoblastine", *Journal of the American Chemical Society*, vol. 96, no. 21, pp. 6806–6807, 1974.

146 (a) POTIER P., LANGLOIS N., LANGLOIS Y., *et al.*, "Partial synthsesis of vinblastine-type alkaloids", *Journal of the Chemical Society-Chemical Communications*, vol. 16, pp. 670–671, 1975;
(b) LANGLOIS N., GUÉRITTE F., LANGLOIS Y., *et al.*, "Application of a modification of the Polonovski reaction to the synthesis of vinblastine-type alkaloids", *Journal of American Chemical Society*, vol. 98, no. 22, pp. 7017–24, 1976;

(c) POTIER P., "Recent developments in field of N-oxides chemistry – Synthesis of antitumoral complex alkaloids", *Chimia*, vol. 30, no. 12, pp. 544–545, 1976.

147 KUTNEY J.P., Synthesis of vinblastine, vincristine and related compounds, U.S. Patents Appl. Ser. No. 582,373, 30 May 1975.

148 KUTNEY J.P., RATCLIFFE A.H., TREASURYWALA A.M., *et al.*, "Studies on synthesis of bisindole alkaloids. 2. Synthesis of a 3', 4'-dehydrovinblastine, 4'-deoxovinblastine and related analogues. Biogenetic approach", *Heterocycles*, vol. 3, no. 8, pp. 639–649, 1975.

149 LANGLOIS Y., GUÉRITTE F., ANDRIAMIALISOA R.Z., *et al.*, "Rearrangement of catharanthine skeleton", *Tetrahedron*, vol. 32, no. 8, pp. 945–949, 1976.

150 VUKOVIC J., GOODBODY A.E., KUTNEY J.P., *et al.*, "Production of 3', 4'-anhydrovinblastine – A unique chemical synthesis", *Tetrahedron*, vol. 44, no. 2, pp. 325–331, 1988.

151 SUNDBERG R.J., GADAMASETTI K.G., HUNT P.J., "Mechanistic aspects of the formation of anhydrovinblastine by Potier-Polonovski oxidative coupling of catharanthine and vindoline. Spectroscopic observation and chemical reactions of intermediates", *Tetrahedron*, vol. 48, no. 2, pp. 277–296, 1992.

152 MANGENEY P., Application de la réaction de Polonovski à l'hémisynthèse de la vinblastine, PhD thesis, Université de Paris-Sud, centre d'Orsay, 1979.

153 (a) GUÉRITTE F., Hémisynthèse d'analogues structuraux de la vinblastine, PhD thesis, Université de Paris-Sud, 1976;
(b) GUÉRITTE F., Dérivés antitumoraux de la vinblastine. Hémisynthèse et Biosynthèse, PhD thesis, Université de Paris-Sud, centre d'Orsay, 1980.

154 LANGLOIS Y., LANGLOIS N., MANGENEY P., *et al.*, "Semi-synthesis of leurosine. Anticarcinogenic alkaloid isolated from *Catharanthus roseus* G.Don (Apocynaceae)", *Tetrahedron Letters*, vol. 44, pp. 3945–3948, 1976.

155 ANDRIAMIALISOA R.Z., LANGLOIS Y., LANGLOIS N., *et al.*, "16-decarbomethoxy catharanthine. Preparation and coupling reaction with vindoline. Structural revision of one of dimeric compounds", *Comptes rendus hebdomadaires des séances de l'Académie des Sciences*, Série C, vol. 284, no. 18, pp. 751–754, 1977.

156 (a) KUTNEY J.P., JOSHUA A.V., LIAO P.H., *et al.*, "Total synthesis of indole and dihydroindole alkaloids. XI. Synthesis of leurosine and coupling of 3α, 4α –substituted catharanthine with vindoline", *Canadian Journal of Chemistry-Revue Canadienne de Chimie*, vol. 55, no. 18, pp. 3235–3242, 1977;
(b) KUTNEY J.P., HIBINO T., JAHNGEN E., *et al.*, "Total synthesis of indole and dihydroindole alkaloids. IX. Studies on synthesis of bisindole alkaloids in vinblastine-vincristine series. Biogenetic approach", *Helvetica Chimica Acta*, vol. 59, no. 8, pp. 2858–2882, 1976.

157 ATTA-UR-RAHMAN, BASHA A., GHAZALA M., "Synthetic studies of anti-leukemic alkaloids. VII. Partial synthesis of vinblastine", *Tetrahedron Letters*, Vol. 17, no. 27, pp. 2351–2354, 1976.

158 HONMA Y., BAN Y., "Coupling of 3-acetoxycatharanthine derivatives with vindoline. Partial synthesis of isovinblastine O-acetate", *Tetrahedron Letters*, vol. 19, no. 2, pp. 155–158, 1978.

159 KUTNEY J.P., GREGONIS D.E., IMHOF R., *et al.*, "Absolute stereochemistry of bisindole alkaloids of vinblastine type. Circular dichroism studies", *Journal of the American Chemical Society*, vol. 97, no. 17, pp. 5013–5015, 1975.

160 PARISH C.A., DONG J.G., BORNMANN W.G., *et al.*, "Circular dichroism studies of bisindole *Vinca* alkaloids", *Tetrahedron*, vol. 54, no. 52, pp. 15739–15758, 1998.

161 CUTTS J.H., "Effect of vincaleukoblastine on dividing cells in vivo", *Cancer Research*, vol. 21, no. 2, pp. 168–172, 1961.

162 OWELLEN R.J., OWENS A.H., DONIGIAN D.W., "Binding of vincristine, vinblastine and colchicine to tubulin", *Biochemical and Biophysical Research Communications*, vol. 47, no. 4, pp. 685–691, 1972.

163 (a) BORISY G.G., TAYLOR E.W., "Mechanism of action of colchicine. Binding of cochicine ^{3}H to cellular protein", *Journal of Cell Biology*, vol. 34, no. 2, pp. 525–533, 1967;
(b) BORISY G.G., TAYLOR E.W., "Mechanism of action of colchicine. Colchicine binding to sea urchin eggs and mitotic apparatus", *Journal of Cell Biology*, vol. 34, no. 2, pp. 535–548, 1967.

164 SHELANSKI M.L., GASKIN F., CANTOR C.R., "Microtubule assembly in absence of added nucleotides", *Proceedings of the National Academy of Sciences of the United States of America*, vol. 70, no. 3, pp. 765–768, 1973.

165 GASKIN F., CANTOR C.R., SHELANSKI M.L., "Turbidimetric studies of *in vitro* assembly and disassembly of porcine neurotubules", *Journal of Molecular Biology*, vol. 89, no. 4, pp. 737–755, 1974.

166 VENTILLA M., CANTOR C.R., SHELANSKI M.L., "Some features of vinblastine-induced assembly of porcine tubulin", *Archives of Biochemistry and Biophysic*, vol. 171, no. 1, pp. 154–162, 1975.

167 HIMES R.H., KERSEY R.N., HELLERBETTINGER I., *et al.*, "Action of *Vinca* alkaloids vincristine, vinblastine, and desacetyl vinblastine amide on microtubules *in vitro*", *Cancer Research*, vol. 36, no. 10, pp. 3798–3802, 1976.

168 BHATTACHARYYA B., WOLFF J., "Tubulin aggregation and disaggregation: mediation by two distinct vinblastine-binding sites", *Proceedings of the National Academy of Sciences of the United States of America*, vol. 73, no. 7, pp. 2375–2378, 1976.

169 ZAVALA F., Étude des interactions de certaines substances à vocation antitumorale, avec la tubuline, PhD thesis, Paris VII,, 1979.

170 ZAVALA F., GUÉNARD D., POTIER P., "Interaction of vinblastine analogues with tubulin", *Experientia*, vol. 34, no. 11, pp. 1497–1499, 1978.

171 SCOTT A.I., "Biogenetic-type synthesis of the indole alkaloids", *Bioorganic Chemistry*, vol. 3, no. 4, pp. 398–429, 1974.

172 SCOTT A.I., GUÉRITTE F., LEE S.L., "Role of anhydrovinblastine in the biosynthesis of the antitumor dimeric indole alkaloids", *Journal of American Chemical Society*, vol. 100, no. 19, pp. 6253–6255, 1978.

173 STUART K.L., KUTNEY J.P., HONDA T., *et al.*, "Intermediacy of 3', 4'-dehydrovinblastine in the biosynthesis of vinblastine-type alkaloids", *Heterocycles*, vol. 9, no. 10, pp. 1419–1427, 1978.

174 BAXTER R.L., DORSCHEL C.A., LEE S.L., *et al.*, "Biosynthesis of the antitumor *Catharanthus* alkaloids. Conversion of anhydrovinblastine into vinblastine", *Journal of the Chemical Society, Chemical Communications*, no. 24, pp. 257–259, 1979.

175 GUÉRITTE F., BAC N.V., LANGLOIS Y., *et al.*, "Biosynthesis of antitumor alkaloids from *Catharanthus roseus*. Conversion of 20'-deoxyleurosidine into vinblastine", *Journal of the Chemical Society, Chemical Communications*, no. 10, pp. 452–453, 1980.

176 KRIES H., O'CONNOR S.E., "Biocatalysts from alkaloid producing plants", *Current Opinion in Chemical Biology*, vol. 31, pp. 22–30, 2016.

177 (a) SOTTOMAYOR M., LOPEZ-SERRANO M., DICOSMO F., *et al.*, "Purification and characterization of alpha-3', 4'-anhydrovinblastine synthase (peroxidase-like) from *Catharanthus roseus* (L) G. Don", *FEBS Letters*, vol. 428, no. 3, pp. 299–303, 1998;
(b) SOTTOMAYOR M., BARCELO A.R., "Peroxidase from *Catharanthus roseus* (L.) G. Don and the biosynthesis of alpha-3', 4'-anhydrovinblastine: a specific role for a multifunctional enzyme", *Protoplasma*, vol. 222, nos 1–2, pp. 97–105, 2003.

178 JOVANOVICS K., FEKETE G., DEZSERI E., *et al.*, Process for the isolation of alkaloid components from the plant *Vinca rosea* L., US Patent 4172077, 23 October 1979; Appl 908584; Filed 22 May 1978; Priority data 31 May 1977.

179 (a) LANGLOIS N., POTIER P., "Antitumor alkaloids of vinblastine-type. Is leurosine an artifact?", *Journal of the Chemical Society, Chemical Communications*, no. 3, pp. 102–103, 1978;
(b) LANGLOIS N., POTIER P., "Antitumor alkaloids of the vinblastine-type: air oxidation of anhydrovinblastine", *Journal of the Chemical Society, Chemical Communications*, no. 13, pp. 582–584, 1979.

180 GOODBODY A.E., WATSON C.D., CHAPPLE C.C.S., *et al.*, "Extraction of 3′,4′-anhydrovinblastine from *Catharanthus roseus*", *Phytochemistry*, vol. 27, no. 6, pp. 1713–1717, 1988.

181 KUTNEY J.P., BALSEVICH J., BOKELMAN G.H., *et al.*, "Studies on synthesis of bisindole alkaloids. III. Synthesis of leurosine and 3'-hydroxyvinblastine", *Heterocycles*, vol. 4, no. 5, pp. 997–1005, 1976.

182 (a) MANGENEY P., ANDRIAMIALISOA R.Z., LANGLOIS N., *et al.*, "Hemisynthesis of vinblastine, vincristine and leurosidine, antitumor alkaloids from *Catharanthus roseus* (Apocynaceae)", *Comptes rendus hebdomadaires des séances de l'Académie des Sciences*, Serie C, vol. 288, no. 3, pp. 129–132, 1979;
(b) MANGENEY P., ANDRIAMIALISOA R.Z., LANGLOIS N., *et al.*, "Preparation of vinblastine, vincristine and leurosidine, antitumor alkaloids from *Catharanthus* spp. (Apocynaceae)", *Journal of the American Chemical Society*, vol. 101, no. 8, pp. 2243–2245, 1979.

183 LANGLOIS N., LANGLOIS Y., MANGENEY P., *et al.*, Nouveau procédé de synthèse de la vinblastine et de la leurosidine, FR 7834599, 8 December 1978.

184 MANGENEY P., ANDRIAMIALISOA R.Z., LALLEMAND J.Y., *et al.*, "5'-Nor anhydrovinblastine. Prototype of a new class of vinblastine derivatives", *Tetrahedron*, vol. 35, no. 18, pp. 2175–2179, 1979.

185 BOMMER P., MCMURRAY W., BIEMANN K., "High resolution mass spectra of natural products. Vinblastine and derivatives", *Journal of the American Chemical Society*, vol. 86, no. 7, pp. 1439–1440, 1964.

186 POTIER P., LANGLOIS N., LANGLOIS Y., *et al.*, Nouveaux composés bis-indoliques utiles comme médicaments et procédé pour leur préparation, FR 7824568, 24 August 1978.

187 MANGENEY P., ANDRIAMIALISOA R.Z., LANGLOIS N., *et al.*, "A new class of antitumor compounds: 5'-nor and 5', 6'-seco derivatives of vinblastine-type alkaloids", *Journal of Organic Chemistry*, vol. 44, no. 22, pp. 3765–3768, 1979.

188 POTIER P., GUENARD D., ZAVALA F., "Résultats récents dans le domaine des alcaloïdes antitumoraux du groupe de la vinblastine. Etudes biochimiques", *Comptes rendus des séances de la Société de biologie et de ses filiales*, vol. 173, no. 2, pp. 414–424, 1979.

189 MARAL R., BOURUT C., CHENU E., *et al.*, "Experimental *in vivo* cross-resistance of *Vinca* alkaloid drugs", *Cancer Chemotherapy and Pharmacology*, vol. 5, pp. 197–199, 1981.

190 RIBAUD P., GOUVEIA J., MARAL R., *et al.*, "Phase I study of 5'-noranhydrovinblastine (Navelbine, NVB)", *Proceedings of the American Association for Cancer Research*, vol. 22, no. March, pp. 368–368, 1981.

191 ANDRIAMIALISOA R.Z., LANGLOIS N., LANGLOIS Y., *et al.*, "Rearrangement of catharanthine skeleton. IV Nor-5 catharanthine and coupling with vindoline", *Canadian Journal of Chemistry - Revue canadienne de chimie*, vol. 57, no. 19, pp. 2572–2577, 1979.

192 (a) ANDRIAMIALISOA R.Z., LANGLOIS N., LANGLOIS Y., *et al.*, "Composés antitumoraux du groupe de la vinblastine: nouvelle méthode de préparation", *Tetrahedron*, vol. 36, nos 20–21, pp. 3053–3060, 1980;
(b) LANGLOIS N., ANDRIAMIALISOA R.Z., LANGLOIS Y., *et al.*, Procédé de préparation de nouveaux composés bis-indoliques, FR 79 02981, 6 February 1979;
(c) LANGLOIS N., LANGLOIS Y., ANDRIAMIALISOA R.Z., *et al.*, Nor bis-indole compounds usable as medicaments, US Patent 4307100 A, 22 December 1981; Appl. 67439, 20 August 1979; Priority data 24 August 1978.

193 GUÉRITTE F., POUILHES A., MANGENEY P., *et al.*, "Antitumor compounds in vinblastine group. Nor-5' anhydrovinblastine derivatives", *European Journal of Medicinal Chemistry*, vol. 18, no. 5, pp. 419–424, 1983.

194 POTIER P., "Synthesis of the antitumor dimeric indole alkaloids from *Catharanthus* species (vinblastine group)", *Journal of Natural Products*, vol. 43, no. 1, pp. 72–86, 1980.

195 (a) RAHMANI R., MARTIN M., BARBET J., *et al.*, "Radioimmunoassay and preliminary pharmacokinetic studies in rats of 5'-noranhydrovinblastine (Navelbine)", *Cancer Research*, vol. 44, pp. 5609–5613, 1984;
(b) RAHMANI R., GUÉRITTE F., MARTIN M., *et al.*, "Comparative pharmacokinetics of antitumor *Vinca* alkaloids: intravenous bolus injections of navelbine and related alkaloids to cancer patients and rats", *Cancer Chemotherapy and Pharmacology*, vol. 16, pp. 223–228, 1986.

196 MARAL R., BOURUT C., CHENU E., *et al.*, "Experimental antitumor-activity of 5'-nor-anhydrovinblastine navelbine", *Cancer Letters*, vol. 22, no. 1, pp. 49–54, 1984.

197 RIBAUD P., GOUVEIA J., LANGLOIS Y., *et al.*, "Phase-I study of 5'-nor-anhydrovinblastine (navelbine, nvb)", *Investigational New Drugs*, vol. 2, no. 1, pp. 127–127, 1984.

198 CROS S., TAKOUDJU M., SCHEPELYNCK-LATASTE H., *et al.*, "Study of naveline ditartrate (nor-5' anhydrovinblastine) with the two antitumor compounds, vinblastine and vincristine", in ISHIGAMI J. (ed.), *Recent Advances in Chemotherapy, Anticancer Comparative* in vitro *and* in vivo, Tokyo University Press, Tokyo, pp. 477-478, 1985.

199 MATHÉ G., REIZENSTEIN P., "Phase I pharmacologic study of a new *Vinca* alkaloid – navelbine", *Cancer Letters*, vol. 27, no. 3, pp. 285–293, 1985.

200 WANG Y.-F., SHI Q.-W., DONG M., *et al.*, "Natural taxanes: developments since 1828", *Chemical Reviews*, vol. 111, pp. 7652–7709, 2011.

201 SPJUT R.W., "Taxonomy and nomenclature of *Taxus* (Taxaceae)", *Journal of the Botanical Research Institute of Texas*, vol. 1, pp. 203–289, 2007.

202 ROQUES J., *Phytographie Médicale. L'histoire des poisons tirés du règne végétale*, vol. 2, Didot le Jeune, Paris, 1821.

203 LUCAS H., "Ueber ein in den Blättern von *Taxus baccata* L. enthaltenes Alkaloid (das Taxin)", *Archiv der Pharmazie*, vol. 135, no. 2, pp. 145–149, 1856.

204 MARME W., "Taxina", *American Journal of Pharmacy*, vol. 48, p. 353, 1876.

205 AMATO D., CAPPARELLI A., "*Taxus baccata*", *American Journal of Pharmacy*, vol. 53, p. 56, 1881.

206 (a) HILGER A., BRANDE F., "Ueber Taxin, das Alkaloïd des Eibenbaumes (*Taxus baccata*)", *Berichte der deutschen chemischen Gesellschaft*, vol. 23, no. 1, pp. 464–468, 1890;
(b) HILGER A., BRANDE F., "On taxine", *American Journal of Pharmacy*, vol. 62, p. 297, 1890.

207 (a) WINTERSTEIN E., IATRIDES D., "Ueber das aus '*Taxus baccata*', Eibe, darstellbare Alkaloid, Taxin", *Zeitschrift Fur Physiologische Chemie*, vol. 117, no. 5/6, pp. 240–283, 1921;
(b) WINTERSTEIN E., GUYER A., "Weitere Beitraege zur Kenntnis des Taxins", *Zeitschrift Fur Physiologische Chemie*, vol. 128, nos 4-6, pp. 175–229, 1923.

208 (a) GRAF E., "Zur chemie des taxins", *Angewandte Chemie*, vol. 68, pp. 249–250, 1956;
(b) GRAF E., BERTHOLDT H., "Amorphous taxine & crystalline taxine A; *Taxus* alkaloids. II", *Pharmazeutische Zentralhalle*, vol. 96, nos 8–9, pp. 385–395, 1957;
(c) GRAF E., "Taxin B, das Hauptalkaloid von *Taxus baccata* L. 4. Mitteilung: *Taxus*-Alkaloide", *Archiv der Pharmazie*, vol. 291, no. 9, pp. 443–449, 1958.

209 (a) GRAF E., KIRFEL A., WOLFF G.J., *et al.*, "The elucidation of taxine A from *Taxus baccata* L.", *Liebigs Annalen Der Chemie*, no. 2, pp. 376–381, 1982;
(b) ETTOUATTI L., AHOND A., POUPAT C., *et al.*, "Révision structurale de la taxine B, alcaloïde majoritaire des feuilles de l'if d'Europe, *Taxus baccata* L.", *Journal of Natural Products*, vol. 54, no. 5, pp. 1455–1458, 1991.

210 TEKOL Y., GOGUSTEN B., "Comparative determination of the cardioselectivity of taxine and verapamil in the isolated aorta, atrium and jejunum preparations of rabbits", *Arzneimittel-Forschung*, vol. 49, no. 8, pp. 673–678, 1999.

211 WILSON C.R., SAUER J.M., HOOSER S.B., "Taxines: a review of the mechanism and toxicity of yew (*Taxus* spp.) alkaloids", *Toxicon*, vol. 39, nos 2–3, pp. 175–185, 2001.

212 LYTHGOE B., "The *Taxus* alkaloids", in MANSKE R.H.F. (ed.), *The Alkaloids*, vol. 10, Academic Press, New York, pp. 597–626, 1968.

213 (a) DELLA CASA DE MARCANO D.P., HALSALL T.G., CASTELLANO E., *et al.*, "Crystallographic structure determination of diterpenoid Baccatin V, a naturally occuring oxetan with a taxane skeleton", *Journal of the Chemical Society D: Chemical Communications*, no. 21, pp. 1382–1383, 1970;
(b) DELLA CASA DE MARCANO D.P., HALSALL T.G., HORNBY G.M., "Structure of baccatin-III, a partially esterified octahydroxy-monoketo-taxane derivative lacking a double bond at C-4", *Journal of the Chemical Society D: Chemical Communications*, no. 4, pp. 216–217, 1970;
(c) DELLA CASA DE MARCANO D.P., HALSALL T.G., "Structures of some taxane diterpenoids, baccatins-III, -IV, -VI, and -VII and 1-dehydroxybaccatin-IV, possessing an oxetan ring", *Journal of the Chemical Society: Chemical Communications*, no. 9, pp. 365–366, 1975.

214 MILLER R.W., "A brief survey of *Taxus* alkaloids and other taxane derivatives", *Journal of Natural Products*, vol. 43, no. 4, pp. 425–437, 1980.

215 WANI M.C., TAYLOR H.L., WALL M.E., *et al.*, "Plant antitumor agents. VI. Isolation and structure of Taxol, a novel antileukemic and antitumor agent from *Taxus brevifolia*", *Journal of the American Chemical Society*, vol. 93, no. 9, pp. 2325–2327, 1971.

216 PERDUE R.E., HARTWELL J.L., "The search for plant sources for anticancer drugs", *Morris Arboretum Bulletin*, vol. 20, pp. 35–53, 1969.

217 DOUROS J., SUFFNESS M., "New anti-tumor substances of natural origin", *Cancer Treatment Reviews*, vol. 8, no. 1, pp. 63–87, 1981.

218 SUFFNESS M., WALL M.E., "Discovery and development of Taxol", in SUFFNESS M. (ed.), *Taxol®: Science and Applications*, CRC Press, LLC, pp. 3–22, 1995.

219 WALL M.E., WANI M.C., "Taxol", in PELLETIER S.W. (ed.), *Alkaloids: Chemical and Biological Perspectives*, vol. 9, Pergamon, New York, pp. 1–21, 1995.

220 WANI M.C., HORWITZ S.B., "Nature as a remarkable chemist: a personal story of the discovery and development of Taxol", *Anti-Cancer Drugs*, vol. 25, no. 5, pp. 482–487, 2014.

221 STATZ D., COON F.B., "Preparation of plant extracts for antitumor screening", *Cancer Treatment Reports*, vol. 60, no. 8, pp. 999–1005, 1976.

222 WALL M.E., WANI M.C., "Recent progress in plant anti-tumor agents", *153rd National Meeting*, American Chemical Society, Miami Beach, 1967.

223 CHAN W.R., HALSALL T.G., HORNBY G.M., *et al.*, "Taxa-4(16), 11-diene-5a,9a,10b,13a-tetraol, a new taxane derivative from the heartwood of yew (*T. baccata* L.): X-ray analysis of a p-bromobenzoate derivative", *Chemical Communications*, no. 24, pp. 923–925, 1966.

224 FUCHS D.A., JOHNSON R.K., "Cytologic evidence that taxol, an anti-neoplastic agent from *Taxus brevifolia*, acts as a mitotic spindle poison", *Cancer Treatment Reports*, vol. 62, no. 8, pp. 1219–1222, 1978.

225 SCHIFF P.B., FANT J., HORWITZ S.B., "Promotion of microtubule assembly *in vitro* by taxol", *Nature*, vol. 277, no. 5698, pp. 665–667, 1979.

226 ROWINSKY E.K., CAZENAVE L.A., DONEHOWER R.C., "Taxol. A novel investigational antimicrotubule agent", *Journal of the National Cancer Institute*, vol. 82, no. 15, pp. 1247–1259, 1990.

227 BLUME E., "Investigators seek to increase taxol supply", *Journal of the National Cancer Institute*, vol. 81, no. 15, pp. 1122–1123, 1989.

228 GENTRY R., "Intensive effort under way to develop taxol supplies", *Journal of the National Cancer Institute*, vol. 83, no. 9, pp. 603–604, 1991.

229 WALSH V., GOODMAN J., "Cancer chemotherapy, biodiversity, public and private property: the case of the anti-cancer drug Taxol", *Social Science & Medicine*, vol. 49, pp. 1215–1225, 1999.

230 Nature (editorial) "Names for hi-jacking" *Nature*, vol. 373, p. 370, 1995.

231 CHAUVIERE G., GUENARD D., PICOT F., *et al.*, "Analyse structurale et étude biochimique de produits isolés de l'if: *Taxus baccata* L. (Taxacées)", *Comptes Rendus de l'Académie des Sciences*, vol. 293, no. 7, pp. 501–503, 1981.

232 SENILH V., Étude des constituants de l'if: *Taxus baccata* L. Relations structure-activité antitumorale *in vitro*, PhD thesis, Université de Paris-Sud Orsay, 1984.

233 CHAUVIERE G., GUENARD D., PASCARD C., *et al.*, "Taxagifine. New taxane derivative from *Taxus baccata* L. (Taxaceae)", *Journal of the Chemical Society-Chemical Communications*, no. 9, pp. 495–496, 1982.

234 SENILH V., BLECHERT S., COLIN M., *et al.*, "Mise en évidence de nouveaux analogues du taxol extraits de *Taxus baccata*", *Journal of Natural Products*, vol. 47, no. 1, pp. 131–137, 1984.

235 LATASTE H., SENILH V., WRIGHT M., *et al.*, "Relationships between the structures of taxol and baccatin III derivatives and their *in vitro* action on the disassembly of mammalian brain and physarum amebal microtubules", *Proceedings of the National Academy of Sciences of the United States of America-Biological Sciences*, vol. 81, no. 13, pp. 4090–4094, 1984.

236 MCLAUGHLIN J.L., MILLER R.W., POWELL R.G., *et al.*, "19-hydroxybaccatin III, 10-deacetylcephalomannine and 10-deacetyltaxol, new antitumor taxanes from *Taxus wallichiana*", *Journal of Natural Products*, vol. 44, no. 3, pp. 312–319, 1981.

237 MILLER R.W., POWELL R.G., SMITH C.R., *et al.*, "Antileukemic alkaloids from *Taxus wallichiana* Zucc", *Journal of Organic Chemistry*, vol. 46, no. 7, pp. 1469–1474, 1981.

238 POWELL R.G., MILLER R.W., SMITH C.R., "Cephalomannine; a new antitumour alkaloid from *Cephalotaxus mannii*", *Journal of the Chemical Society, Chemical Communications*, no. 3, pp. 102–104, 1979.

239 KINGSTON D.G.I., HAWKINS D.R., OVINGTON L., "New taxanes from *Taxus brevifolia*", *Journal of Natural Products*, vol. 45, no. 4, pp. 466–470, 1982.

240 PARNESS J., KINGSTON D.G.I., POWELL R.G., *et al.*, "Structure-activity study of cytotoxicityand microtubule assembly *in vitro* by taxol and related taxanes", *Biochemical and Biophysical Research Communications*, vol. 105, no. 3, pp. 1082–1089, 1982.

241 RIONDEL J., JACROT M., PICOT F., *et al.*, "Therapeutic response to taxol of 6 human tumors xenografted into nude-mice", *Cancer Chemotherapy and Pharmacology*, vol. 17, no. 2, pp. 137–142, 1986.

242 SENILH V., GUÉRITTE F., GUENARD D., *et al.*, "Hémisynthèse de nouveaux analogues du taxol. Etude de leur interaction avec la tubuline", *Comptes rendus de l'Académie des Sciences*, vol. 299, no. 15, pp. 1039–1043, 1984.

243 WINDHOLZ T.B., JOHNSTON D.B., "Trichloroethoxycarbonyl, a generally applicable protecting group", *Tetrahedron Letters*, vol. 8, no. 27, pp. 2555–2557, 1967.

244 GUÉRITTE-VOEGELEIN F., SÉNILH V., DAVID B., *et al.*, "Chemical studies of 10-deacetyl baccatin III. Hemisynthesis of taxol derivatives", *Tetrahedron*, vol. 42, no. 16, pp. 4451–4460, 1986.

245 DARZENS G., "Méthode générale de synthèse des aldéhydes à l'aide des acides glycidiques substitués", *Comptes rendus hebdomadaires des séances de l'Académie des sciences*, vol. 139, pp. 1214–1215, 1904.

246 TAKIMOTO S., INANAGA J., KATSUKI T., *et al.*, "Preparation of hindered esters from acid chlorides and alcohols in presence of silver cyanide", *Bulletin of the Chemical Society of Japan*, vol. 49, no. 8, pp. 2335–2336, 1976.

247 NEISES B., STEGLICH W., "4-dialkylaminopyridines as acylation catalysts. V. Simple method for esterification of carboxylic acids", *Angewandte Chemie-International Edition*, vol. 17, no. 7, pp. 522–524, 1978.

248 (a) SHARPLESS K.B., CHONG A.O., OSHIMA K., "Osmium-catalyzed vicinal oxyaminations of olefins by chloramine-T", *Journal of Organic Chemistry*, vol. 41, no. 1, pp. 177–179, 1976;
(b) HERRANZ E., SHARPLESS K.B., "Improvements in osmium-catalyzed oxyamination of olefins by chloramine-T", *Journal of Organic Chemistry*, vol. 43, no. 12, pp. 2544–2548, 1978.

249 (a) HERRANZ E., BILLER S.A., SHARPLESS K.B., "Osmium-catalyzed vicinal oxyamination of olefins by N-chloro-N-argentocarbamates", *Journal of the American Chemical Society*, vol. 100, no. 11, pp. 3596–3598, 1978;
(b) HERRANZ E., SHARPLESS K.B., "Osmium-catalyzed vicinal oxyamination of olefins by N-chloro-N-metallocarbamates", *Journal of Organic Chemistry*, vol. 45, no. 13, pp. 2710–2713, 1980.

250 DAVID B., Hémisynthèse dans la série Taxol. Etudes des relations structure-activité *in vitro* sur la tubuline, Master of Advanced Studies, Université de Paris-Sud, faculté de pharmacie, Chatenay-Malabry, 1985.

251 MANGATAL L., ADELINE M.T., GUÉNARD D., *et al.*, "Application of the vicinal oxyamination reaction with asymmetric induction to the hemisynthesis of taxol and analogs", *Tetrahedron*, vol. 45, no. 13, pp. 4177–4190, 1989.

252 MANGATAL L., Dérivés antitumoraux du Taxol. Hémisynthèse et relations structure-activité, PhD thesis, Université Paris XI Orsay, 1989.

253 COLIN M., GUENARD D., GUÉRITTE-VOEGELEIN F., *et al.*, Procédé de préparation du taxol et du désacétyl-10 taxol. Eur. Pat. Appl. EP 253 739, 20th January 1988; Fr. Appl. 86/10,401, 17 July 1986.

254 GUÉRITTE-VOEGELEIN F., GUÉNARD D., MANGATAL L., *et al.*, "Structure of a synthetic taxol precursor: N-*tert*-Butoxycarbonyl-10-deacetyl-*N*-debenzoyltaxol", *Acta Crystallographica Section C. Crystal Structure Communications*, vol. 46, pp. 781–784, 1990.

255 COLIN M., GUENARD D., GUÉRITTE-VOEGELEIN F., *et al.*, Dérivés du taxol, leur préparation et les compositions pharmaceutiques qui les contiennent. Eur. Pat. Appl. EP 253 739, 20th January 1988; Fr. Appl. 86/10,401, 17 July 1986.

256 GUÉRITTE-VOEGELEIN F., GUÉNARD D., LAVELLE F., *et al.*, "Relationships between the structure of taxol analogs and their antimitotic activity", *Journal of Medicinal Chemistry*, vol. 34, no. 3, pp. 992–998, 1991.

257 DENIS J.N., GREENE A.E., SERRA A.A., *et al.*, "An efficient, enantioselective synthesis of the taxol side chain", *Journal of Organic Chemistry*, vol. 51, no. 1, pp. 46–50, 1986.

258 KATSUKI T., SHARPLESS K.B., "The first practical method for asymmetric epoxidation", *Journal of the American Chemical Society*, vol. 102, no. 18, pp. 5974–5976, 1980.

259 DENIS J.-N., GREENE A.-E., GUENARD D., *et al.*, Procédé de préparation du taxol. Eur. Pat. Appl. EP 336840, 5 April 1989; Fr. Appl. 88/4512, 6 April 1988.

260 DENIS J.N., GREENE A.E., GUÉNARD D., *et al.*, "A highly efficient, practical approach to natural taxol", *Journal of the American Chemical Society*, vol. 110, no. 17, pp. 5917–5919, 1988.

261 (a) DENIS J.N., CORREA A., GREENE A.E., "An improved synthesis of the Taxol side-chain and of RP 56976", *Journal of Organic Chemistry*, vol. 55, no. 6, pp. 1957–1959, 1990;

(b) DENIS J.N., CORREA A., GREENE A.E., "Direct, highly efficient synthesis from (*S*)-(+)-phenylglycine of the Taxol and Taxotere side chains", *Journal of Organic Chemistry*, vol. 56, no. 24, pp. 6939–6942, 1991.

262 KANAZAWA A.M., DENIS J.N., GREENE A.E., "Direct, stereoselective synthesis of the protected paclitaxel (taxol) side chain and high-yield transformation to paclitaxel", *Journal of the Chemical Society-Chemical Communications*, no. 22, pp. 2591–2592, 1994.

263 HOLTON R.A., Method of preparation of Taxol using an oxazoninone. Eur. Pat. Appl. EP 400,971 (1990); US Patent 5,015,744 (1991), Filed: 14 November 1989.

264 HOLTON R.A., Method for preparation of Taxol using β-Lactam. Eur. Pat. Appl. EP 428,376 (1991); US Patent 5,175,315 (1992), Filed: 29 September 1989.

265 (a) OJIMA I., HABUS I., ZHAO M.Z., *et al.*, "Efficient and practical asymmetric synthesis of the taxol C-13 side-chain, N-benzoyl-(2*R*,3*S*)-3-phenylisoserine, and its analogs via chiral 3-hydroxy-4-aryl-β-lactams through chiral ester enolate-imine cyclocondensation", *Journal of Organic Chemistry*, vol. 56, no. 5, pp. 1681–1683, 1991;
(b) OJIMA I., HABUS I., ZHAO M., *et al.*, "New and efficient approaches to the semisynthesis of taxol and its C-13 side chain analogs by means of β-lactam synthon method", *Tetrahedron*, vol. 48, no. 34, pp. 6985–7012, 1992.

266 GEORG G.I., MASHAVA P.M., AKGUN E., *et al.*, "Asymmetric synthesis of β-lactams and N-benzoyl-3-phenylisoserines via the staudinger reaction", *Tetrahedron Letters*, vol. 32, no. 27, pp. 3151–3154, 1991.

267 NICOLAOU K.C, DAI W.-M., GUY R.K., "Chemistry and Biology of Taxol", *Angewandte Chemie International Edition*, vol. 33, no. 1, pp. 15–44, 1994.

268 BACHELOR F.W., BANSAL R.K., "Darzens glycidic ester condensation", *Journal of Organic Chemistry*, vol. 34, no. 11, pp. 3600–3604, 1969.

269 COLIN M., GUENARD D., GUÉRITTE-VOEGELEIN F., *et al.*, Procédé de préparation de dérivés de la baccatine III et de la désacétyl-10 baccatine III. Eur. Pat. Appl. EP 0336841, 11th October 1989; Fr. Appl. 88/04513, 6 April 1988.

270 (a) DENIS J.N., KANAZAWA A.M., GREENE A.E., "Taxotere by esterification with stereochemically wrong (2*S*,3*S*)-phenylisoserine derivatives", *Tetrahedron Letters*, vol. 35, no. 1, pp. 105–108, 1994;
(b) KANAZAWA A.M., DENIS J.N., GREENE A.E., "Highly stereocontrolled and efficient preparation of the protected, esterification-ready docetaxel (Taxotere) side-chain", *The Journal of Organic Chemistry*, vol. 59, no. 6, pp. 1238–1240, 1994.

271 COMMERCON A., BÉZARD D., BERNARD F., *et al.*, "Improved protection and esterification of a precursor of the Taxotere and Taxol side-chains", *Tetrahedron Letters*, vol. 33, no. 36, pp. 5185–5188, 1992.

272 LAVELLE F., FIZAMES C., GUÉRITTE-VOEGELEIN F., *et al.*, "Experimental properties of RP 56976, a Taxol derivative", *Proceedings of the American Association for Cancer Research*, vol. 30, p. 2254, 1989.

273 BISSERY M.C., GUÉNARD D., GUÉRITTE-VOEGELEIN F., *et al.*, "Experimental antitumor-activity of Taxotere (RP 56976, NSC 628503), a Taxol analog", *Cancer Research*, vol. 51, no. 18, pp. 4845–4852, 1991.

274 (a) EXTRA J.-M., ROUSSEAU F., BOURHIS J., *et al.*, "Phase I trial of Taxotere (RP 56976, NSC 628 503)", *Proceedings of the American Association for Cancer Research*, vol. 32, p. 1225, 1991;
(b) ROUSSEAU F., EXTRA J.-M., CULINE S., *et al.*, "Phase I and pharmacological study of Taxotere, a newtaxol analog", *European Journal of Cancer*, vol. 27, no. 2, p. 1238, 1991;
(c) TOMIAK E., PICCART M.-J., KERGER J., *et al.*, "A phase I study of Taxotere (RP 56976 NSC 628503) administered as a one hour intravenous infusion on a weekly basis", *European Journal of Cancer*, vol. 27, no. 2, p. 1184, 1991.

275 GROSSETTI M., BES M.-P., "Encastrement et découplages dans les relations science-industrie", *Revue Française de Sociologie*, vol. 42, no. 2, pp. 327–355, 2001.

276 LE ROUX M., "Recherche industrielle et recherche publique. État des lieux des années 1990 à Pechiney", *Histoire Économie et Société*, vol. 4, pp. 489–498, 2001.

277 VEYNE P., *Palmyre – L'irremplaçable trésor*, Albin Michel, Paris, 2015.

Index

G, H, I

L, M, N

O, P, R

T, U, V

FSC
www.fsc.org
MIX
Papier | Fördert gute Waldnutzung
FSC® C083411

Kolibri 360 GmbH
Ferdinand-Jühlke-Straße 7
99095 Erfurt, Deutschland
produktsicherheit@kolibri360.de